Korean Language

Grammar Pattern

Cholho Choe

Draft2Digital

Korean Language: Grammar Pattern

Table of Contents

Korean Language: Grammar Pattern

UNIT 11. MODIFYING VERB
       1. modifying verb in past tense
       2. modifying verb in present tense
       3. modifying verb in future tense
       4. modifying verb in past progressive tense
       5. modifying verb in present progressive tense
       6. modifying verb in future progressive tense

UNIT 12. CONJUNCTION
       1. and
       2. but
       3. or
       4. when as adverb clause
       5. when as noun clause
       6. before
       7. after
       8. as soon as
       9. until
       10. while
       11. because
       12. although
       13. if

UNIT 1. NUMBER: Sino Korean and pure Korean number

※Sino Korean means words or numbers which are originated from Chinese characters but can be transcribed in Hangeul.

Number	Pure Korean (number as noun)	Pure Korean (number as adjective)	Sino Korean (noun & adjective)
1	*하나	*한 __one__ person(사람): 한 사람　*하나 사람	일
2	*둘	*두 __two__ people(사람): 두 사람　*둘 사람	이
3	*셋	*세 __three__ people: 세 사람　*셋 사람	삼
4	*넷	*네 __four__ people: 네 사람　*넷 사람	사
5	다섯	다섯	오
6	여섯	여섯	육
7	일곱	일곱	칠
8	여덟 *ㅂ is silent. 여덜 is pronounced.	여덟	팔

Korean Language: Grammar Pattern

9	아홉	아홉	구
10	열	열	십
20	*스물	*스무 __twenty__ people: __스무__ 사람 *_스물_ _사람_	이십
30	서른	서른	삼십
40	마흔	마흔	사십
50	쉰	쉰	오십
60	예순	예순	육십
70	일흔	일흔	칠십
80	여든	여든	팔십
90	아흔	아흔	구십
100	백	백	백
1,000	천	천	천
10,000	만	만	만
100,000	십만	십만	십만(10x 만)
1,000,000	백만	백만	백만(100x 만)
10,000,000	천만	천만	천만(1,000x 만)

Examples:

Number	Pure Korean (noun)	Pure Korean + noun (adjective)	Sino Korean (noun and adjective)
15	열다섯	열다섯	십오

Korean Language: Grammar Pattern

22	*스물둘	*스물두	이십이
31	*서른하나	*서른한	삼십일
45	마흔다섯	마흔여섯	사십육
57	쉰일곱	쉰일곱	오십칠
68	예순여덟	예순여덟	육십팔
73	*일흔셋	*일흔세	칠십삼
84	*여든넷	*여든네	팔십사
96	아흔여섯	아흔여섯	구십육
109	백아홉	백아홉	백구
1,150	천백쉰	천백쉰	천백오십
27,589	이만 칠천오백여든아홉	이만 칠천오백여든아홉	이만 칠천오백팔십구
472,905	사십칠만 이천구백다섯	사십칠만 이천구백다섯	사십칠만 이천구백오
9,143,851	*구백십사만 삼천팔백쉰하나	*구백십사만 삼천팔백쉰한	구백십사만 삼천팔백오십일
75,361,494	*칠천오백삼십육만 천사백아흔넷	*칠천오백삼십육만 천사백아흔네	칠천오백삼십육만 천사백구십사

Exercise 1. Fill in the blanks with appropriate Korean numbers.

Number	pure Korean (noun)	pure Korean (adjective)	Sino Korean (noun and adjective)
19	열아홉	열아홉	십구
25	스무다섯	스무다섯	이십오
36	스른여섯	스른여섯	삼십육

[여기에 입력]
Korean Language: Grammar Pattern

48	마흔여덟	마흔여덟	사십팔
51	쉰하나	*쉰한	오십일
63	예순셋	*예순세	육십삼
72	일흔둘	*일흔두	칠십이
87	여든일곱	여든일곱	팔십칠
94	아흔넷	*아흔네	구십사
161	백예순하나	*백예순한	백육십일
284	이백여든넷	*이백여든네	이백팔십사
392	삼백아흔둘	*삼백아흔두	삼백구십이
433	사백서른셋	*사백서른세	사백삼십삼
3,269	삼천이백예순아홉	삼천이백예순아홉	삼천이백육십구
5,081	오천여든하나	*오천여든한	오천팔십일
8,720	팔천칠백스물둘	*팔천칠백스물두	팔천칠백이십
9,457	구천사백쉰일곱	구천사백쉰일곱	구천사백오십칠

UNIT 2. PRONOUN

1. personal pronoun

※For more information on marker, refer to UNIT 5. MARKER.

person	number	subject case: -vowel ending + 는 -consonant ending + 은	possessive case: -vowel or consonant ending + 의	object case: -vowel ending + 를 -consonant ending + 을
1st person I: 나 or 저	singular *저 is used to respect a listener you are talking to.	I: 나는 or 저는 *나 ends in vowel ㅏ. ※은/는 is subject marker.	my: 나의 or 저의 -나의 행동: my action(행동) ※의 is possessive marker.	me: 나를 or 저를 ※을/를 is object marker.
we: 우리 or 저희	plural *저희 is used to respect a listener.	we: 우리는/저희는 *리 ends in vowel ㅣ.	our: 우리의/저희의 -우리의 나라: our country(나라)	us: 우리를/저희를
2nd person you: 너/당신 or 너희들/당신들	singular	you: 너/당신	you: 너는/당신은	your: 너의/당신의 -당신의 결정: your decision(결정)	you: 너를/당신을
	plural	you:	your:	you:

Korean Language: Grammar Pattern

	너희들/당신들 ※들 is the plural suffix.	너희들은/당신들은 *들 ends in consonant ㄹ.	너희들의/당신들의 -너희들의 실수: your mistake(실수)	너희들을/당신들을
3rd person he: 그 she: 그녀 they: 그들	singular 그/그녀	he: 그는 *그 ends in vowel ㅡ. she: 그녀는 *녀 ends in vowel ㅕ.	his: 그의 her: 그녀의 -그의/그녀의 소망: his/her wish(소망)	him: 그를 her: 그녀를
	plural: 그들	they: 그들은 *들 ends in consonant ㄹ.	their: 그들의 -그들의 습관: their habit(습관)	them: 그들을

2. demonstrative pronoun

number	subject case: 은 or 는	possessive case: 의	object case: 을 or 를
singular: this: 이것	이것은 *것 ends in consonant ㅅ.	이것의 -이것의 용도: the usage(용도) of this	이것을
plural: these: 이것들 ※것 means 'a thing'	이것들은	이것들의 -이것들의 목적: the goal(목적) of these	이것들을
singular:	그것은	그것의	그것을

Korean Language: Grammar Pattern

it: 그것			
plural: they: 그것들	그것들은 ※그들(they) is also plural form of 3rd person.	그것들의 -그것들의 위치: the location(위치) of them	그것들을
singular: that: 저것	저것은	저것의 -저것의 정체: the identity(정체) of that	저것을
plural: those: 저것들	저것들은	저것들의 -저것들의 행방: the whereabouts(행방) of those	저것들을

※이것(this) refers to something that is close to a speaker.

그것(it) refers to something that is close to a listener.

저것(that) refers to something that is away from both a speaker and a listener.

3. indefinite pronoun

indefinite pronoun	usage	subject case: 은 or 는	possessive case: 의	object case: 을 or 를
all	as pronoun: 모두/전부 *두 ends in vowel ㅜ.	모두는/전부는 *두 ends in vowel ㅜ.	모두의/전부의 *모든 is adjective: -모든 돈: all the money(돈)	모두를/전부를

Korean Language: Grammar Pattern

both	as pronoun: 둘 다 ※둘 means pure Korean number 2 and 다 means 'all'.	둘 다<u>는</u> *다 ends in vowel ㅏ.	둘 다<u>의</u> -둘 다의 집: the house(집) <u>of</u> both	둘 다<u>를</u>
each	as pronoun: 각자/각각	각자<u>는</u>/각각<u>은</u> *자 ends in vowel ㅏ. *각 ends in consonant ㄱ.	각자<u>의</u>/각각<u>의</u> -각자의 선택: the choice(선택) <u>of</u> each	각자<u>를</u>/각각<u>을</u>
some	as pronoun: 몇몇 + countable noun 약간 + amount	몇몇<u>은</u>/약간<u>은</u> *몇 ends in consonant ㅊ. *간 ends in consonant ㄴ.	몇몇<u>의</u>/약간<u>의</u> -몇몇의 사람: some people(사람) -약간의 물: some water(물)	몇몇<u>을</u>/약간<u>을</u>
such	as pronoun: 그런 사람(such a person) or 그런 것(such a thing)	그런 사람<u>은</u>/그런 것<u>은</u>	*그런 is adjective: -그런 집: such a house(집)	그런 사람<u>을</u>/그런 것<u>을</u>
the same	as pronoun: 같은 사람(the same person) or 같은 것(he same thing)	같은 사람<u>은</u>/같은 것<u>은</u>	*같은 is adjective: 같은 모자: the same hat(모자)	같은 사람<u>을</u>/같은 것<u>을</u>

Korean Language: Grammar Pattern

another	as pronoun: 또 다른 사람(another person) or 또 다른 것(another thing)	또 다른 사람은 /또 다른 것은	*또 다른 is adjective: -또 다른 컴퓨터: another computer	또 다른 사람을 /또 다른 것을
one another /each other	as pronoun: 서로	서로는 *로 ends in vowel ㅗ.	서로의 -서로의 인생: life(인생) <u>of</u> each other	서로를

4. interrogative pronoun

interrogative pronouns	subjective case: 은 or 는	possessive case or as adjective: 의	objective case: 을 or 를
who 누구	누가: who *누구가 sounds awkward.	누구의: whose -누구의 돈: whose money(돈) -누구의 대답: whose answer(대답)	누구를: whom
which: 어떤 것: which thing	어떤 것이	*어떤 is adjective: 어떤 차: which car(차) 어떤 커피: which coffee	어떤 것을
what:	무엇이	*무엇의 is possessive case	무엇을

Korean Language: Grammar Pattern

무엇		and 무슨 is adjective: -무엇의 질문: the question(질문) of what -무슨 학교: what school(학교) -무슨 문제: what problem(문제)	

UNIT 3. GERUND: root verb stem + 기

※Drop 다 from the root verb stem and add 기.   The gerund form of English looks exactly like present participle.

Examples:

•하다(to do): 하기(doing)   ※Drop 다 and add 기.

•쓰다(to write): 쓰기(writing)

•마시다(to drink): 마시기(drinking)

•읽다(to read): 읽기(reading)

•잡다(to catch): 잡기(catching)

•자다(to sleep): 자기(sleeping)

•찾다(to find): 찾기(finding)

•집어 들다(to pick up): 집어 들기(picking up)

•살다(to live): 살기(living)

•사다(to buy): 사기(buying)

•팔다(to sell): 팔기(selling)

•닫다(to close): 닫기(closing)

•알다(to know): 알기(knowing)

Exercise 2. Rewrite the gerund forms in Korean.

root verb stem	gerund form in Korean: 기
잃다	잃기

Korean Language: Grammar Pattern

*to lose	losing
이기다 *to win	이기기 winning
벌다 *to earn	벌기 earning
일하다 *to work	일하기 working
걷다 *to walk	걷기 walking
당기다 *to pull	당기기 pulling
밀다 *to push	밀기 pushing
듣다 *to listen	듣기 listening
읽다 *to read	읽기 reading
노래하다 *to sing	노래하기 singing
입다 *to wear	입기 wearing
믿다 *to believe	믿기 believing
타다	타기

Korean Language: Grammar Pattern

*to ride	riding
물다 *to bite	물기 biting
마시다 *to drink	마시기 drinking
보다 *to see	보기 seeing
먹다 *to eat	먹기 eating
열다 *to open	열기 opening
돕다 *to help	돕기 helping

UNIT 4. TO-INFINITIVE as a role of noun: 는 것

1) root verb stem ending in consonant or vowel + 는 것

※Drop 다 from root verb stem and add 는 것. 것 means 'a thing'.

Examples:

•<u>To do</u>(하다) is good: 하는 것.   Drop 다 from root verb stem and add 는 것.

*to be good: 좋다   하는 것 = the thing that (you) do

•It is good <u>to walk</u>(걷다): 걷는 것

•<u>To come</u>(오다) is good: 오는 것

•It is good <u>to go</u>(가다): 가는 것

•<u>To wash</u>(씻다) is good: 씻는 것

•It is good <u>to learn</u>(배우다): 배우는 것

2) root verb stem ending in ㄹ: Drop ㄹ and add 는 것.

※For more detailed information, refer to UNIT 11. MODIFYING VERB 2-2).

•<u>To hang</u>(걸다) is good: 거는 것   *걸는 것   ※Drop ㄹ and add 는 것.

*거는 것=The thing that (you) hang

•It is good <u>to sell</u>(팔다): 파는 것   *팔는 것

•<u>To open</u>(열다) is good: 여는 것   *열는 것

3) root verb stem of static verbs ending in ㅂ: Drop ㅂ and add 운 것.

[여기에 입력]
Korean Language: Grammar Pattern

※For more detailed information, see UNIT 8. Adjective 1-4) and UNIT 11. MODIFYING VERB 2-3).

•To be spicy(맵다) is good: 매운 것   *맵는 것   맵 ends in consonant ㅂ. Drop ㅂ and add 운 것.   매운 것: the thing that is spicy = spicy thing

Exercise 3. Rewrite the underlined English 'to-infinity' in Korean.

to-infinity as noun role	to-infinity in Korean: 는 것 or 운 것
To write is good. *to write: 쓰다	쓰는 것
To ask is good. *to ask: 묻다	묻는 것
To be close is good. *to be close: 가깝다	가까운 것 *가깝은 것 *Drop ㅂ and add 운 것
To lie down is good. *to lie down: 눕다	눕는 것
To grind is good. *to grind: 갈다	가는 것 *갈는 것 *Drop ㄹ and add 는 것.
To be cold is good. *to be cold: 춥다	추운 것 *춥은 것 *Drop ㅂ and add 운 것.
To read is good. *to read: 읽다	읽는 것
To fix a bike is good.	고치는 것/수리하는 것

Korean Language: Grammar Pattern

*to fix: 고치다(pure Korean)/수리하다(Sino Korean)	
<u>To build</u> a house is good. *to build: 짓다	짓는 것
<u>To stay overnight</u> is not good. *to stay overnight: 밤샘하다	밤샘하는 것
<u>To push</u> a cart is good. *to push: 밀다	미는 것 *밀는 것 *Drop ㄹ and add 는 것

UNIT 5. MARKER

types of markers	markers in Korean
subject/ subject compliment/topic marker	**은 or 는/이 or 가** -consonant ending + 은 or 이 -vowel ending + 는 or 가 ※은/는 is subject marker. 이/가 is subject compliment or topic marker. ※A subject in a sentence is followed by a subject marker with NO exception.
object marker	**을 or 를** -consonant ending + 을 -vowel ending + 를 ※An object in a sentence is followed by an object marker with NO exception.
possessive marker	**의** *The possessive preposition 'OF' is the English equivalent.
location marker	**에 or 에서** *'AT/IN/ON' is the English equivalent. -active verb + 에서 -static verb + 에

Korean Language: Grammar Pattern

direction marker	에게 or 한테/에 or (으)로
*Person is combined with 에게 or 한테(TO)/에게서 한테서(FROM)	*'TO/TOWARD' is the English equivalent. *to a PERSON: 에게 or 한테 *to a PLACE: 에 or (으)로 -consonant ending + 으로 -vowel ending + 로
*Place is combined with 에 or (으)로(TO)/에서 or (으)로부터(FROM) ※한테/한테서/에/에서 is informal. 에게/에게서/(으)로/(으)로부터 is formal.	에게서 or 한테서 에서 or (으)로부터 *'FROM' is the English equivalent. *from a PERSON: 에게서 or 한테서 *from a PLACE: 에서 or (으)로부터 -consonant ending + 으로부터 -vowel ending + 로부터
comparison marker	보다 *'THAN' is the English equivalent. He is taller <u>than</u> me.
	처럼 *'LIKE' as a preposition is the English equivalent. It is sweet <u>like</u> a candy.
method marker	*noun + (으)로 -consonant ending + 으로

[여기에 입력]
Korean Language: Grammar Pattern

	-vowel ending + 로 *로 is like 'by means of'/'through'/'in the method of'

1. subject/subject compliment/topic marker: 은/는 or 이/가

※은/는 is a subject marker while 이/가 is a topic marker. It is better to use 이/가 if you want to emphasize the subject. However, 은/는 and 이/가 are not different in terms of its meaning and usage.

* In the sentence of 'I want you to go', the subject is 'I' and the topic is 'you'. In this sentence, the topic 'you(너)' is focused on. Therefore, 가 is the better marker to identify 'you'. *너**가**

1) subject ending in consonant + 은 or 이

•집(house): 집(house)은 or 집이   *집 ends in consonant ㅂ and 은 or 이 should be a marker.

2) subject ending in vowel + 는 or 가

•모자(hat): 모자(hat)는 or 모자가   *자 ends in vowel ㅏ and 는 or 가 will be subject marker.

Examples:

•차(car): 차는 or 차가

•쌀(rice): 쌀은 or 쌀이

•고양이(cat): 고양이는 or 고양이가

•한국말(Korean language): 한국말은 or 한국말이

[여기에 입력]
Korean Language: Grammar Pattern

Exercise 4. Fill in the blanks with the appropriate subject and topic marker.

noun as subject	subject marker/topic marker in Korean: 은 or 는(subject marker) 이 or 가(topic marker)
책(book)	책은 or 책이 *책 ends in consonant ㄱ.
공기(air)	공기는 or 공기가 *기 ends in vowel ㅣ.
컴퓨터(computer)	컴퓨터는/컴퓨터가
휴대폰(cell phone)	휴대폰은/휴대폰이
음악(music)	음악은/음악이
편지(letter)	편지는/편지가
부모(parents)	부모는/부모가
산(mountain)	산은/산이
바다(ocean)	바다는/바다가
사람(person)	사람은/사람이
연필(pencil)	연필은/연필이
신용카드(credit card)	신용카드는/신용카드가
사진(photo)	사진은/사진이
축구(soccer)	축구는/축구가
그림(picture)	그림은/그림이
사랑(love)	사랑은/사랑이
취미(hobby)	취미는/취미가

Korean Language: Grammar Pattern

커피(coffee)	커피는/커피가
한류(Korean wave)	한류는/한류가
빛(light)	빛은/빛이

2. object marker: 을 or 를

1) object ending in consonant + 을

•책(book): 책을   *책 ends in consonant ㄱ and the object marker is 을.

2) vowel ending + 를

•커피(coffee): 커피를   *피 ends in vowel ㅣ and the object marker is 를.

Examples:

•그녀(she): 그녀를

•음식(food): 음식을

•책상(table): 책상을

*상 ends in consonant ㅇ and the object marker is 을.   Ending ㅇ is a consonant while beginning ㅇ is a vowel.

•의자(chair): 의자를

Exercise 5. Fill in the blanks with the appropriate object marker in Korean.

noun as an object	object marker in Korean: 을 or 를
책(book)	책을

Korean Language: Grammar Pattern

	*책 ends in consonant ㄱ.
공기(air)	공기를 *기 ends in vowel ㅣ.
컴퓨터(computer)	컴퓨터를
휴대폰(cell phone)	휴대폰을
음악(music)	음악을
편지(letter)	편지를
부모(parents)	부모를
산(mountain)	산을
바다(ocean)	바다를
사람(person)	사람을
연필(pencil)	연필을
신용카드(credit card)	신용카드를
사진(photo)	사진을
축구(soccer)	축구를
그림(picture)	그림을
사랑(love)	사랑을
취미(hobby)	취미를
커피(coffee)	커피를
한류(Korean wave)	한류를
빛(light)	빛을

3. possessive marker: 의

Korean Language: Grammar Pattern

*Noun ending in consonant or vowel + 의

Examples:

•돈(money): 돈의(of the money)　　*돈 ends in a consonant ㄴ and the possessive marker is 의.

•그(he): 그의(his)　　*그 ends in a vowel ㅡ and the possessive marker is 의.

Exercise 6. Fill in the blanks with the possessive marker in Korean.

noun	possessive marker in Korean: 의
숲(forest)	숲의
비(rain)	비의
학교(school)	학교의
화장실(bathroom)	화장실의
극장(movie theater)	극장의
고속도로(freeway)	고속도로의
친구(friend)	친구의
결혼식(wedding ceremony)	결혼식의
책(book)	책의
의자(chair)	의자의
부모(parents)	부모의
편지(letter)	편지의
돈(money)	돈의

우리(we)	우리의

4. location marker: 에 or 에서

1) action verb + 에서

•to play <u>in</u>(에서) the field   *'To play' is an action verb and the location marker is 에서.

2) static verb(to be-verb) +에

•to <u>be at</u>(에) a café   *'To be' is a static verb and the location marker is 에.

Examples:

•to swim <u>in</u> the river(강): 강<u>에서</u>   *to swim: 수영하다

•to live <u>in</u> Korea(한국): 한국<u>에서</u>   *to live: 살다

•to be <u>on</u> the tree(나무): 나무위<u>에</u>   *to be: 있다

•to be <u>at</u> home(집): 집<u>에</u>

•to eat <u>at</u> the restaurant(식당): 식당<u>에서</u>   *to eat: 먹다

•to be in the box(상자): 상자안<u>에</u>

※Regardless of verb type, 에 is always combined with special event, time, date, day, month or year which are not locations.

•to meet <u>on</u> 3 o'clock(세시): 세시<u>에</u>   *to meet: 만나다   3 o'clock is not a location.

•to go hiking <u>on</u> Sunday(일요일): 일요일<u>에</u>   *to go hiking: 등산가다

•to eat out <u>on</u> (에) Christmas(성탄절)/New Year(새해)/my birthday(나의 생일): 성탄절/새해/나의 생일<u>에</u>   *to eat: 먹다

Korean Language: Grammar Pattern

※'to sit(앉다)/to stand(서다)/to lie down(눕다)' is combined with 에.

•to sit <u>on</u> the chair(의자): 의자에   *의자에서

•to stand up <u>on</u> the floor(바닥): 바닥에   *바닥에서

•to lie down on the bed(침대): 침대에 눕다   *침대에서

Exercise 7. Rewrite the underlined part with the appropriate location marker in Korean.

location	location marker in Korean: 에 or 에서
to study <u>in</u> the library(도서관) *to study: 공부하다	에서 'to study' is an action verb.
to sail <u>in</u> the ocean(바다) *to sail: 항해하다	에서 'to sail' is an action verb.
to be <u>on</u> top of the mountain(산꼭대기) *to be: 있다	에 *static verb + 에
to stop <u>at</u> the red light(빨간 등) *to stop: 멈추다	에서 'to stop' is an action verb.
to take a rest <u>on</u> Monday(월요일) *to take a rest: 쉬다	에 *Monday is not a location.
to sleep <u>on</u> bed(침대) *to sleep: 자다	에서 'to sleep' is an action verb.
to be <u>on</u> the left side(왼쪽)	에
to walk <u>at</u> the sidewalk(보도)	에서

Korean Language: Grammar Pattern

*to walk: 걷다	'to walk' is an action verb.
to have a party <u>on</u> X-mas eve(성탄전야) *to have a party: 파티하다	에 *X-mas is not a location.
to dine out <u>at</u> a restaurant(식당) *to dine: 식사하다	에서 'to dine out' is an action verb.
to be <u>under(밑)</u> the bridge(다리)	에 'to be' is a static verb.
to fly <u>up in(위)</u> the sky(하늘) *to fly: 날다	에서 'to fly' is an action verb.
to see a movie <u>on</u> weekend(주말) *to see a movie: 영화보다	에 'weekend' is not a location.

5. direction marker: person + 에게 or 한테/place + 에 or (으)로

1-1) <u>TO/TOWARD/INTO</u> + person ending in consonant or vowel: <u>에게</u> or <u>한테</u>

•<u>to</u> me (나): 나<u>에게</u>/나<u>한테</u>   *나 ends in vowel ㅏ.   Just add 에게 or 한테

•<u>to</u> my son (아들): 아들<u>에게</u>/아들<u>한테</u>   *들 ends in consonant ㄹ.   Just add 에게/한테

•<u>to</u> my supervisor (상관): 상관<u>에게</u>/상관<u>한테</u>   *관 ends in consonant ㄴ.

1-2) <u>TO/TOWARD/INTO</u> + place ending in consonant: <u>에</u> or <u>으로</u>

•<u>to</u> a foreign country(외국): 외국<u>에</u>/외국<u>으로</u>   *국 ends in consonant ㄱ.   Add 에 or 으로

[여기에 입력]
Korean Language: Grammar Pattern

•<u>to</u> the beach (해변): 해변<u>에</u>/해변<u>으로</u>   *변 ends in consonant ㄴ. Add 으로 or 에.

1-3) <u>TO/TOWARD/INTO</u> + place ending in vowel or ㄹ: 에 or 로

•<u>to</u> the classroom (교실): 교실<u>에</u>/교실<u>로</u>   *실 ends in ㄹ.   Add just 로 or 에.

•<u>to</u> Hawaii: 하와이에/하와이로   *이 ends in vowel ㅣ.   Add 로 or 에

※에게 and (으)로 is formal and 한테 and 에 is informal. It is better to use 에게 and (으)로 when written and when spoken, 한테 and 에 is better.

2-1) <u>FROM/OUT OF</u> + person ending in consonant: <u>한테서</u> or <u>에게서</u> or <u>으로부터</u>

•<u>from</u> my uncle(삼촌): 삼촌<u>한테서</u>/삼촌<u>에게서</u>/삼촌<u>으로부터</u>

*촌 ends in consonant ㄴ.   Add 한테서/에게서/으로부터

•<u>from</u> the police officer(경찰관): 경찰관<u>한테서</u>/경찰관<u>에게서</u>/경찰관<u>으로부터</u>

*관 ends in consonant ㄴ.

2-2) <u>FROM/OUT OF</u> + person ending in vowel or ㄹ: <u>한테서</u> or <u>에게서</u> or <u>로부터</u>

•<u>from</u> my aunt(이모/고모): 이모<u>한테서</u>/이모<u>에게서</u>/이모<u>로부터</u>

*모 ends in vowel ㅗ.   Add 한테서

•<u>from</u> my mom(엄마): 엄마<u>한테서</u>/엄마<u>에게서</u>/엄마<u>로부터</u>   *마 ends in vowel ㅏ.

※(으)로부터 is the most formal and 한테서 is the most informal expression. However, (으)로부터 is commonly used for both person and place.

2-3) <u>FROM/OUT OF</u> + place ending in consonant: <u>으로부터</u> or <u>에서</u>

•<u>from</u> the airport(공항): 공항<u>으로부터</u>/공항<u>에서</u>   *항 ends in consonant ㅇ.

•<u>from</u> the kitchen(부엌): 부엌<u>으로부터</u>/부엌<u>에서</u>   *엌 ends in consonant ㅋ.

2-4) <u>FROM</u>/<u>OUT OF</u> + place ending in vowel or ㄹ: <u>로부터</u> or <u>에서</u>

•<u>from</u> the road(도로): 도로<u>로부터</u>/도로<u>에서</u>

*로 ends in the vowel of ㅗ.   Add just 로부터 or 에서.

•<u>from</u> the living room(거실): 거실<u>로부터</u>/거실<u>에서</u>   *실 ends in ㄹ.

•<u>from</u> Seoul(서울): 서울<u>로부터</u>/서울<u>에서</u>   *울 ends in ㄹ.   Add just 로부터 or 에서.

※(으)로부터 is so formal that it sometimes sounds awkward.   However, it is never incorrect to speak or write.

Examples:

•<u>to</u> my son(아들): 아들<u>에게</u>/아들<u>한테</u>   *들 ends in ㄹ.

*아들<u>로</u> is awkward because 아들 is NOT a place.

•<u>to</u> my family(가족): 가족<u>에게</u>/가족<u>한테</u>   *족 ends in consonant ㄱ.

•<u>to</u> Korea(한국): 한국<u>에</u>/한국<u>으로</u>   *국 ends in consonant ㄱ.

•<u>from</u> the sky(하늘): 하늘<u>로부터</u>/하늘<u>에서</u>   *늘 ends in ㄹ.

•<u>from</u> my aunt(이모): 이모<u>에게서</u>/이모<u>한테서</u>/이모<u>로부터</u>   *모 ends in vowel ㅗ.

•<u>from</u> the roof(지붕): 지붕<u>에서</u>/지붕<u>으로부터</u>   *붕 ends in consonant ㅇ.

6. comparison marker: 보다(than) and 처럼(like)

1) THAN + person or place: 보다

[여기에 입력]
Korean Language: Grammar Pattern

•<u>than</u> a flower(꽃): 꽃<u>보다</u>

•<u>than</u> the car(차): 차<u>보다</u>

•<u>than</u> him(그): 그<u>보다</u>   *그를 보다 is incorrect.

2) LIKE + person or place: 처럼

•<u>like</u> a bee(벌): 벌<u>처럼</u>

•<u>like</u> a player(선수): 선수<u>처럼</u>

Exercise 8. Fill in the blanks with the appropriate Korean equivalent to the underlined marker.

direction and comparison marker TO & FROM	direction and comparison marker in Korean: -person + 에게 or 한테(TO)/에게서 or 한테서 or (으)로부터(FROM) -place + 에 or (으)로(TO)/에서 or (으)로부터(FROM)
<u>to</u> my father(아버지)	아버지<u>에게</u>/아버지<u>한테</u>
<u>to</u> the school(학교)	학교<u>에</u>/학교<u>로</u>
<u>from</u> you(너)	너<u>에게서</u>/너<u>한테서</u>/너<u>로부터</u>
<u>from</u> Europe(유럽)	유럽<u>에서</u>/유럽<u>으로부터</u>
<u>from</u> the station(역)	역<u>에서</u>/역<u>으로부터</u>
<u>to</u> my daughter(딸)	딸<u>에게</u>/딸<u>한테</u>
<u>to</u> the criminal(범인)	범인<u>에게</u>/범인<u>한테</u>
<u>to</u> us(우리)	우리<u>에게</u>/우리<u>한테</u>
<u>to</u> America(미국)	미국<u>에</u>/미국<u>으로</u>
<u>from</u> the driver(운전자)	운전자<u>에게서</u>/운전자<u>한테서</u>

Korean Language: Grammar Pattern

<u>from</u> the parking lot(주차장)	주차장<u>에서</u>/주차장<u>으로부터</u>
<u>to</u> the singer(가수)	가수<u>에게</u>/가수<u>한테</u>
<u>to</u> the hometown(고향)	고향<u>에</u>/고향<u>으로</u>
<u>from</u> the friend(친구)	친구<u>한테서</u>/친구<u>에게서</u>/친구<u>로부터</u>
<u>from</u> the office(사무실)	사무실<u>에서</u>/사무실<u>로부터</u>

7. method marker: noun + (으)로

※Method marker 로 is 'by means of + noun' or 'through the method of + noun'.

1) noun ending in consonant + 으로

•to learn <u>through</u> books(책): 책<u>으로</u>   *책 ends in consonant ㄱ and add 으로.

2) noun ending in vowel or ㄹ+ 로

•to go <u>by</u> bicycle(자전거): 자전거<u>로</u>   *거 ends in vowel ㅓ and add 로.

•to cut <u>with</u> a knife(칼): 칼로   *칼 ends in ㄹ and add just 로.

Examples:

•to commute <u>in</u> a car(차): 차로

•to write <u>with</u> a pencil(연필): 연필<u>로</u>

•to pay <u>by</u> credit card(신용카드): 신용카드<u>로</u>

•to light up <u>with</u> a candle(촛불): 촛불<u>로</u>

Exercise 9. Fill in the blank with method marker in Korean.

Korean Language: Grammar Pattern

noun as method	method marker in Korean: 로 or 으로
얼음 ice	얼음<u>으로</u> *음 ends in consonant ㅁ.
공 ball	공<u>으로</u> *The ending ㅇ is a consonant.
돈 money	돈<u>으로</u> *돈 ends in consonant ㄴ.
비행기 airplane	비행기<u>로</u> *기 ends in vowel ㅣ.
총 gun	총<u>으로</u> *총 ends in consonant ㅇ.
컴퓨터 computer	컴퓨터<u>로</u> *터 ends in vowel ㅓ.
한국어 Korean language	한국어<u>로</u> *어 ends in vowel ㅓ.
지식 knowledge	지식<u>으로</u> *식 ends in consonant ㄱ.
휴식 relaxation	휴식<u>으로</u> *식 ends in consonant ㄱ.
수건 towel	수건<u>으로</u> *건 ends in consonant ㄴ.
사진	사진<u>으로</u>

Korean Language: Grammar Pattern

photo	*진 ends in consonant ㄴ.
그림 painting	그림<u>으로</u> *림 ends in consonant ㅁ.
바위 rock	바위<u>로</u> *위 ends in vowel ㅟ.
돌 stone	돌<u>로</u> *돌 ends in ㄹ.
사과 apple	사과<u>로</u> *과 ends in vowel ㅘ.
고기 meat	고기<u>로</u> *기 ends in vowel ㅣ.
지하철 subway train	지하철<u>로</u> *철 ends in ㄹ.
대중교통 public transportation	대중교통<u>으로</u> *통 ends in consonant ㅇ.
영화 movie	영화<u>로</u> *화 ends in vowel ㅘ.
관광 tour	관광<u>으로</u> *광 ends in consonant ㅇ.

UNIT 6. LINKING SUFFIX

types of suffix	suffix in Korean
quotation suffix	*statement quotation + 고
	*request quotation + 라고 or 으라고 -consonant ending + 으라고 -vowel ending + 라고
	*question quotation + 냐고 or 는지
supplement suffix	*'ONLY or EXCLUSIVELY' is the English equivalent to 만 or 기만. -noun + 만 -verb + 기만
	*'ALSO' is the English equivalent to 도 -noun + 도 -verb stem in positive sentence + 기도 *'not---even' is the English equivalent to 지도. -cannot even + verb: 지도 못하다

	-do not even + verb: 지도 안한다 ※못 implies a lack of ability and 안 means a lack of effort.
conjunctive suffix	*'noun + AND + noun' is the English equivalent. -vowel ending + 와 or 랑 or 하고 -consonant ending +과 or 이랑 or 하고 ※ (이)랑 sounds cute like a baby talk. 와/과 is better when written because it is formal. 하고 is better when spoken because it is informal.
purpose suffix	러 or 으러 *'IN ORDER TO' is the English equivalent. -consonant ending + 으러 -vowel ending + 러

1. suffix for statement quotation: 고

※If necessary, refer to 'UNIT 7. VERB STEM & TENSES' for more detailed information on verb stem and tense.

1) statement quotation in present tense + 고

*The ending syllable 다 should not be dropped from the verb stem in present tense.

Examples:

[여기에 입력]
Korean Language: Grammar Pattern

•He said, "I <u>love</u> you": 사랑한다고　　*to love: 사랑하다

*the verb stem in present tense: 사랑한다

•They said, "Korea <u>is beautiful</u>": 아름답다고　　*to be beautiful: 아름답다

*the verb stem in present tense: 아름답다　　※In the case of static verb, the root verb stem is the same as the verb stem in present tense.

•I think that he <u>looks</u>: 본다고　　*to look: 보다

*the verb stem in present tense is 본다

•It is said that Hangeul <u>is easy</u>: 쉽다고　　*to be easy: 쉽다　　쉽다 is a static verb.

•She said that she <u>knows</u>: 안다고　　*to know: 알다

*the verb stem in present tense: 안다

2) statement quotation in past tense + 고

*verb stem in past tense ends in ㅆ다 or 었다 or 았다.　The ending syllable 다 should not be dropped from the verb stem in past tense.

Examples:

•I think that he <u>chose</u>: 골랐다고/선택했다고　　*to choose: 고르다(pure Korean)/선택하다(Sino Korean)

*verb stem in past tense(=to have chosen): 골랐다/선택했다.

•I think that he <u>disliked</u>: 싫어 했다고　　*to dislike: 싫어하다

*verb stem in past tense: 싫어했다.

•I think that he <u>forgot</u>: 잊었다고　　*to forget: 잊다

*verb stem in past tense: 잊었다.

•I remember that I <u>heard</u>: 들었다고　　*to hear: 듣다

*verb stem in past tense: 들었다

[여기에 입력]
Korean Language: Grammar Pattern

•He said that he <u>knew</u>: 알았다고   *to know: 알다   *verb stem in past tense: 알았다

3) statement quotation in future tense + 고

*Verb stem in future tense ends in 겠다/ㄹ(을) 것이다/ㄹ(을)거다.   The ending syllable 다 should not be dropped from the verb stem in future tense.

※In the case of 것이다/거다, 라고 is also acceptable for statement quotation.

•He said that he <u>will go</u>: 갈 것이**다고**(or 갈 것이**라고**)/갈 거**다고**(or 갈 거**라고**)

•He said that he <u>will be going</u>: 가고 있을 것이**다고**(or 것이**라고**)/가고 있을 거**다고**(or 거**라고**)

Examples:

•He said that he <u>will come</u>: 오겠다고/올 것이**다고**(라고)/올 거**다고**(라고)

*to come: 오다

*verb stem in future tense: 오겠다/올 것이다/올 거다.   Just add 고 at the end of the verb stem.

•He said, "I <u>will marry</u> her": 결혼하겠다고/결혼할 것이**다고**(라고)/결혼할 거**다고**(라고)

*to marry: 결혼하다

*he verb stem in future tense: 결혼하겠다/결혼할 것이다/결혼할 거다

•I think that he <u>will drive</u>: 운전하겠다고/운전할 것이**다고**(라고)/운전할 거**다고**(라고)

*to drive: 운전하다

*verb stem in future tense: 운전하겠다/운전할 것이다/운전할 거다

•I think that he <u>will teach</u>: 가르치겠다고/가르칠 것이**다고**(라고)/가르칠 거**다고**(라고)

*to teach: 가르치다

*verb stem in future tense is 가르치겠다/가르칠 것이다/가르칠 거다

Korean Language: Grammar Pattern

•I think that he <u>will clean up</u>: 청소하겠다고/청소할 것이<u>다고</u>(라고)/청소할 거<u>다고</u>(라고)

*to clean up: 청소하다

*verb stem in future tense: 청소하겠다/청소할 것이다/청소할 거다

4) statement quotation in past progressive tense + 고

*Verb stem in past progressive tense ends in 고 있었다.   The ending syllable 다 should not be dropped from the verb stem in past progressive tense.

Examples:

•I think that he <u>was walking</u>: 걷고 있었다고   *to walk: 걷다

*verb stem in past progressive tense: 걷고 있었다

•I think that he <u>was working</u>: 일하고 있었다고

*to work: 일하다

*verb stem in past progressive tense: 일하고 있었다

•I think that he <u>was helping</u>: 돕고 있었다고   *to help: 돕다

*verb stem in past progressive tense: 돕고 있었다

•I think that he <u>was leaving</u>: 떠나고 있었다고   *to leave: 떠나다

*verb stem in past progressive tense: 떠나고 있었다

•I know that he <u>was talking</u>: 말하고 있었다고   *to talk: 말하다

*verb stem in past progressive tense: 말하고 있었다

5) statement quotation in present progressive tense + 고

*Verb stem in present progressive tense ends in 고 있다.   The ending syllable 다 should not be dropped from the verb stem in present progressive tense.

Examples:

•I think that he <u>is dancing</u>: 춤추고 있다고   *to dance: 춤추다

*verb stem in present progressive tense: 춤추고 있다

•I think that he <u>is listening</u>: 듣고 있다고   *to listen: 듣다

*verb stem in present progressive tense: 듣고 있다

•I think that he <u>is catching</u>: 잡고 있다고   *to catch: 잡다

*verb stem in present progressive tense: 잡고 있다

•I think that he <u>is arriving</u>: 도착하고 있다고   *to arrive: 도착하다

*verb stem in present progressive tense: 도착하고 있다

•I think that he <u>is swimming</u>: 수영하고 있다고   *swim: 수영하다

*verb stem in present progressive tense: 수영하고 있다

6) statement quotation in future progressive tense + 고

*Verb stem in future progressive tense ends in 고 있겠다/고 있을 것이다/고 있을 거다.   The ending syllable 다 should not be dropped from the verb stem in future progressive tense.

Examples:

•I think that he <u>will be sleeping</u>: 자고 있겠다고/자고 있을 것이<u>다고</u>(라고)/자고 있을 거<u>다고</u>(라고)

*to sleep: 자다   *verb stem in future progressive tense: 자고 있겠다/자고 있을 것이다/자고 있을 거다

•I think that he <u>will be breaking</u>: 부수고 있겠다고/부수고 있을 것이<u>다고</u>(라고)/부수고 있을 거<u>다고</u>(라고)   *to break: 부수다

[여기에 입력]
Korean Language: Grammar Pattern

*verb stem in future progressive tense: 부수고 있겠다/부수고 있을 것이다/부수고 있을 거다

※고 implies progressive action and 겠 indicates future tense. UNIT 7 has more details.

•I think that he <u>will be hiking</u>: 등산하고 있겠다고/등산하고 있을 것이다고(라고)/등산하고 있을 거다고(라고)   *to hike: 등산하다

*verb stem in future progressive tense: 등산하겠다/등산할 것이다/등산할 거다.

•I think that he <u>will be departing</u>: 출발하고 있겠다고/출발하고 있을 거다고(라고)/출발하고 있을 거다고(라고)   *to depart: 출발하다

*verb stem in future progressive tense: 출발하고 있겠다/출발하고 있을 것이다/출발하고 있을 거다

•He said that he <u>will be boiling</u>: 끓이고 있겠다고(라고)/끓이고 있을 것이다고(라고)/끓이고 있을 거다고(라고)   *to boil: 끓이다

*verb stem in future progressive tense: 끓이고 있겠다/끓이고 있을 것이다/끓이고 있을 거다

Exercise 10. Rewrite the statement quotation in Korean.

statement quotation	statement quotation in Korean: 고
said that--<u>played golf</u> *to play golf: 골프를 치다	골프를 쳤다고 *to have played golf: 골프를 쳤다
said that--<u>touches</u> *to touch: 만지다	만진다고 *verb stem in present tense: 만진다
said that--<u>will like</u> *to like: 좋아하다	좋아하겠다고/좋아할 것이다고/좋아할 거다고 *to be going to like: 좋아하겠다/좋아할 것이다/좋아할 거다

Korean Language: Grammar Pattern

said that--<u>fished</u> *to fish: 낚시하다	낚시했다고 *to have fished: 낚시했다
said that--<u>sends</u> *to send: 보내다	보낸다고 *verb stem in present tense: 보낸다
said that--<u>will receive</u> *to receive: 받다	받겠다고/받을 것이다고/받을 거다고 *to be going to receive: 받겠다/받을 것이다/받을 거다
said that--<u>changed</u> *to change: 바꾸다	바꿨다고 = 바꾸었다고 *to have changed: 바꿨다 = 바꾸었다
said that--<u>hits</u> *to hit: 때리다	때린다고/친다고 *verb stem in present tense: 때린다/친다
said that--<u>will use</u> *to use: 사용하다	사용하겠다고/사용할 것이다고/사용할 거다고 *to be going to use: 사용하겠다/사용할 것이다/사용할 거다
said that--<u>is shopping</u> *to shop: 쇼핑하다	쇼핑하고 있다고 *to be shopping: 쇼핑하고 있다
said that--<u>was shouting</u> *to shout: 외치다/소리치다	외치고 있었다고/소리치고 있었다고 *to have been shouting: 외치고 있었다/소리치고 있었다
said that--<u>will be waiting</u> *to wait: 기다리다	기다리고 있겠다고/기다리고 있을 것이다고/기다리고 있을 거다고 *to be going to be waiting: 기다리고 있겠다/기다리고 있을 것이다/기다리고 있을 거다
said that--<u>can write</u>	쓸 수 있다고

Korean Language: Grammar Pattern

*to write: 쓰다	*to be able to write: 쓸 수 있다
said that--<u>will say</u> *to say: 말하다	말하겠다고/말할 것이다고/말할 거다고 *to be going to say: 말하겠다/말할 것이다/말할 거다
said that---<u>must enjoy</u> *to enjoy: 즐기다	즐겨야 한다고 *to have to enjoy: 즐겨야 하다
said that--<u>could draw</u> *draw: 그리다	그릴 수 있었다고 *to have been able to draw: 그릴 수 있었다
said that--<u>had to use</u> *to use: 쓰다(pure Korean)/사용하다(Sino Korean)	쓰야 했다고/사용해야 했다고 *had to use: 쓰야 했다/사용해야 했다
said that--<u>raises</u> *to raise: 올리다	올린다고 *verb stem in present tense: 올린다
said that--<u>can throw away</u> *to throw away: 버리다	버릴 수 있다고 *to be able to throw away: 버릴 수 있다
said that--<u>had to chew</u> *to chew: 씹다	씹어야 했다고 *had to chew: 씹어야 했다
said that--<u>pulled</u> *to pull: 당기다	당겼다고 *to have pulled: 당겼다
said that--<u>will be washing</u> *to wash: 씻다	씻고 있겠다고/씻고 있을 것이다고/씻고 있을 거다고 *to be going to be washing: 씻고 있겠다/씻고 있을 것이다/씻고 있을 거다
said that--<u>could donate</u> *to donate: 기부하다	기부할 수 있었다고

Korean Language: Grammar Pattern

	*to have been able to donate: 기부할 수 있었다
said that--<u>must stop</u> *to stop: 멈추다(pure Korean)/정지하다(Sino Korean)	멈춰야 한다고 = 멈추어야 한다고/정지해야 한다고 *to have to stop: 멈춰야 하다/정지해야 하다
said that--<u>can boil</u> *to boil: 끓이다	끓일 수 있다고 *to be able to boil: 끓일 수 있다

2. suffix for request/command/order quotation: 라고 or 으라고 or 우라고

1) root verb stem ending in vowel + 라고

*Drop 다 from root verb stem and add 라고.

•He recommended that I <u>swim</u>. = He recommended me <u>to swim</u>: 수영하라<u>고</u>

*to swim: 수영하다   하 ends in vowel ㅏ. Drop 다 from root verb stem and add 라고.

•He told me <u>to go</u>: 가라고   *to go: 가다   가 ends in vowel ㅏ. Drop 다 and add 라고.

2) root verb stem ending in consonant + 으라고

*Drop 다 from the root verb stem and add 으라고

•He advised that I <u>catch</u> the ball. = He advised me <u>to catch</u> the ball: 잡으라<u>고</u>

*to catch: 잡다   잡 ends in consonant ㅂ. Drop 다 and add 으라고.

•He recommended that I <u>eat</u>. = He recommended me <u>to eat</u>: 먹으라고

*to eat: 먹다   먹 ends in consonant ㄱ.   Drop 다 and add 으라고.

Korean Language: Grammar Pattern

3) root verb stem ending in ㄷ: Irregular change rule applies to 듣다(to listen)/싣다(to load)/걷다(to walk)/묻다(to bury).   In this case, ㄷ is dropped root verb stem and ㄹ으라고 is added.   For the other verbs, regular change rule applies.   See the following Table 1 for more.

•He requested that I <u>listen</u>: 들으라고   *to listen: 듣다   Drop 다 from root verb stem and add 으라고.

Table 1.   *Marks in Italics* are incorrect.

root verbs ending in ㄷ	suffix for request/command/order quotation: ㄹ으라고 or 으라고
듣다 *to listen	들으라고 *듣으라고 *ㄷ is dropped and ㄹ으라고 is added.
싣다 *to load	실으라고 *싣으라고
걷다 *to walk	걸으라고 *걷으라고
묻다 *to ask	물으라고 *묻으라고
받다 *to receive	받으라고
믿다 *to believe	믿으라고
얻다 *to gain/obtain	얻으라고
딛다	딛으라고

Korean Language: Grammar Pattern

*to step	
걷다 *to collect	걷으라고
닫다 *to close	닫으라고
묻다 *to bury	묻으라고

4) root verb stem ending in ㄹ: 라고　Drop 다 from root verb stem and add just 라고.

•He requested that I <u>roll</u> Kimbap. = He requested me <u>to roll</u> Kimbap: 말라고

*to roll: 말다　Drop 다 from root verb stem and add just 라고.

•He asked that I <u>grind</u> coffee beans. = He asked me <u>to grind</u> coffee beans: 갈라고

*to grind: 갈다　Drop 다 from root verb stem and add just 라고.

5) root verb stem of static verbs ending in ㅂ: Drop ㅂ and add just 우라고.

*This rule applies to static verbs only except for 눕다(to lie down) and 깁다(to sew) and 돕다(to help) which are action verbs.　To the other verbs ending in ㅂ, regular change rule applies.　He told me <u>to catch</u>: 잡으라고　*to catch: 잡다

•The doctor told me <u>to lie down</u>: 누우라고　*to lie down: 눕다

*ㅂ is dropped and 우라고 is added.　*눕으라고* is incorrect.

•He asked me <u>to help</u>: 도우라고　*to help: 돕다

*ㅂ is dropped and 우라고 is added.　*돕으라고* is incorrect.

•He recommended me <u>to be happy</u>: 즐거우라고

*to be happy: 즐겁다　겁 ends in consonant ㅂ.　Drop ㅂ and add 우라고 is added.　*즐겁으라고* is incorrect.

[여기에 입력]
Korean Language: Grammar Pattern

Examples:

•He advised me <u>to swim</u>: 수영하라고   *to swim: 수영하다   *하 ends in vowel ㅏ.

•She requested that we <u>plant</u> a tree: 심으라고   *to plant: 심다

*심 ends in consonant ㅁ.

•He recommended that I <u>close</u> the window: 닫으라고   *to close: 닫다

*닫 ends in consonant ㄷ.

•He told me <u>to sleep</u>: 자라고   *to sleep: 자다   *자 ends in vowel ㅏ.

•He advised me that I <u>choose</u>: 고르라고/선택하라고

*to choose: 고르다(pure Korean)/선택하다(Sino Korean)

*르 ends in vowel ㅡ and 하 ends in vowel ㅏ.

•He ordered me <u>to watch</u>: 지켜보라고   *to watch: 지켜보다   *보 ends in vowel ㅗ.

•He recommended that I <u>work</u>: 일하라고   *to work: 일하다   *하 ends in vowel ㅏ.

•He asked me <u>to teach</u>: 가르치라고   *to teach: 가르치다   *치 ends in vowel ㅣ.

•He requested that I <u>call</u>: 부르라고   *to call: 부르다   *르 ends in vowel ㅡ.

•He recommended <u>to forget</u>: 잊으라고   *to forget: 잊다   *잊 ends in consonant ㅈ.

Exercise 11. Rewrite the underlined request/command/order quotation in Korean.

request/command/order quotation	request/command/order quotation in Korean: 라고 or 으라고 or 우라고 or ㄹ으라고
requested <u>to dislike</u>	싫어하라고

Korean Language: Grammar Pattern

*to dislike: 싫어하다	*Drop 다 from the verb stem and add 라고 or 으라고 or 우라고
advised <u>to lose</u> *to lose: 잃다	잃으라고
ordered <u>to catch</u> *to catch: 잡다	잡으라고
recommended <u>to go hiking</u> *to go hiking: 등산가다	등산가라고
requested <u>to arrive</u> *to arrive: 도착하다	도착하라고
asked <u>to wait</u> *to wait: 기다리다	기다리라고
ordered <u>to bury</u> *to bury: 묻다	묻으라고
requested <u>to push</u> *to push: 밀다	밀라고 *밀으라고
asked <u>to buy</u> *to buy: 사다	사라고
advised <u>to live</u> *to live: 살다	살라고 *살으라고
requested <u>to sit down</u> *to sit down: 앉다	앉으라고
recommended <u>to sell</u> *to sell: 팔다	팔라고 *팔으라고

Korean Language: Grammar Pattern

advised <u>to lie down</u> *to lie down: 눕다	누우라고 *Drop ㅂ and add 우라고.
requested <u>to promise</u> *to promise: 약속하다	약속하라고
asked <u>to load</u> *to load: 싣다	실으라고 *ㄷ is dropped and 르으라고 is added.
advised <u>to walk</u> *to walk: 걷다	걸으라고 *걷으라고
recommended <u>to receive</u> *to receive: 받다	받으라고 *Regular change rule applies to 받다.
told me <u>to be happy</u> *to be happy: 즐겁다	즐거우라고 즐겁으라고

3. suffix for question quotation: 냐고 or 는지

※냐고 sounds just a little bit more informal than 는지.   However, both are perfect to write or speak.

※If necessary, refer to UNIT 7. VERB STEM & TENSE for more detailed information on tenses.

1-1) root verb stems + <u>냐고</u> or 는지 for present tense.

*Drop 다 from root verb stem and add 냐고 or 는지.

Examples:

Korean Language: Grammar Pattern

•He asked me if I <u>go</u>: 가냐고/가<u>는지</u>   *to go: 가다

*Drop 다 from root verb stem and add 냐고/는지

•He asked what I <u>eat</u>: 먹<u>냐고</u>/먹<u>는지</u>   *to eat: 먹다

*Drop 다 from root verb stem and add 냐고/는지

•He asked where I <u>study</u>: 공부하<u>냐고</u>/공부하<u>는지</u>   *to study: 공부하다

•He asked how long I <u>walk</u>: 걷<u>냐고</u>/걷<u>는지</u>   *to walk: 걷다

•He asked how fast I <u>run</u>: 달리<u>냐고</u> or 뛰<u>냐고</u>/달리<u>는지</u> or 뛰<u>는지</u>

*to run: 달리다/뛰다   *Drop 다 from root verb stem and add 냐고/는지

•He asked what I <u>like</u>: 좋아하<u>냐고</u>/좋아하<u>는지</u>   *to like: 좋아하다

1-2) root verb stem ending in ㄹ: Drop ㄹ and add 냐고 or 는지 for present tense.

See the following Table 2 for more information.

Table 2   *Marks in Italic* are incorrect.

root verb stem ending in ㄹ	question quotation in present tense *Drop ㄹ and add 냐고 or 는지
asked if--<u>sells</u> *to sell: 팔다	파냐고/파는지 *팔냐고/팔는지* ※Drop ㄹ and add 냐고 or 는지
asked if--<u>cries</u> *to cry: 울다	우냐고/우는지 *울냐고/울는지* cries
asked if--<u>blows</u> *to blow: 불다	부냐고/부는지 *불냐고/불는지*
asked if--<u>pushes</u> *to push: 밀다	미냐고/미는지 *밀냐고/밀는지*

Korean Language: Grammar Pattern

asked if--<u>opens</u> *to open: 열다	여냐고/여는지　*열냐고/열는지
asked if--<u>drives</u> *to drive: 몰다	모냐고/모는지　*몰냐고/몰는지
asked if--<u>is far</u> *to be far: 멀다	머냐고/머는지　*멀냐고/멀는지 ※This verb is a static verb.
asked if--<u>knows</u> *to know: 알다	아냐고/아는지　*알냐고/알는지
asked if--<u>plays/hangs out</u> *to play/to hang out: 놀다	노냐고/노는지　*놀냐고/놀는지
asked if--<u>decreases</u> *to decrease: 줄다	주냐고/주는지　*줄냐고/줄는지
asked if--<u>stays</u> *to stay: 머물다	머무냐고/머무는지　*머물냐고/머물는지
asked if--<u>turns</u> *to turn: 돌다	도냐고/도는지　*돌냐고/돌는지
asked if--<u>begs</u> *to beg: 빌다	비냐고/비는지　*빌냐고/빌는지
asked if--<u>makes</u> *to make: 만들다	만드냐고/만드는지　*만들냐고/만들는지
asked if--<u>drags</u> *to drag: 끌다	끄냐고/끄는지　*끌냐고/끌는지
asked if--<u>grinds/changes</u> *to grind/to change: 갈다	가냐고/가는지　*갈냐고/갈는지

Korean Language: Grammar Pattern

asked if--<u>picks up/raises</u> *to pick up/to raise: 들다	드냐고/드는지　　*들냐고/들는지
asked if--<u>is long</u> *to be long: 길다	기냐고/기는지　　*길냐고/길는지 ※This is a static verb.
asked if--<u>freezes</u> *to freeze: 얼다	어냐고/어는지　　*얼냐고/얼는지
asked if--<u>dozes off</u> *to doze off: 졸다	조냐고/조는지　　*졸냐고/졸는지
asked if--<u>shakes</u> *to shake: 흔들다	흔드냐고/흔다는지　　*흔들냐고/흔들는지
asked if--<u>is tired</u> *to be tired: 힘들다	힘드냐고/힘드는지　　*힘들냐고/힘들는지 ※This is a static verb.
asked if--<u>solves/unties</u> *to solve/to untie: 풀다	푸냐고/푸는지　　*풀냐고/풀는지
asked if--<u>lives</u> *to live: 살다	사냐고/사는지　　*살냐고/살는지
asked if--<u>earns</u> *to earn: 벌다	버냐고/버는지　　*벌냐고/벌는지
asked if--<u>bites</u> *to bite: 물다	무냐고/무는지　　*물냐고/물는지
asked if--<u>hangs</u> *to hang: 걸다	거냐고/거는지　　*걸냐고/걸는지
asked if--<u>rolls</u> *to roll: 말다	마냐고/마는지　　*말냐고/말는지

Korean Language: Grammar Pattern

asked if--<u>flies</u> *to fly: 날다	나냐고/나는지 *날냐고/날는지
asked if--<u>washes/sucks</u> *to wash/to suck: 빨다	빠냐고/빠는지 *빨냐고/빨는지
asked if--<u>increases</u> *to increase: 늘다	느냐고/느는지 *늘냐고/늘는지
asked if--<u>swells</u> *to swell: 부풀다	부푸냐고/부푸는지 *부풀냐고/부풀는지
asked if--<u>inclines</u> *to incline: 기울다	기우냐고/기우는지 *기울냐고/기울는지

2) verb stem in past tense + 냐고 or 는지.

*Verb stem in past tense ends in 썼다 or 았다 or 었다. Drop 다 from verb stem in past tense and add 냐고 or 는지.

Examples:

•He asked what I <u>saw</u>: 보았냐고/보았<u>는지</u>   *to see: 보다

*verb stem in past tense: 보았다. Drop 다 and add 냐고/는지.

•He asked if I <u>walked</u>: 걸었냐고/걸었<u>는지</u>   *to walk: 걷다

*verb stem in past tense: 걸었다. Drop 다 and add 냐고/는지.

•He asked where I <u>went</u>: 갔냐고/갔<u>는지</u>   *to go: 가다

*verb stem in past tense: 갔다

•He asked what I <u>broke</u>: 부쉈<u>냐고</u>(부수었냐고)/부쉈<u>는지</u>(부수었는지)

*to break: 부수다   *verb stem in past tense: 부쉈다(부수었다)

•He asked when I <u>saw</u>: 봤<u>냐고</u>(보았냐고)/봤<u>는지</u>(보았는지)   *to see: 보다

[여기에 입력]
Korean Language: Grammar Pattern

*verb stem in past tense: 봤다(보았다)

3) verb stem in future tense + 냐고 or 는지.

*Verb stem in future tense ends in 겠다/ㄹ(을) 것이다/ㄹ(을) 거다. Drop 다 from verb stem in past tense and add 냐고 or 는지.

Examples:

•He asked if I <u>will give up</u>: 포기하겠<u>냐고</u> or 포기할 것이<u>냐고</u> or 포기할 거<u>냐고</u>/포기하겠<u>는지</u> or 포기할 것<u>인지</u> or 포기할 <u>건지</u>   *to give up: 포기하다

*This is the only irregular change.   Just add ㄴ지.   *포기할 것이는지/포기할 거는지 is incorrect.

*The verb stem in future tense: 포기하겠다/포기할 것이다/포기할 거다

•He asked when I <u>will finish</u>: 끝내겠<u>냐고</u> or 끝낼 것이<u>냐고</u> or 끝낼 거<u>냐고</u>/끝내겠<u>는지</u> or 끝낼 것<u>인지</u> or 끝낼 <u>건지</u>   *to finish: 끝내다

*verb stem in future tense: 끝내겠다/끝낼 것이다/끝낼 거다

•He asked how I <u>will win</u>: 이기겠<u>냐고</u> or 이길 것이<u>냐고</u> or 이길 거<u>냐고</u>/이기겠<u>는지</u> or 이길 것<u>인지</u> or 이길 <u>건지</u>   *to win: 이기다

*verb stem in future tense: 이기겠다/이길 것이다/이길 거다

•He asked if I <u>will continue</u>: 계속하겠<u>냐고</u> or 계속할 것이<u>냐고</u> or 계속할 거<u>냐고</u>/계속하겠<u>는지</u> or 계속할 것<u>인지</u> or 계속할 <u>건지</u>   *to continue: 계속하다

*verb stem in future tense: 계속하겠다/계속할 것이다/계속할 거다

•He asked if I <u>will help</u>: 돕겠<u>냐고</u> or 도울 것이<u>냐고</u> or 도울 거<u>냐고</u>/돕겠<u>는지</u> or 도울 것<u>인지</u> or 도울 <u>건지</u>   *to help: 돕다

*verb stem in future tense: 돕겠다/도울 것이다/도울 거다

•I asked when she <u>will come</u>: 오겠<u>냐고</u> or 올 것이<u>냐고</u> or 올 거<u>냐고</u>/오겠<u>는지</u> or 올 것<u>인지</u> or 올 <u>건지</u>

*to come: 오다   The verb stem in future tense is 오겠다/올 것이다/올 거다

56

4) verb stem in past progressive tense + 냐고 or 는지

*Verb stem in past progressive tense ends in 고 있었다. Drop 다 from verb stem in past tense and add 냐고 or 는지.

Examples:

•He asked when I <u>was swimming</u>: 수영하고 있었<u>냐고</u>/수영하고 있었<u>는지</u>

*to swim: 수영하다   The verb stem in past progressive tense: 수영하고 있었다.
Drop 다 and add 냐고/는지. Drop 다 from verb stem and add 냐고/는지.

•He asked where I <u>was eating out</u>: 외식하고 있었<u>냐고</u>/외식하고 있었<u>는지</u>

*to eat out: 외식하다   *verb stem in past tense: 외식하고 있었다

•He asked what I <u>was pulling</u>: 당기고 있었냐고/당기고 있었는지   *to pull: 당기다

*verb stem in past progressive tense: 당기고 있었다

•He asked what I <u>was wearing</u>: 입고 있었냐고/입고 있었는지   *to wear: 입다

*verb stem in past progressive tense: 입고 있었다

•He asked how I <u>was building</u>: 짓고 있었냐고/짓고 있었는지   *to build: 짓다

*verb stem in past progressive tense: 짓고 있었다

•He asked why I <u>was drawing</u>: 그리고 있었<u>냐고</u>/그리고 있었<u>는지</u>

*to draw: 그리다   *verb stem in past progressive tense: 그리고 있었다

5) verb stem in present progressive tense + 냐고 or 는지

*Verb stem in present progressive tense ends in 고 있다. Drop 다 from verb stem in present tense and add 냐고 or 는지.

Examples:

Korean Language: Grammar Pattern

•He asked why I <u>am drinking</u>: 마시고 있<u>냐고</u>/마시고 있<u>는지</u>   *to drink: 마시다

*verb stem in present progressive tense: 마시고 있다. Drop 다 and add 냐고/는지.

•He asked whom I <u>am teasing</u>: 놀리고 있<u>냐고</u>/놀리고 있<u>는지</u>   *to tease: 놀리다

*verb stem in present progressive tense: 놀리고 있다

•He asked where I <u>am climbing</u>: 오르고 있<u>냐고</u>/오르고 있<u>는지</u>   *to climb: 오르다

*verb stem in present progressive tense: 오르고 있다

•He asked what I <u>am writing</u>: 쓰고 있<u>냐고</u>/쓰고 있<u>는지</u>   *to write: 쓰다

*verb stem in present progressive tense: 쓰고 있다

•He asked if I am attaching: 붙이고 있냐고/붙이고 있는지   *to attach: 붙이다

*verb stem in present progressive tense: 붙이고 있다

•He asked what I <u>am throwing away</u>: 버리고 있<u>냐고</u>/버리고 있<u>는지</u>

*to throw away: 버리다   *verb stem in present progressive tense: 버리고 있다

6) verb stem in future progressive tense + 냐고 or 는지

*Future progressive tense ends in 고 있겠다/고 있을 것이다/고 있을 거다.   Drop 다 from verb stem in present tense and add 냐고 or 는지 or ㄴ지 for 것이다 and 거다.

Examples:

•He asked if I <u>will be running</u>: 뛰고 있겠<u>냐고</u> or 뛰고 있을 것이<u>냐고</u> or 뛰고 있을 거<u>냐고</u>/뛰고 있겠는지 or 뛰고 있을 것*인지* or 뛰고 있을 *건지*   *to run: 뛰다

*verb stem in future progressive tense: 뛰고 있겠다/뛰고 있을 것이다/뛰고 있을 거다   Drop 다 from the verb stem and add 냐고 or 는지.

•He asked if I will be drawing; 그리고 있겠<u>냐고</u> or 그리고 있을 것이<u>냐고</u> or 그리고 있을 거<u>냐고</u>/그리고 있겠<u>는지</u> or 그리고 있을 것*인지* or 그리고 있을 *건지*

Korean Language: Grammar Pattern

*to draw: 그리다   *verb stem in future progressive tense: 그리고 있겠다/그리고 있을 것이다/그리고 있을 거다

•He asked how I will be preparing: 준비하고 있겠냐고 or 준비하고 있을 것이냐고 or 준비하고 있을 거냐고/준비하고 있겠는지 or 준비하고 있을 것인지 or 준비하고 있을 건지   *to prepare: 준비하다

*verb stem in future progressive tense: 준비하고 있겠다/준비하고 있을 것이다/준비하고 있을 거다

•He asked where I will be travelling: 여행하고 있겠냐고 or 여행하고 있을 것이냐고 or 여행하고 있을 거냐고/여행하고 있겠는지 or 여행하고 있을 것인지 or 여행하고 있을 건지   *to travel: 여행하다

*verb stem in future progressive tense: 여행하고 있겠다/여행하고 있을 것이다/여행하고 있을 거다

•He asked whom I will be calling: 부르고 있겠냐고 or 부르고 있을 것이냐고 or 부르고 있을 거냐고/부르고 있겠는지 or 부르고 있을 것인지 or 부르고 있을 건지

*to call: 부르다   *verb stem in future progressive tense: 부르고 있겠다/부르고 있을 것이다/부르고 있을 거다

•He asked why I <u>will be crying</u>: 울고 있겠<u>냐고</u> or 울고 있을 것이냐고 or 울고 있을 거<u>냐고</u>/울고 있겠<u>는지</u> or 울고 있을 것<u>인지</u> or 울고 있을 <u>건지</u>   *to cry: 울다

*verb stem in future progressive tense: 울고 있겠다/울고 있을 것이다/울고 있을 거다

Exercise 12. Rewrite the underlined question quotation in Korean.

question quotation	question quotation in Korean: 냐고 or 는지 *냐고 is more informal than 는지
asked when I <u>departed</u> *to depart: 출발하다	출발했냐고/출발했는지 *to have departed: 출발했다

Korean Language: Grammar Pattern

asked why I <u>push</u> the cart *to push: 밀다	미냐고/미는지　*밀냐고/밀는지
asked where I <u>will wait</u> *to wait: 기다리다	기다리겠냐고/기다릴 것이냐고/기다릴 거냐고 or 기다리겠는지/기다릴 것인지/기다릴 건지 *to be going to wait: 기다리겠다/기다릴 것이다/기다릴 거다
asked if I <u>was chewing</u> *to chew: 씹다	씹고 있었냐고/씹고 있었는지 *to have been chewing: 씹고 있었다
asked if I <u>am boiling</u> *to boil: 끓이다	끓이고 있냐고/끓이고 있는지 *to be boiling: 끓이고 있다
asked if I <u>will be attaching</u> *to attach: 붙이다	붙이고 있겠냐고/붙이고 있을 것이냐고/붙이고 있을 거냐고 or 붙이고 있겠는지/붙이고 있을 것인지/붙이고 있을 건지 *to be going to be attaching: 붙이고 있겠다/붙이고 있을 것이다/붙이고 있을 거다
asked what I <u>wore</u> *to wear: 입다	입었냐고/입었는지 *to have worn: 입었다
asked where I <u>buy</u> *to buy: 사다	사냐고/사는지
asked why I <u>will laugh</u> *to laugh: 웃다	웃겠냐고/웃을 것이냐고/웃을 거냐고 or 웃겠는지/웃을 것인지/웃을 건지 *to be going to laugh: 웃겠다/웃을 것이다/웃을 거다
asked what I <u>was making</u>	만들고 있었냐고/만들고 있었는지

Korean Language: Grammar Pattern

*to make: 만들다	*to have been making: 만들고 있었다
asked where I <u>am living</u> *to live: 살다	살고 있냐고/살고 있는지 *to be living: 살고 있다
asked why I <u>will be staying</u> *to stay: 머물다	머물고 있겠냐고/머물고 있을 것이냐고/머물고 있을 거냐고 or 머물고 있겠는지/머물고 있을 것*인지*/머물고 있을 *건지* *to be going to be staying: 머물고 있겠다/머물고 있을 것이다/머물고 있을 거다
asked if I <u>sat down</u> *to sit down: 앉다	앉았냐고/앉았는지 *to have sat down: 앉았다
asked if I <u>stand up</u> *to stand up: 서다	서냐고/서는지
asked how I <u>will learn</u> *to learn: 배우다	배우겠냐고/배울 것이냐고/배울 거냐고 or 배우겠는지/배울 것*인지*/배울 *건지* *to be going to learn: 배우겠다/배울 것이다/배울 거다
asked where I <u>was washing</u> *to wash: 씻다	씻고 있었냐고/씻고 있었는지 *to have been washing: 씻고 있었다
asked why I <u>was bending</u> *to bend: 굽히다	굽히고 있었냐고/굽히고 있었는지 *to have been bending: 굽히고 있었다
asked what I <u>am reading</u> *to read: 읽다	읽고 있냐고/읽고 있는지 *to be reading: 읽고 있다
asked if I <u>will be dozing off</u> *to doze off: 졸다	졸고 있겠냐고/졸고 있을 것이냐고/졸고 있을 거냐고 or 졸고 있겠는지/졸고 있을 것*인지*/졸고 있을 *건지*

Korean Language: Grammar Pattern

	*to be going to be dozing off: 졸고 있겠다/졸고 있을 것이다/졸고 있을 거다

Exercise 13. Write the underlined part with the appropriate Korean quotation suffix.

sentence with a quotation	quotation suffix in Korean: -다고: for statement -냐고 or 는지: for question -라고: for command/request
They said that she <u>is cute</u>. *to be cute: 귀엽다	귀엽<u>다고</u>
He requested that I <u>read</u> the book. *to read: 읽다	읽<u>으라고</u>
She asked when I <u>returned</u>. *to return: 돌아오다	돌아왔<u>냐고</u>/돌아왔<u>는지</u> *to have returned: 돌아왔다
We agree that Korean language <u>is difficult</u>. *to be difficult: 어렵다	어렵다고
She answered that he <u>went</u>. *to go: 가다	갔다고 *to have gone: 갔다
He complained that it <u>is cold</u>. *to be cold: 춥다	춥다고
She told me <u>to clean up</u> my room. *to clean up: 청소하다	청소하라고
I asked her <u>to open</u> the window. *to open: 열다	열라고

Korean Language: Grammar Pattern

He recommended me <u>to work out</u>. *to work out: 운동하다	운동하라고
The commander ordered the soldiers <u>to move</u>. *to move: 움직이다	움직이라고
I asked her how she <u>pushed</u>. *to push: 밀다	밀었냐고/밀었는지 *to have pushed: 밀었다
She asked me why I <u>called</u>. *to call: 부르다	불렀냐고/불렀는지 *to have called: 불렀다
He asked her how much she <u>drank</u>. *to drink: 마시다	마셨냐고/마셨는지 *to have drunk: 마셨다
I asked him where he <u>studied</u>. *to study: 공부하다	공부했냐고/공부했는지 *to have studied: 공부했다
He said <u>that</u> he <u>will succeed</u>. *to succeed: 성공하다	성공하겠다고/성공할 것이다고/성공할 거다고 *to be going to succeed: 성공하겠다/성공할 것이다/성공할 거다
She told us <u>to leave</u>. *to leave: 떠나다	떠나라고
I asked when I <u>can eat</u>. *to eat: 갈 수 있다	먹을 수 있냐고/먹을 수 있는지 *to be able to eat: 먹을 수 있다
He thought that she <u>was watching</u> TV. *to watch: 보다	보고 있었다고 *to have been watching: 보고 있었다
The owner ordered his dog <u>to stop</u>.	멈추라고

Korean Language: Grammar Pattern

*to stop: 멈추다	
She asked what I <u>would eat</u>. *to eat: 먹다	먹겠냐고/먹을 것이냐고/먹을 거냐고 or 먹겠는지/먹을 것*인지*/ or /먹을 *건지* *to be going to eat: 먹겠다/먹을 것이다/먹을 거다
Mother believed <u>that</u> I <u>broke</u> the window. *to break: 깼다	깼다고 *to have broken: 깼다
He requested that we all <u>stand up</u>. *to stand up: 일어서다	일어서라고
She asked if she <u>could swim</u>. *to swim: 수영하다	수영할 수 있었냐고/수영할 수 있었는지 *to have been able to swim: 수영할 수 있었다
We knew that he <u>is hiking</u>. *to hike: 등산하다	등산하고 있다고 *to be hiking: 등산하고 있다
He ordered me <u>to finish</u>. *to finish: 끝내다	끝내라고
They asked when the new semester <u>begins</u>. *to begin: 시작하다	시작하냐고/시작하는지
I agreed that the game <u>was exciting</u>. *to be exciting: 흥미 있다	흥미 있었다고 *to have been exciting: 흥미 있었다
She told me <u>to close</u> the door. *to close: 닫다	닫으라고

Korean Language: Grammar Pattern

| He asked how I <u>could arrive</u>.

*to arrive: 도착하다 | 도착할 수 있었냐고/도착할 수 있었는지

*to have been able to arrive: 도착할 수 있었다 |

4. supplement suffix:

1-1) noun + 만(=only/exclusively)

•한국어(Korean language)<u>만</u> 쉽다(to be easy): 만 emphasizes Korean language.

•여름(summer)만 덥다(to be hot): 만 emphasizes a noun from behind.

1-2) root verb stem + 기만 하다 as 'only or exclusively'

*Drop 다 from root verb stem and add 기만.

•먹<u>기만 하다</u> = to do nothing but eat or to eat only   *to eat: 먹다

*Drop 다 from root verb stem and add 기만 하다.

•보<u>기만 하다</u> = to do nothing but see   *to see: 보다

2-1) noun + 도(= also or even)

•한국어(Korean language)<u>도</u> 쉽다(to be easy).   도 emphasizes Korean language.

•아이(kid)<u>도</u> 할 수 있다(to be able to do).   도 emphasizes a noun from behind.

2-2) root verb stem + 기도 하다 as 'also or even'

*Drop 다 from root verb stem and add 기도 하다.

•운동하<u>기도 하다</u> = to even work out   *to work out: 운동하다

•앉<u>기도 하다</u> = to even sit down   *to sit down: 앉다

[여기에 입력]
Korean Language: Grammar Pattern

3-1) cannot even + verb: 지도 못하다(due to a lack of ability)

*Drop 다 from root verb stem and add 지도 못하다.

•먹지도 못하다 = cannot even eat   *to eat: 먹다

•말하지도 못하다 = cannot even talk   *to talk: 말하다

3-2) do not even + verb: 지도 안 하다(due to a lack of effort)

*Drop 다 from root verb stem and add 지도 안 하다.

•인사하지도 안 하다 = do not even say hello   *to say hello: 인사하다

•마시지도 안 하다 = do not even drink   *to drink: 마시다

※기만 or 기도 are combined with '하다-verb' and 지도 must be followed by either 못하다 or 안 하다.

*만 and 도 emphasize noun and 기만 and 지도 emphasize verb. Drop 다 from root verb stem and add 기만 하다 or 기도 하다.

Examples:

•I (나) was the only one who cried: 나만   *만 emphasizes noun or pronoun.

•It was exclusively the house(집) which was burnt: 집만

•He did nothing but drink: 마시기만 했다   *to drink: 마시다   했다 is in past tense.

*기만 emphasizes verb. Drop 다 from root verb stem and add 기만.

•She just looks at it: 보기만   *to look: 보다

•The house(집) also was burnt: 집도   *'also' emphasizes the house.

Korean Language: Grammar Pattern

•The dog <u>also</u> <u>ate</u> grass: 먹<u>기도</u>   *'also' emphasizes the verb, 'ate'.   *to eat: 먹다

•He ca<u>nnot even</u> <u>write</u>: 쓰<u>지도 못하다</u>   *to write: 쓰다

•He does <u>not even</u> <u>read</u>: 읽<u>지도 안 하다</u>   *to read: 읽다

•<u>She(그녀) also</u> laughed: 그녀<u>도</u>

•The <u>trees(나무) also</u> fell down: 나무<u>도</u>

•He <u>also</u> <u>paints</u> a picture: 그리<u>기도</u>   *to paint: 그리다

*Drop 다 from root verb stem and add 기도.   It implies that he not only paints a picture but also does something else.

•He paints <u>even</u> a <u>person</u>(사람): 사람<u>도</u>

*It implies that he paints not only a person but also something else.

•He <u>also</u> <u>drive</u>: 운전하<u>기도 하다</u>   *to drive: 운전하다

•She <u>cannot even</u> <u>eat</u>: 먹<u>지도 못하다</u>   *to eat: 먹다

•He <u>cannot even write</u> his own name: 쓰<u>지도 못하다</u>   *to write: 쓰다   It implies that he can't read his name and can't even write it, either.   Drop 다 from the verb stem and add 지도.

•He <u>did not even</u> <u>breathe</u>(숨쉬다): 숨쉬<u>지도 안 했다</u>   *했다 is in past tense.   Drop 다 from the verb stem and add 지도 안 하다.   It implies that he didn't move and even breathe, either.

Exercise 14. Write the underlined part with the appropriate marker in Korean.

sentence with supplementary marker	supplementary marker in Korean: -noun + 만 or 도 -verb + 기만 하다 or 기도 하다 or 지도 못하다 or 지도 안 하다
I saw <u>nothing but</u> <u>the ocean</u>(바다).	바다만

[여기에 입력]
Korean Language: Grammar Pattern

<u>Only</u> <u>you</u>(너) can do it.	너만
He ate only the chicken breast(닭가슴).	닭가슴만
I did <u>nothing but</u> smile. *to smile: 웃다	웃기만 했다
We <u>just</u> <u>walked</u>. *to walk: 걷다	걷기만 했다
<u>Even</u> <u>a kid</u>(아이) can do it.	아이도
I <u>also</u> <u>fix</u> a bike(자전거). *to fix: 고치다	고치기도
I can eat <u>even</u> <u>Kimchi</u>(김치).	김치도
She can drive not only a car <u>but also a truck</u>(트럭).	트럭도
<u>My mother</u>(어머니) <u>also</u> can play golf.	어머니도
I can speak not only Korean <u>but also</u> <u>English</u>(영어).	영어도
She didn't <u>even</u> <u>speak</u> to me. *to speak: 말하다	말하지도 안했다 ※안 means a lack of effort.
I couldn't <u>even</u> <u>drink</u>(마시다) water. *to drink: 마시다	마시지도 못했다 ※못 means a lack of ability.
He doesn't <u>even</u> <u>try</u>(시도하다). *to try: 시도하다	시도하지도 안하다 *to not try: 시도하지 않다
It isn't <u>even</u> <u>funny</u>. *to be funny: 웃기다	웃기지도 않다 *not to be funny: 웃기지 않다
I am not <u>even</u> <u>hungry</u>.	배고프지도

*to be hungry: 배고프다	*not to be hungry: 배고프지 않다

5. conjunctive suffix: noun+ And(와/과 or (이)랑 or 하고) +Noun

1) noun ending in consonant + 과 or 이랑 or 하고

•the mountain(산) <u>and</u> the ocean(바다): 산<u>과</u> 바다/산<u>이랑</u> 바다/산<u>하고</u> 바다

*산 ends in consonant ㄴ.

2) noun ending in vowel + 와 or 랑 or 하고

•a paper(종이) <u>and</u> a pencil(연필): 종이<u>와</u> 연필/종<u>이랑</u> 연필/종이<u>하고</u> 연필

*이 ends in vowel ㅣ.

※랑 is the most informal expression while 와/과 is very formal. 와/과 is the most commonly written expression. 하고 is placed between 랑 and 와 in terms of its formality. 하고 is most frequently spoken expression.

Examples:

•You(너) <u>and</u> I(나): 너<u>와</u> 나/너<u>랑</u> 나/너<u>하고</u> 나   *너 ends in vowel ㅓ.

•a house(집) <u>and</u> a car(차): 집<u>과</u> 차/집<u>이랑</u> 차/집<u>하고</u> 차

*집 ends in consonant ㅂ.

•my friend(친구) <u>and</u> family(가족): 친구<u>와</u> 가족/친구<u>랑</u> 가족/친구<u>하고</u> 가족

•relaxation(휴식) <u>and</u> workout(운동): 휴식<u>과</u> 운동/휴식<u>이랑</u> 운동/휴식<u>하고</u> 운동

Exercise 15. Fill in the blanks with the appropriate Korean equivalent to the underlined marker.

Korean Language: Grammar Pattern

conjunctive suffix AND	conjunctive suffix AND in Korean: (이)랑 or 와/과 or 하고
the King(왕) <u>and</u> I(나)	왕과 나/왕이랑 나/왕하고 나
Beauty(미녀) <u>and</u> the Beast(야수)	미녀와 야수/미녀랑 야수/미녀하고 야수
football(축구) <u>and</u> baseball(야구)	축구와 야구/축구랑 야구/축구하고 야구
a drum(드럼) <u>and</u> a guitar(기타)	드럼과 기타/드럼이랑 기타/드럼하고 기타
Korea(한국) <u>and</u> Korean(한국어)	한국과 한국어/한국이랑 한국어/한국하고 한국어
coffee(커피) <u>and</u> tea(차)	키피와 차/커피랑 차/커피하고 차
the cause(원인) <u>and</u> the effect(결과)	원인과 결과/원인이랑 결과/원인하고 결과

6. suffix for purpose/intention: 러 or 으러

※The English equivalent to (으)러 is 'IN ORDER TO.

1) root verb stem ending in consonant + 으러

•in order to catch: 잡으러   *to catch: 잡다

*잡 ends in consonant ㅂ. Drop 다 from the root verb stem and add 으러.

2) root verb stem ending in vowel or consonant ㄹ + 러

•in order to give: 주러   *to give: 주다

*주 ends in vowel ㅜ. Drop 다 from the root verb stem and add just 러.

•in order to grind: 갈러   *to grind: 갈다

Korean Language: Grammar Pattern

*갈 ends in consonant ㄹ. Drop 다 from root verb stem and add just 러.

3) root verb stem ending in consonant ㄷ: Irregular change rule applies to only 듣다(to listen)/싣다(to load)/걷다(to walk)/묻다(to ask). In this case, ㄷ is dropped and ㄹ으러 is added. For the other verbs ending in ㄷ, regular change rule applies. See the following Table 3 for more information.

Table 3   *Marks in Italic* are incorrect.

root verb stem ending in ㄷ	suffix for purpose/intention=in order to: 으러 or ㄹ으러
듣다 to listen	들으러 *듣으러* *ㄷ is dropped and ㄹ으러 is added.
싣다 to load	실으러 *싣으러*
걷다 to walk	걸으러 *걷으러*
묻다 to ask	물으러 *묻으러*
받다 to receive	받으러
믿다 to believe	믿으러
얻다 to gain/to obtain	얻으러
딛다 to step	딛으러

Korean Language: Grammar Pattern

걷다 to collect/to pick up	걷<u>으러</u>
닫다 to close	닫<u>으러</u>
묻다 to bury	묻<u>으러</u>

4) root verb stem ending in ㅂ: Irregular change rule applies to mostly static verbs. In this case, ㅂ is dropped and 우러 is added.   Among action verbs, 깁다(to sew)/눕다(to lie down)/돕다(to help) fall in this case.

•in order to sew/lie down/help(깁다/눕다/돕다): 기<u>우러</u>/누<u>우러</u>/도<u>우러</u>

*ㅂ is dropped and 우러 is added.   *깁으러/눕으러/돕으러 is incorrect.

•in order to be happy(즐겁다): 즐거우러

*즐겁다(to be happy) is static verb. 겁 ends in consonant ㅂ. Drop 다 from root verb stem and add 우러.

Examples:

•in order <u>to see</u>: 보러   *to see: 보다

•in order <u>to catch</u>: 잡<u>으러</u>   *to catch: 잡다

•in order <u>to study</u>: 공부하<u>러</u>   *to study: 공부하다

•in order <u>to make</u>: 만들<u>러</u>   *만들으러 is incorrect.   *to make: 만들다

•in order <u>to read</u>: 읽<u>으러</u>   *to read: 읽다

•in order <u>to open</u>: 열<u>러</u>   *열으러 is incorrect.   *to open: 열다

•in order <u>to close</u>: 닫<u>으러</u>   *to close: 닫다

Korean Language: Grammar Pattern

Exercise 16. Write the underlined part with the appropriate purpose marker in Korean.

suffix for purpose = (in order) to + verb	suffix for purpose in Korean: 으러 or 러 or ㄹ으러
in order <u>to run</u> *to run: 달리다	달리러　　*vowel ending + 러
in order <u>to bark</u> *to bark: 짖다	짖으러　　*consonant ending + 으러
in order <u>to block</u> *to block: 막다	막으러
in order <u>to eat</u> *to eat: 먹다	먹으러
in order <u>to cut</u> *to cut: 자르다	자르러
in order <u>to do</u> *to do: 하다	하러
in order <u>to win</u> *to win: 이기다	이기러
in order <u>to run</u> *to run: 달리다	달리러
in order <u>to boil</u> *to boil: 삶다/끓이다	삶으러/끓이러
in order <u>to receive</u> *to receive: 받다	받으러
in order <u>to roll</u>	말러　　*말으러

[여기에 입력]
Korean Language: Grammar Pattern

*to roll: 말다	
in order <u>to ask</u> *to ask: 묻다	묻으러
in order <u>to forget</u> *to forget: 잊다	잊으러
in order <u>to pay back</u> *to pay back: 갚다	갚으러
in order <u>to tell</u> *to tell: 말하다	말하러
in order <u>to write</u> *to write: 쓰다	쓰러

Exercise 17. Read the following sentences and draw a line under the markers or suffixes.

나<u>는</u> 학교<u>에</u> 갔습니다. *나: I/학교: school/갔습니다: went	*는: subject marker *에: direction marker
그<u>는</u> 그녀<u>를</u> 사랑합니다. *그: he/그녀: her/사랑합니다: loves	*는: subject marker/를: object marker
당신<u>의</u> 취미<u>는</u> 무엇입니까? *당신: you/취미: hobby 무엇: what	*의: possessive marker *는: subject marker
한국어<u>를</u> 배우<u>러</u> 한국<u>으로</u> 오세요. *한국어: Korean language/한국: Korea/배우다: to learn/오다: to come	*를: object marker *러: method marker *으러: direction marker
한국어<u>는</u> 어렵<u>다고</u> 말합니다.	*는: subject marker

Korean Language: Grammar Pattern

*어렵다: to be difficult/말하다: to say	*다고: statement quotation suffix
어머니**는** 나**의** 방**을** 청소하**라고** 나**에게** 말했습니다. *어머니: mother/나: I/방: room/청소하다: to clean up/말했다: to have said	*는: subject marker *의: possessive marker *을: object marker *라고: command quotation suffix *에게: direction marker
어디**에서** 점심**을** 먹었**냐고** 친구**가** 물었습니다. *어디: where/점심: lunch/친구: friend/먹다: to eat/묻다: to ask	*에서: location marker *을: object marker * 냐고: question quotation suffix *가: subject marker
저**는** 한국**에서** 왔습니다. *한국: Korea/왔다: to have come	*는: subject marker *에서: direction marker
부산**보다** 서울**이** 더 춥습니다. *부산: Busan/서울: Seoul/춥다: to be cold/더: more	*보다: comparison marker *이: topic marker
소금**이** 눈**처럼** 보입니다. *소금: salt/눈: snow/보이다: to be seen	*이: topic marker *처럼: comparison marker
나**만** 왕따**가** 되었습니다. *왕따: bullied person/되다:to become	*만: supplement marker *가: subject marker
그녀**는** 바다**를** 바라보**기만** 했습니다. *그녀: she/바다: ocean/바라보다: to look at	*는: subject marker *를: object marker *기만: supplement suffix
우리**도** 동의했습니다. *우리: we/동의하다: to agree	*도: supplement suffix

Korean Language: Grammar Pattern

쥐**는** 고양이 앞**에서** 조금**도** 움직이지도 못했습니다. *쥐: rat/고양이: cat/앞: front/움직이다: to move/조금: a little/못하다: can not	*는: subject marker *에서: location marker *도: supplement suffix *지도: supplement suffix ※조금도: even a little
그**는** 항상 나**와** 커피**를** 마시고 싶어 합니다. *그: he/항상: always/커피: coffee/마시다: to drink/싶어 하다: to like to	*는: subject marker *와: conjunctive suffix *를: object marker
그들**은** 친구들**이랑** 등산**을** 갔습니다. *그들: they/친구들: friends/등산: hiking/갔다: to have gone	*은: subject marker *이랑: conjunctive suffix *을: object marker
우리**하고** 갈래요? *우리: we/가다: to go/...래요?: would you like to?	*하고: conjunctive suffix
나**는** 컴퓨터**로** 일합니다. *나: I/컴퓨터: computer/일하다: to work	*는: subject marker *로: method marker
우리들**은** 바다**를** 보**러** 부산**에** 갔습니다. *우리들: we/바다: sea/보다: to see/부산: Busan/갔다: to have gone(=went)	*은: subject marker *를: object marker *러: purpose suffix *에: direction marker
그**는** 내**가** 학생이**냐고** 물었습니다. *그: he/내: I/학생: student/물었다: to have asked	*는: subject marker *가: topic marker *냐고: question quotation suffix

Korean Language: Grammar Pattern

무엇**으로** 과일**을** 자릅니까? *무엇: what/과일: fruit/자르다: to cut	*으로: method marker *을: object marker
개**와** 산책하**러** 밖**에** 나갔습니다. *개: dog/산책하다: to take a walk/밖: outside/나갔다: to have gone	*와: conjunctive suffix *러: purpose suffix *에: direction marker
엄마**가** 나**에게** 방**을** 청소하**라고** 말했습니다. *엄마: mom/나: I/방: room/청소하다: to clean up/말했다: to have told	*가: subject marker *에게: direction marker *을: object marker *라고: command suffix
친구**가** 학교**에서** 나**를** 기다립니다. *친구: friend/학교: school/나: I/기다리다: to wait	*가: subject marker *에서: location marker *를: object marker

UNIT 7. VERB STEM & TENSE

Root verb stem and verb stem in 6 other tenses (past, present, future, past progressive, present progressive and future progressive tense) are critically important because the changes in verb endings are entirely based on the verb stem. In other words, root verb stem and verb stem in various tenses are the starting points of all types of verb endings including but not limited to formal and informal statement/question/ command/order, modifying verbs, adjectives and adverbs, conjunctions, gerund, subjunctive mood, passive voice, auxiliary verbs, etc. It is required to have the knowledge of root verb stem and the other verb stems in order to have a good command of creating appropriate verb endings. It is not a root verb stem or a verb stem in various tenses which will be actually spoken or written to be communicated in real life situation.   Verb stems are not the final products to be spoken or written but provide the important basis of verb endings for the finally spoken or written statement, question and command.

There are two types of verb stems; one is root verb stem and the others are verb stems in various tenses.

Root verb stem is the original form of verb before a change is applied to verb endings. Compared with English grammar, root verb stem is like infinitives with or without 'to' such as 'to eat', 'to run', etc. Verb stems in various tenses are modified from the root verb stem to reflect each tense because root verb stem implies no information on tense at all.   The root verb stem of 'to do'(하다) has no clue on tense.   'To have done'(했다) is in past tense.   'To be going to do'(하겠다/할 것이다/할 거다) is in future tense.   'To have been doing'(하고 있었다) is in past progressive tense.   'To be doing'(하고 있다) is in present progressive tense.   'To be going to be doing'(하고 있겠다/하고 있을 것이다/하고 있을 거다) is in future progressive tense.

There are 7 different types of verb stems:

1. root verb stem (to + original verb):

Korean Language: Grammar Pattern

•가다: to go

•오다: to come

•잡다: to catch

•먹다: to eat

•보다: to see

2. verb stem in past tense (to have + past particle):

ㅆ다 or 었다 or 았다

•갔다: to have gone = went

•왔다: to have come = came

•잡았다: to have caught = caught

•먹었다: to have eaten = ate

•봤다(보았다): to have seen = saw

※ㅆ or 았 or 었 implies an action in the past.

3. verb stem in present tense: ㄴ다 or 는다

•간다: goes

•온다: comes

•잡는다: catches

•먹는다: eats

•본다: sees

※ㄴ or 는 implies an action in the present.

4. verb stem in future tense (to be going to + verb = will + verb):

겠다 or (ㄹ/을) 것이다 or (ㄹ/을) 거다

• 가겠다/갈 것이다/갈 거다: to be going to go = will go

• 오겠다/올 것이다/올 거다: to be going to come = will come

• 잡겠다/잡을 것이다/잡을 거다: to be going to catch = will catch

• 먹겠다/먹을 것이다/먹을 거다: to be going to eat = will eat

• 보겠다/볼 것이다/볼 거다: to be going to see = will see

※ㄹ or 을 implies an action the future.   implies an intention in the future.

5. verb stem in past progressive tense (to have been + present particle =was/were + present particle): 고 있었다

• 가고 있었다: to have been going = was going

• 오고 있었다: to have been coming = was coming

• 잡고 있었다: to have been catching = was catching

• 먹고 있었다: to have been eating = was eating

• 보고 있었다: to have been seeing = was seeing

※고 implies a progressive action and 었 implies an action in the past.

6. verb stem in present progressive tense (to be + present particle = am/are/is + present particle): 고 있다

• 가고 있다: to be going = am/are/is going

• 오고 있다: to be coming = am/are/is coming

• 잡고 있다: to be catching = am/are/is catching

• 먹고 있다: to be eating = am/are/is eating

•보고 있다: to be seeing = am/are/is seeing

※고 implies a progressive action.

7. verb stem in future progressive tense (to be going to be + present particle = will be + present particle): 고 있겠다 or 고 있을 것이다 or 고 있을 거다

•가고 있겠다/가고 있을 것이다/가고 있을 거다: to be going to be going = will be going

•오고 있겠다/오고 있을 것이다/있을 거다: to be going to be coming = will be coming

•잡고 있겠다/잡고 있을 것이다/잡고 있을 거다: to be going to be catching = will be catching

※고 implies a progressive action. 겠 implies a future intention and 을 implies an action in the future. 있겠다 is the most formal and 있을 거다 is the most informal expression. When written, 있겠다 is better and when spoken, 있을 거다 is better. Both are perfect to write and speak.

※Korean root verb stems are equivalent to English root infinitives like (to) go, (to) come, or (to) speak, etc.   Refer to the following grid for the examples of root verb stems.   The final syllable 다 of verb stems will be dropped to modify various verb endings.

1. root verb stems: '(to)+ original verb'

root verb stem: *to + original verb	Korean root verb stem ending in 다 *다 will be dropped for various verb endings.
to cry	울다

Korean Language: Grammar Pattern

to study	공부하다
to have	가지다
to agree	동의하다
to hit	때리다/치다
to walk	걷다
to work	일하다
to enjoy	즐기다
to eat	먹다
to drink	마시다
to send	보내다
to begin	시작하다
to earn	벌다
to edit	편집하다
to meet	만나다
to ride	타다
to be high	높다
to be heavy	무겁다
to be cold	춥다
to die	죽다
to be angry	화나다
to be difficult	어렵다
to be easy	쉽다
to borrow	빌리다

Korean Language: Grammar Pattern

to wear	입다
to connect	연결하다
to be sad	슬프다
to be good	좋다
to be dark	어둡다
to be expensive	비싸다
to wash	씻다
to know	알다

※There are six major tenses which include past, present, future, past progressive, present progressive and future progressive tense.   The followings are the verb stem in each tense. The verb endings will be modified from the verb stem for the finally spoken and written statement, question and command.

2. verb stems in past tense: 썼다 or 았다 or 었다

※ㅆ or 았 or 었 implies an action in the past.

※The linking vowel decides on either 았다 or 었다.

1) root verb stem ending in the linking vowels of ㅗ or ㅛ WITH or WITHOUT ending consonant + 았다

•보다(to see): 보았다 or shortly 봤다(to have seen = saw)

*보 ends in linking vowel ㅗ and has no ending consonant.   Drop 다 and add 았다.   봤다 is a short form of 보았다. 봤다 sounds more natural and informal than 보았다.

Korean Language: Grammar Pattern

•녹다(to melt down): 녹았다(to have melted down = melted down)

*The linking vowel of 녹 is ㅗ and it has an ending consonant of ㄱ. Drop 다 and add 았다.

2-1) root verb stem ending in the linking vowels of ㅏ or ㅑ WITH ending consonant + 았다

•막다(to block): 막았다(to have blocked=blocked)

*막 ends in vowel ㅏ and has ending consonant ㄱ. Drop 다 and add 았다.

2-2) root verb stem ending in the linking vowels of ㅏ or ㅑ WITHOUT ending consonant + ㅆ다

•사다(to buy): 샀다(to have bought=bought)

*사 ends in vowel ㅏ and has no ending consonant. Drop 다 and add just ㅆ다.

3) root verb stem ending in the linking vowels of ㅜ or ㅠ or ― or ㅣ WITH or WITHOUT ending consonant + 었다

•비우다 (to empty): 비웠다=비우었다(to have emptied=emptied)

*우 ends in vowel ㅜ and has no ending consonant. Drop 다 and add just 었다.

•이기다 (to win): 이겼다=이기었다(to have won=won)

*기 ends in vowel ㅣ. Drop 다 and add just 었다. 비웠다 and 이겼다 are short forms which are preferably spoken or written.

•숨다 (to hide): 숨었다 (to have hidden = hid)

*숨 ends in linking vowel ㅜ and has ending consonant ㅁ. Drop 다 and add 었다.

4-1) root verb stem ending in the linking vowels of ㅓ or ㅕ WITH ending consonant + 었다

Korean Language: Grammar Pattern

•접다(to fold): 접었다(to have folded=folded)

*접 ends in vowel ㅓ and has ending consonant ㅂ. Drop 다 and add 었다.

4-2) root verb stem ending in the linking vowels of ㅓ or ㅕ WITHOUT ending consonant + ㅆ다

*서다(to stand up): 섰다(to have stood up=stood up)   *서었다 is incorrect.

*서 ends in vowel ㅓ and has no ending consonant. Drop 다 and simply add ㅆ다.

5) root verb stem ending in consonant of ㄷ:

Irregular change rule applies to 듣다(to listen)/싣다(to load)/걷다(to walk)/묻다(to ask). In this case, ㄷ is dropped and ㄹ 었다 is added. To the other verbs ending in ㄷ, regular change rule applies, in which ㄷ is kept and 았다 or 었다 is added. See the following Table 4 for the comparison of the verb stems ending in ㄷ in past tense.

Table 4   *Marks in Italic are incorrect.

root verb stem ending in ㄷ	verb stem in past tense: ㅆ다 or 았다 or 었다 ※The linking vowel decides on either 았다 or 었다.
듣다 *to listen	들었다 *듣었다 to have listened
싣다 *to load	실었다 *싣었다 to have loaded
걷다 *to walk	걸었다 *걷었다 to have walked

Korean Language: Grammar Pattern

묻다 *to ask	물었다　　*묻었다 to have asked
받다 *to receive	받았다 to have received
믿다 *to believe	믿었다 to have believed
얻다 *to gain/to obtain	얻었다 to have gained/obtained
딛다 *to step	딛었다 to have stepped
걷다 *to collect/to pick up	걷었다 to have collected/picked up
닫다 *to close	닫았다 to have closed
묻다 *to bury	묻었다 to have buried

6) root verb stem ending in ㅂ:

Irregular change rule applies to mostly but not all static verbs(to be + adjective) ending in ㅂ.　In this case, ㅂ is dropped and 우었다(=shortly 웠다) or 오았다(=shortly 왔다) is added.　Even though 깁다(to sew) and 눕다(to lie down) and 돕다(to help) are action verbs, irregular change rule applies. For the other ㅂ ending verbs, regular change rule applies.　See the following Table 5 for the comparison of the verb stems ending in ㅂ in past tense.

Table 5　　*Marks in Italic are incorrect.

root verb stems ending in ㅂ	verb stems in past tense:

Korean Language: Grammar Pattern

	았다 or 었다 or 웠다 *Pay attention to linking vowels.
잡다 *to catch	잡았다 to have caught
업다 *to carry on the back	업었다 to have carried on the back
입다 *to wear	입었다 to have worn
좁다 *to be narrow ※This is a static verb but regular change rule applies.	좁았다 to have been narrow
접다 *to fold	접었다 to have folded
뽑다 *to select	뽑았다 to have selected
씹다 *to chew	씹었다 to have chewed
맵다 *to be spicy *Hereafter irregular change rule applies.	매웠다　　*맵었다 to have been spicy *매웠다 is a short form of 매우었다. Short forms of speech sound much more natural and are more generally written and spoken.
춥다 *to be cold	추웠다　　*춥었다 to have been cold

Korean Language: Grammar Pattern

덥다 *to be hot	더웠다 **덥었다* to have been hot
답다 *to be like	다웠다 **답았다* to have been like
무겁다 *to be heavy	무거웠다 **무겁었다* to have heavy
가렵다 *to be itchy	가려웠다 **가렵었다* to have itchy
가엽다 *to be pathetic	가여웠다 **가엽었다* to have pathetic
눕다 *to lie down ※This is an active verb but irregular change rule applies.	누웠다 **눕었다* to have lain down
가소롭다 *to be ridiculous	가소로웠다 **가소롭았다* to have been ridiculous
어렵다 *to be difficult	어려웠다 **어렵었다* to have been difficult
쉽다 *to be easy	쉬웠다 **쉽었다* to have been easy
돕다 *to help ※This is an active verbs but irregular change rule applies.	도왔다 **돕았다* to have helped ※vowel ㅏ + 왔다

Korean Language: Grammar Pattern

더럽다 *to be dirty	더러웠다 *더럽었다 to have been dirty
우습다 *to be funny	우스웠다 to have been funny *우습었다
고맙다 *to be thankful	고마웠다 *고맙았다 to have been thankful
밉다 *to be hateful	미웠다 *밉었다 to have been hateful
무섭다 *to be scary	무서웠다 *무섭었다 to have been scary
귀엽다 *to be cute	귀여웠다 *귀엽었다 to have been cute
즐겁다 *to be happy	즐거웠다 *즐겁었다 to have been happy

7-1) linking vowels of ㅏ or ㅑ or ㅗ or ㅛ + 르다: Drop 르다 and add ㄹ랐다.

•바르다(to apply): 발랐다(to have applied)

*바 ends in vowel ㅏ. Drop 르다 from the verb stem and add ㄹ랐다.   바렀다 or 바랐다 is incorrect.

7-2) linking vowels of ㅜ or ㅠ or ㅓ or ㅕ or ㅡ or ㅣ + 르다: Drop 르다 and add ㄹ렀다.

•부르다(to call): 불렀다(to have called)

*부 ends in the linking vowel of ㅜ. Drop 르다 from the verb stem and add ㄹ렀다. 부렀다 is incorrect.   See the following Table 6 for more details.

Korean Language: Grammar Pattern

Table 6   *Marks in Italic are incorrect

root verb stem ending in 르다	verb stem in past tense: ㄹ랐다 or ㄹ렀다 ※A linking vowel decides on either 랐다 or 렀다
바르다 *to apply	발랐다 *바랐다 to have applied See 7-1)
부르다 *to call	불렀다 *부렀다 to have called See 7-2)
자르다 *to cut	잘랐다 *자랐다 to have cut
노래 부르다 *to sing	노래 불렀다 *노래 부렀다 to have sung
마르다 *to be skinny	말랐다 *마랐다 to have been skinny
오르다 *to rise/to climb	올랐다 *오랐다 to have risen/to have climbed
소리지르다 *to shout	소리질렀다 *소리지렀다 to have shouted
흐르다 *to flow	흘렀다 *흐렀다 to have flown
이르다 *to be early	일렀다 *이렀다 to have been early
벼르다	별렀다 *벼렀다

Korean Language: Grammar Pattern

*to be determined	to have been determined

※Drop 다 from root verb stem and add 씼다 or 았다 or 었다 for verb stems in past tense.   Short forms of verbs are preferred to regular forms.

Examples:

•붙이다(to attach): 붙이었다 or shortly 붙였다(to have attached)

*linking vowel ㅣ with no ending consonant + 었다

•이다(to be): 이었다 or shortly 였다(to have been)

*linking vowel ㅣ with no ending consonant + 었다

•되다(to become): 되었다 or shortly 됐다(to have become)

*linking vowel ㅣ with no ending consonant + 었다

•믿다(to believe): 믿었다(to have believed)

*linking vowel ㅣ with ending consonant ㄷ + 었다

•부수다(to break): 부수었다 or shortly 부쉈다(to have broken)

*linking vowel ㅜ with no ending consonant + 었다

•가져오다(to bring): 가져왔다(to have brought)   *왔다 is the short form of 오았다.

*linking vowel ㅗ with no ending consonant + 았다

•사다(to buy): 샀다(to have bought)   *사 ends in vowel ㅏ with no ending consonant.   In this case, just add 씼다.   *사았다 is incorrect.

•씹다(to chew): 씹었다(to have chewed)

*linking vowel ㅣ with ending consonant ㅂ + 었다

•울다(to cry): 울었다(to have cried)

*linking vowel ㅜ with ending consonant ㄹ + 었다

•출발하다(to depart): 출발했다(to have departed)

[여기에 입력]
Korean Language: Grammar Pattern

*하 ends in the vowel ㅏ with no ending consonant. So just add 했다. *_핬다_ or _하았다_ is incorrect. This rule applies to all the '하다-verbs'.

•하다(to do): 했다(to have done)

•말리다(to dry): 말리었다 or shortly 말렸다(to have dried)

*linking vowel ㅣ with no ending consonant + 었다

•지우다(to erase): 지우었다 or shortly 지웠다(to have erased)

*linking vowel ㅜ with no ending consonant + 었다

•있다(to exist): 있었다(to have existed)

*linking vowel ㅣ with ending consonant ㅆ + 었다

•볶다(to fry): 볶았다(to have fried)

*linking vowel ㅗ with ending consonant ㄲ + 았다

•가다(to go): 갔다(to have gone)

*가 ends in vowel ㅏ with no ending consonant. In this case, just add ㅆ다. _가았다_ is incorrect.

•갈다(to grind): 갈았다(to have ground)

*linking vowel ㅏ with ending consonant ㄹ + 았다

•걸다(to hang): 걸었다(to have hung)   ※to walk(걷다): to have walked(걸었다)

*linking vowel ㅓ with ending consonant ㄹ + 었다

•즐겁다(to be happy): 즐거우었다 or 즐거웠다(to have been happy)

*In the case of static verb ending in ㅂ, ㅂ is dropped and 웠다.

•붙잡다(to hold): 붙잡았다(to have held)

*linking vowel ㅏ with ending consonant ㅂ + 았다

•배고프다(to be hungry): 배고팠다(to have been hungry)

※This is an irregular change. _배고펐다_ is incorrect.

[여기에 입력]
Korean Language: Grammar Pattern

•웃다(to laugh): 웃었다(to have laughed)

*linking vowel ㅜ with ending consonant ㅅ + 었다

•배우다(to learn): 배우었다 or shortly 배웠다(to have learned)

*linking vowel ㅜ with no ending consonant + 었다

•살다(to live): 살았다(to have lived)

*linking vowel ㅏ with ending consonant ㄹ + 았다

•만들다(to make): 만들었다(to have made)

*linking vowel ㅡ with ending consonant ㄹ + 었다

•채굴하다(to mine): 채굴했다(to have mined)   *This is one of the '하다-verbs'.

•열다(to open): 열었다(to have opened)

*linking vowel ㅕ with ending consonant ㄹ + 었다

•준비하다(to prepare): 준비했다(to have prepared)   *This is also '하다-verb'.

•받다(to receive): 받았다(to have received)

*linking vowel ㅏ with ending consonant ㄷ + 았다

•말다(to roll): 말았다(to have rolled)

*linking vowel ㅏ with ending consonant ㄹ + 았다

•슬프다(to be sad)→슬펐다(to have been sad)

*linking vowel ㅡ with no ending consonant + 었다   *슬프었다 is incorrect.

•보다(to see): 보았다 or shortly 봤다(to have seen)

*linking vowel ㅗ with no ending consonant + 았다

•앉다(to sit): 앉았다(to have sat)

*linking vowel ㅏ with ending consonant ㄵ + 았다

•뽑다(to select): 뽑았다(to have selected)

*linking vowel ㅗ with ending consonant ㅂ + 았다

•서다(to stand): 섰다(to have stood)

*서 ends in vowel ㅓ with no ending consonant. Therefore, just add 쎴다.
서었다 is not correct.

•입다(to wear): 입었다(to have worn)

*linking vowel ㅣ with ending consonant ㅂ + 었다

3. verb stem in present tense: ㄴ다 or 는다

Verb stems have their value only when their endings are modified to fit the right
sentence types including but not limited to statement, question and command. The
right sentence means the one with the honorific endings and will be finally written
and spoken in real life situation. Verb stems in various tenses are like blunt
expression and they sound rude and impolite. However, learning verb stems is a
critically important process which cannot be skipped for the acquisition of the
honorific sentences. It is available only by modifying the ending of verb stems to
create a honorific sentence which is the final goal of Korean language acquisition.

1) root verb stem ending in consonant + 는다

•먹다(to eat): 먹는다

*먹 ends in consonant ㄱ. Drop 다 from root verb stem and add 는다.

2) root verb stem ending in vowel + ㄴ다

•보다(to see): 본다

*보 ends in vowel ㅗ. Just add ㄴ다.

3) root verb stem ending in the consonant of ㄹ: ㄹ is dropped and ㄴ다 is added.
The following verbs end in ㄹ. Ending ㄹ is dropped and ㄴ다 is added for verb
stem in present tense. If the verb is a static verb, the verb stem in present tense is

Korean Language: Grammar Pattern

the same as the root verb stem.   See the following Table 7 for more information on verb stems in present tense.

Table 7   *Marks in Italic* are incorrect.

root verb stem ending in ㄹ	verb stem in present tense *Drop the ending consonant ㄹ and add ㄴ다.
팔다 *to sell	판다 **팔는다* sells
울다 *to cry	운다 **울는다* cries
불다 *to blow	분다 **불는다* blows
밀다 *to push	민다 **밀는다* pushes
열다 *to open	연다 **열는다* opens
몰다 *to drive	몬다 **몰는다* drives
멀다 *to be far	멀다 **멀는다* ※This is a static verb. am/are/is far
알다 *to know	안다 **알는다* knows
놀다 *to play/to hang out	논다 **놀는다* plays/hangs out
줄다	준다 **줄는다*

Korean Language: Grammar Pattern

*to decrease	decreases
머물다 *to stay	머문다 *머무는다 stays
돌다 *to turn	돈다 *도는다 turns
빌다 *to beg	빈다 *비는다 begs
만들다 *to make	만든다 *만드는다 makes
끌다 *to drag	끈다 *끄는다 drags
갈다 *to grind/to change	간다 *가는다 grinds/changes
들다 *to pick up/to raise	든다 *드는다 picks up/raises
길다 *to be long	길다 *길는다/긴다 ※This is a static verb. am/are/is long
얼다 to freeze	언다 *어는다 freezes
졸다 *to doze off	존다 *조는다 dozes off
흔들다 *to shake	흔든다 *흔드는다 shakes
풀다	푼다 *푸는다

Korean Language: Grammar Pattern

*to solve/to untie	solves/unties
살다 *to live	산다　　**살는다* lives
벌다 *to earn	번다　　*벌는다* earns
물다 *to bite	문다　　*물는다* bites
걸다 *to hang	건다　　*걸는다* hangs
말다 *to roll	만다　　*말는다* rolls
날다 *to fly	난다　　*날는다* flies
빨다 *to wash/to suck	빤다　　*빨는다* washes/sucks
늘다 *to increase	는다　　*늘는다* increases
부풀다 *to swell	부푼다　*부풀는다* swells
기울다 *to incline	기운다　*기울는다* inclines

※Verbs ending in the consonant of ㄷ or ㅂ have NO irregular changes.

•걷다(to walk): 걷는다

[여기에 입력]
Korean Language: Grammar Pattern

*걷 ends in consonant. Drop 다 from root verb stem and add 는다.

•돕다(to help): 돕는다

*돕 ends in consonant ㅂ. Drop 다 from root verb stem and add 는다.

※In the case of 'be-verb(am/are/is)+adjective' or static verb, the verb stem in present tense is the same as the root verb stem.

•am/are/is fast(verb stem in present tense) =t o be fast(root verb stem): 빠르다
*빠른다 is incorrect.

•am/are/is big(verb stem in present tense) = to be big(root verb stem): 크다 *큰다 is incorrect.

•am/are/is deep(verb stem in present tense) = to be big(root verb stem): 깊다
*깊는다 is incorrect.

Examples:

•믿다(to believe): 믿는다(believes)   *consonant ending + 는다

•부수다(to break): 부순다(breaks)   *vowel ending + ㄴ다

•가져오다(to bring): 가져온다(brings)   *vowel ending + ㄴ다

•사다(to buy): 산다(buys)   *vowel ending + ㄴ다

※살다(to live): 산다(lives)   See the verbs ending in ㄹ.

•부르다(to call): 부른다(calls)   *vowel ending + s 다

•씹다(to chew): 씹는다(chews)   *consonant ending + 는다

•자르다(to cut): 자른다(cuts)   *vowel ending + ㄴ다

•하다(to do): 한다(does)   *vowel ending + ㄴ다

•출발하다(to depart): 출발한다(departs)   *vowel ending + ㄴ다

•이르다(to be early): 이르다(is early)   *이르다 is a static verb.

Korean Language: Grammar Pattern

*The verb stem in present tense of a static verb is the same as the root verb stem. *이른다* is incorrect.

• 흐르다(to flow): 흐른다(flows)   *vowel ending + ㄴ다

• 접다(to fold): 접는다(folds)   *consonant ending + 는다

• 볶다(to fry): 볶는다(fries)   *consonant ending + 는다

• 가다(to go): 간다(goes)   *vowel ending + ㄴ다

• 기쁘다(to be happy): 기쁘다(is happy)   *기쁜다 is incorrect.

• 붙잡다(to hold): 붙잡는다(holds)   *consonant ending + 는다

• 배고프다(to be hungry): 배고프다(is hungry)   *배고픈다 is incorrect.

• 웃다(to laugh): 웃는다(laughs)   *consonant ending + 는다

• 싣다(to load): 싣는다(loads)   *consonant ending + 는다

• 슬프다(to be sad): 슬프다(is sad)   *슬픈다 is incorrect.

• 보다(to see): 본다(sees)   *vowel ending + ㄴ다

• 뽑다(to select): 뽑는다(selects)   *consonant ending + 는다

• 배우다(to learn): 배운다(learns)   *vowel ending + ㄴ다

• 채굴하다(to mine): 채굴한다(mines)   *vowel ending + ㄴ다

• 오르다(to rise): 오른다(rises)   *vowel ending + ㄴ다

• 소리지르다(to shout): 소리지른다(shouts)   *vowel ending + ㄴ다

• 서다(to stand): 선다(stands)   *vowel ending + ㄴ다

• 준비하다(to prepare): 준비한다(prepares)   *vowel ending + ㄴ다

• 받다(to receive): 받는다(receives)   *consonant ending + 는다

• 입다(to wear): 입는다(wears)   *consonant ending + 는다

• 귀엽다(to be cute): 귀엽다(is cute)   *귀엽다 is a static verb.   *귀엽는다

4. verb stems in future tense: 겠다 or (ㄹ/을) 것이다 or (ㄹ/을) 거다

*겠 implies future intention or determination rather than future tense.   And ㄹ or 을 means simple future tense. When spoken, ㄹ/을 거다 is preferred for simple future tense. Verb stem in future tense has no irregular changes. ㄹ/을 것이다 sounds too formal and serious.   This is not very frequently used in real life situation.   Instead, formally 겠다 or informally ㄹ/을 거다 can be alternatives.

1) root verb stem ending in consonant + 겠다/을 것이다/을 거다

•읽다(to read): 읽겠다/읽을 것이다/읽을 거다(to be going to read = will read)

*읽 ends in combined consonant ㄹㄱ.   Drop 다 from root verb stem and add 겠다/을 것이다/을 거다.

•녹다(to melt down): 녹겠다/녹을 것이다/녹을 거다(to be going to melt down)

*녹 ends in consonant ㄱ.   Drop 다 and add 겠다/을 것이다/을 거다

2) root verb stem ending in vowel + 겠다/ㄹ 것이다/ㄹ 거다

•사다(to buy): 사겠다/살 것이다/살 거다 (to be going to buy = will buy)

*사 ends in vowel ㅏ.   Drop 다 from root verb stem and add 겠다/ㄹ 것이다/ㄹ 거다.

•마시다(to drink): 마시겠다/마실 것이다/마실 거다 (to be going to drink = will drink)

*시 ends in vowel ㅣ.   Drop 다 from root verb stem and add 겠다/ㄹ 것이다/ㄹ 거다.

3) root verb stem ending in ㄹ + 겠다/것이다/거다

•팔다(to sell): 팔겠다/팔 것이다/팔 거다 (to be going to sell=will sell)

*팔 ends in ㄹ. Add just 것이다.

•알다(to know): 알 겠다/알 것이다/알 거다 (to be going to know = will know)

Korean Language: Grammar Pattern

*알 ends in ㄹ. Drop 다 and simply add 겠다/것이다/거다.

4) root verb stem ending in consonant ㅂ

*The verb stems ending in ㅂ have both regular and irregular verb change in future tense.   Regular verb change rule applies to most action verbs. Irregular verb change rule applies to static verbs ending in ㅂ.   For the irregular change, ㅂ is dropped from root verb stem and 울 것이다 or 울 거다 is added.   Among action verbs ending in ㅂ, irregular change rule is applied to 깁다(to sew) and 눕다(to lie down) and 돕다(to help).   See the following Table 8 for detailed verb stems in future tense.

Table 8   *Marks in Italic are incorrect.

root verb stem ending in ㅂ	verb stem in future tense 겠다 or 을 것이다 or 을 거다 /울 것이다/울 거다
잡다 *to catch	잡겠다/잡을 것이다/잡을 거다 to be going to catch
업다 *to carry on the back	업겠다/업을 것이다/업을 거다 to be going to carry on the back
입다 *to wear	입겠다/입을 것이다/입을 거다 to be going to wear
좁다 *to be narrow *This is a static verb but regular change rule applies.	좁겠다/좁을 것이다/좁을 거다 to be going to be narrow *조울 것이다/조울 거다
접다 *to fold	접겠다/접을 것이다/접을 거다 to be going to fold
뽑다	뽑겠다/뽑을 것이다/뽑을 거다

Korean Language: Grammar Pattern

*to select	to be going to select
씹다 *to chew	씹겠다/씹을 것이다/씹을 거다 to be going to chew
맵다 *to be spicy	맵겠다/매울 것이다/매울 거다 *맵을 것이다/맵을 거다　　*ㅂ is dropped. to be going to be spicy
춥다 *to be cold	춥겠다/추울 것이다/추울 거다 *춥을 것이다/춥을 거다 to be going to be cold
덥다 *to be hot	덥겠다/더울 것이다/더울 거다 *덥을 것이다/덥을 거다 to be going to be hot
무겁다 *to be heavy	무겁겠다/무거울 것이다/무거울 거다 *무겁을 것이다/무겁을 거다 to be going to be heavy
가렵다 *to be itchy	가렵겠다/가려울 것이다/가려울 거다 *가렵을 것이다/가렵을 거다 to be going to be itchy
가엽다 *to be pathetic	가엽겠다/가여울 것이다/가여울 거다 *가엽을 것이다/가렵을 거다 to be going to be pathetic
눕다 *to lie down	눕겠다/누울 것이다/누울 거다 *눕을 것이다/눕을 거다　　*ㅂ is dropped. to be going to lie down

Korean Language: Grammar Pattern

*This is an active verb but irregular change rule applies.	
가소롭다 *to be ridiculous	가소롭겠다/가소로울 것이다/가소로울 거다 *가소롭을 것이다/가소롭을 거다 to be going to be ridiculous
어렵다 *to be difficult	어렵겠다/어려울 것이다/어려울 거다 *어렵을 것이다/어렵을 거다 to be going to be difficult
쉽다 *to be easy	쉽겠다/쉬울 것이다/쉬울 거다 *쉽을 것이다/쉽을 거다 to be going to be easy
돕다 *to help *This is an active verb but irregular change rule applies.	돕겠다/도울 것이다/도울 거다 *돕을 것이다 l돕을 거다 to be going to help
더럽다 *to be dirty	더럽겠다/더러울 것이다/더러울 거다 *더럽을 것이다/더럽을 거다 to be going to be dirty
우습다 *to be funny	우습겠다/우스울 것이다/우스울 거다 *우습을 것이다/우습을 거다 to be going to be funny
고맙다 *to be thankful	고맙겠다/고마울 것이다/고마울 거다 *고맙을 것이다/고맙을 거다 to be going to be thankful
밉다 *to be hateful	밉겠다/미울 것이다/미울 거다 *밉을 것이다/밉을 거다

	to be going to be hateful
무섭다 *to be scary	무섭겠다/무서울 것이다/무서울 거다 *무섭을 것이다/무섭을 거다* to be going to be scary
귀엽다 *to be cute	귀엽겠다/귀여울 것이다/귀여울 거다 *귀엽을 것이다/귀엽을 거다* to be going to be cute
즐겁다 *to be happy	즐겁겠다/즐거울 것이다/즐거울 거다 *즐겁을 것이다/즐겁을 거다* to be going to be happy

5) root verb stem ending in ㄷ

*Among the verbs ending in consonant ㄷ, irregular change rule applies to 듣다(to listen), 싣다(to load), 걷다(to walk) and 묻다(to ask).   In the case of irregular change, ㄷ is dropped from root verb stem and ㄹ을 것이다 or ㄹ을 거다 is added.   Other than these 4 verbs, regular change rule applies to the other verbs ending in ㄷ.   See the following Table 9 for the comparison of the verb stems ending in ㄷ.

Table 9   *Marks in Italic* are wrong.

root verbs ending in ㄷ	verb stems in future tense: 겠다 or (ㄹ/을) 것이다 or (ㄹ/을) 거다
듣다 *to listen	듣겠다/들을 것이다/들을 거다 *듣을 것이다/듣을 거다* *ㄷ is replaced with ㄹ을 것이다/ㄹ을 거다. to be going to listen
싣다	싣겠다/실을 것이다/실을 거다

Korean Language: Grammar Pattern

*to load	*싣을 것이다 /싣을 거다 to be going to load
걷다 *to walk	걷겠다/걸을 것이다/걸을 거다 *걷을 것이다/걷을 거다 to be going to walk
묻다 *to ask	묻겠다/물을 것이다/물을 거다 *묻을 것이다/묻을 거다 to be going to ask
받다 *to receive	받겠다/받을 것이다/받을 거다 to be going to receive
믿다 *to believe	믿겠다/믿을 것이다/믿을 거다 to be going to believe
얻다 *to gain/obtain	얻겠다/얻을 것이다/얻을 거다 to be going to gain/obtain
딛다 *to step	딛겠다/딛을 것이다/딛을 거다 to be going to step
걷다 *to collect	걷겠다/걷을 것이다/걷을 거다 to be going to collect
닫다 *to close	닫겠다/닫을 것이다/닫을 거다 to be going to close
묻다 *to bury	묻겠다/묻을 것이다/묻을 거다 to be going to bury

Examples:

[여기에 입력]
Korean Language: Grammar Pattern

•붙이다(to attach): 붙이겠다/붙일 것이다/붙일 거다(to be going to attach)

•이다(to be): 이겠다/일 것이다/일 거다   *이다 is a typical static verb.

•되다(to become): 되겠다/될 것이다/될 거다(to be going to become)

•믿다(to believe): 믿겠다/믿을 것이다/믿을 거다(to be going to believe)

•부수다(to break): 부수겠다/부술 것이다/부술 거다(to be going to break)

•가져오다(to bring): 가져오겠다/가져올 것이다/가져올 거다(to be going to bring)

•부르다(to call): 부르겠다/부를 것이다/부를 거다(to be going to call)

•씹다(to chew): 씹겠다/씹을 것이다/씹을 거다(to be going to chew)

•울다(to cry): 울겠다/울 것이다/울 거다(to be going to cry)

*울을 것이다/울을 거다 is in correct.

•자르다(to cut): 자르겠다/자를 것이다/자를 거다(to be going to cut)

•출발하다(to depart): 출발하겠다/출발할 것이다/출발할 거다(to be going to depart)

•하다(to do): 하겠다/할 것이다/할 거다(to be going to do)

*'to do' is typical '하다-verb'. 출발하다(to depart)/도착하다(to arrive)/노래하다(to sing)/청소하다(to clean up)/산책하다(to take a walk)/요리하다(to cook)/공부하다(to study)말하다(to speak), etc.

•마르다(to be skinny): 마르겠다/마를 것이다/마를 거다(to be going to be skinny)

•이르다(to be early): 이르겠다/이를 것이다/이를 거다(to be going to be early)

•지우다(to erase): 지우겠다/지울 것이다/지울 거다(to be going to erase)

•있다(to exist): 있겠다/있을 것이다/있을 거다(to be going to exist)

•흐르다(to flow): 흐르겠다/흐를 것이다/흐를 거다(to be going to flow)

•접다(to fold): 접겠다/접을 것이다/접을 거다(to be going to fold)

•볶다(to fry): 볶겠다/볶을 것이다/볶을 거다(to be going to fry)

•가다(to go): 가겠다/갈 것이다/갈 거다(to be going to go)

•갈다(to grind): 갈겠다/갈 것이다/갈 거다(to be going to grind)

Korean Language: Grammar Pattern

갈을 것이다/갈을 거다 is incorrect.

•걸다(to hang): 걸겠다/걸 것이다/걸 거다(to be going to hang)

걸을 것이다/걸을 거다 is incorrect.

•기쁘다(to be happy): 기쁘겠다/기쁠 것이다/기쁠 거다(to be going to be happy)

•붙잡다(to hold): 붙잡겠다/붙잡을 것이다/붙잡을 거다(to be going to hold)

•배고프다(to be hungry): 배고프겠다/배고플 것이다/배고플 거다(to be going to be hungry)

•웃다(to laugh): 웃겠다/웃을 것이다/웃을 거다(to be going to laugh)

•배우다(to learn): 배우겠다/배울 것이다/배울 거다(to be going to learn)

•만들다(to make): 만들겠다/만들 것이다/만들 거다(to be going to make)

만들을 것이다/만들을 거다 is incorrect.

•채굴하다(to mine): 채굴하겠다/채굴할 것이다/채굴할 거다(to be going to mine)

•열다(to open): 열겠다/열 것이다/열 거다(to be going to open)

•준비하다(to prepare): 준비하겠다/준비할 것이다/준비할 거다(to be going to prepare)

•받다(to receive): 받겠다/받을 것이다/받을 거다(to be going to receive)

•오르다(to rise): 오르겠다/오를 것이다/오를 거다(to be going to rise)

•말다(to roll): 말겠다/말 것이다/말 거다(to be going to roll)

말을 것이다/말을 거다 is incorrect.

•슬프다(to be sad): 슬프겠다/슬플 것이다/슬플 거다(to be going to be sad)

•보다(to see): 보겠다/볼 것이다/볼 거다(to be going to see)

•뽑다(to select): 뽑겠다/뽑을 것이다/뽑을 거다(to be going to select)

•소리치다(to shout): 소리치겠다/소리칠 것이다/소리칠 거다(to be going to shout)

•앉다(to sit down): 앉겠다/앉을 것이다/앉을 거다(to be going to sit down)

•서다(to stand up): 서겠다/설 것이다/설 거다(to be going to stand up)

Korean Language: Grammar Pattern

•입다(to wear): 입겠다/입을 것이다/입을 거다(to be going to wear)

*In the following grid, compare the verb stems in past, present and future tense.

※Irregular verb change rule applies to mostly the verbs ending in ㄷ or ㅂ or ㄹ or especially static verbs ending in ㅂ.   It is advised to more attention to them.

root verb stem	verb stem in past tense: ㅆ다/았다/었다/웠다	verb stem in present tense: ㄴ다/는다	verb stem in future tense: 겠다/(ㄹ/을) 것이다 /(ㄹ/을) 거다/울 것이다/울 거다
우습다 *to be funny	우스웠다 to have been funny	우습다 *This is a static verb. ※In the case of static verb, root verb stem is the same as present verb stem.	우습겠다/우스울 것이다/우스울 거다 to be going to be funny
먹다 *to eat	먹었다 to have eaten	먹는다	먹겠다/먹을 것이다/먹을 거다 to be going to eat
보다 *to look	봤다(보았다) to have looked	본다	보겠다/볼 것이다/볼 거다 to be going to look
씻다 *to wash	씻었다 to have washed	씻는다	씻겠다/씻을 것이다/씻을 거다 to be going to wash
돕다 *to help	도왔다 to have helped	돕는다	돕겠다/도울 것이다/도울 거다 to be going to help
깁다 *to sew	기웠다 *깁었다 to have sewn	깁는다	깁겠다/기울 것이다/기울 거다 to be going to sew

Korean Language: Grammar Pattern

빠르다 *to be fast	빨랐다 to have been fast	빠르다	빠르겠다/빠를 것이다 /빠를 거다 to be going to be fast
파다 *to dig	팠다 to have dug	판다	파겠다/팔 것이다/팔 거다 to be going to dig
짖다 *to bark	짖었다 to have barked	짖는다	짖겠다/짖을 것이다/ 짖을 거다 to be going to bark
놀다 *to play	놀았다 to have played	논다	놀겠다/놀 것이다/놀 거다 to be going to play
끓이다 *to boil	끓였다(끓이었다) to have boiled	끓인다	끓이겠다/끓일 것이다 /끓일 거다 to be going to boil
날다 *to fly	날았다 to have flown	난다	날겠다/날 것이다/날 거다 to be going to fly
굽히다 *to bend	굽혔다(굽히었다) to have bent	굽힌다	굽히겠다/굽힐 것이다 /굽힐 거다 to be going to bend
읽다 *to read	읽었다 to have read	읽는다	읽겠다/읽을 것이다/ 읽을 거다 to be going to read
높다 *to be high	높았다 to have been high	높다	높겠다/높을 것이다/ 높을 거다 to be going to be high
낮다 *to be low	낮았다 to have been low	낮다	낮겠다/낮을 것이다/ 낮을 거다 to be going to be low
떨어지다 *to fall down	떨어졌다(떨어지었 다) to have fallen down	떨어진다	떨어지겠다/떨어질 것 이다/떨어질 거다 to be going to fall down
굶다 *to starve	굶었다 to have starved	굶는다	굶겠다/굶을 것이다/ 굶을 거다 to be going to starve

Korean Language: Grammar Pattern

불다 *to blow	불었다 to have blown	분다	불겠다/불 것이다/불 거다 to be going to blow
얻다 *to gain	얻었다 to have gained	얻는다	얻겠다/얻을 것이다/ 얻을 거다 to be going to gain
잃다 *to lose	잃었다 to have lost	잃는다	잃겠다/잃을 것이다/ 잃을 거다 to be going to lose
부풀다 *to swell	부풀었다 to have swollen	부푼다	부풀겠다/부풀 것이다 /부풀 거다 to be going to swell
돕다 *to help	도왔다 to have helped	돕는다	돕겠다/도울 것이다/ 도울 거다 to be going to help
맵다 *to be spicy	매웠다 to have been spicy	맵다	맵겠다/매울 것이다/ 매울 거다 to be going to be spicy

Exercise 18. Fill in the blanks with appropriate verb stems in Korean.

※In the case of static verb, root verb stem is the same as verb stem in present tense.

root verb stem	verb stem in past tense: ㅆ다/았다/었다/왔다/웠다	verb stem in present tense: ㄴ다/는다	verb stem in future tense: 겠다/ㄹ(을) 것이다/ㄹ(을) 거다/울 것이다/울 거다
춤추다 *to dance	춤췄다 = 춤추었다 to have danced	춤춘다 dances	춤추겠다/춤출 것이다/춤출 거다 to be going to dance
말하다 *to tell	말했다 to have told	말한다 tells	말하겠다/말할 것이다/말할 거다 *to be going to tell
고치다 *to fix	고쳤다 = 고치었다 	고친다 fixes	고치겠다/고칠 것이다/고칠 거다 *to be going to fix

Korean Language: Grammar Pattern

	*to have fixed		
자다 *to sleep	잤다 *to have slept	잔다 sleeps	자겠다/잘 것이다/잘 거다 *to be going to sleep
걷다 *to walk	걸었다 *to have walked	걷는다 walks	걷겠다/걸을 것이다/ 걸을 거다 *to be going to sleep
기다리다 *to wait	기다렸다 = 기다리었다 to have waited	기다린다 waits	기다리겠다/기다릴 것이다/기다릴 거다 to be going to wait
쓰다 *to write	썼다 to have wrote	쓴다 writes	쓰겠다/쓸 것이다/쓸 거다 to be going to write
꿈꾸다 *to dream	꿈꿨다 = 꿈꾸었다 to have dreamed	꿈꾼다 dreams	꿈꾸겠다/꿈꿀 것이다/꿈꿀 거다 to be going to dream
만들다 *to make	만들었다 to have made	만든다 makes	만들겠다/만들 것이다/만들 거다 to be going to make
먹다 *to eat	먹었다 to have eaten	먹는다 eats	먹겠다/먹을 것이다/먹을 거다 to be going to eat
닫다 *to close	닫았다 to have closed	닫는다 closes	닫겠다/닫을 것이다/닫을 거다 to be going to close
배우다 *to learn	배웠다 = 배우었다 to have learned	배운다 learns	배우겠다/배울 것이다/배울 거다 to be going to learn
믿다 *to believe	믿었다 to have believed	믿는다 believes	믿겠다/믿을 것이다/믿을 거다 to be going to believe
막다 *to block	막았다 to have blocked	막는다 blocks	막겠다/막을 것이다/막을 거다 to be going to block

Korean Language: Grammar Pattern

접다 *to fold	접었다 to have folded	접는다 folds	접겠다/접을 것이다/접을 거다 to be going to fold
밀다 *to push	밀었다 to have pushed	민다 pushes	밀겠다/밀 것이다/밀 거다 to be going to push
당기다 *to pull	당겼다 = 당기었다 to have pulled	당긴다 pulls	당기겠다/당길 것이다/당길 거다 to be going to pull
웃다 *to laugh	웃었다 to have laughed	웃는다 laughs	웃겠다/웃을 것이다/웃을 거다 to be going to laugh
읽다 *to read	읽었다 to have read	읽는다 reads	읽겠다/읽을 것이다/읽을 거다 to be going to read
낚시하다 *to fish	낚시했다 to have fished	낚시한다 fishes	낚시하겠다/낚시할 것이다/낚시할 거다 to be going to fish
춥다 *to be cold	추웠다 to have been cold	춥다 is cold	춥겠다/추울 것이다/추울 거다 to be going to be cold
삼키다 *to swallow	삼켰다 to have swallowed	삼킨다 swallows	삼키겠다/삼킬 것이다/삼킬 거다 to be going to swallow
재미있다 *to be funny	재미있었다 to have been funny	재미있다 is funny	재미있겠다/재미있을 것이다/재미있을 거다 to be going to be funny
돕다 *to help	도왔다 to have helped	돕는다 helps	돕겠다/도울 것이다/도울 거다 to be going to help
좋다 *to be good	좋았다 to have been good	좋다 is good	좋겠다/좋을 것이다/좋을 거다 to be going to be good

Korean Language: Grammar Pattern

맛있다	맛있었다	맛있다	맛있겠다/맛있을 것이다/맛있을 거다
*to be tasty	to have been tasty	is tasty	to be going to be tasty
눕다	누웠다	눕는다	눕겠다/누울 것이다/누울 거다
*to lie down	to have lied down	lies down	to be going to lie down

5. verb stems in past progressive tense (to have been + present particle = was/were + present particle): root verb stem + 고 있었다

※ 고 implies progressive action and 써/었/았 implies past tense. Drop 다 from the root verb stem and add 고 있었다 for verb stem in past progressive tense.

Examples:

•붙이다(to paste): 붙이고 있었다(to have been pasting)

•되다(to become): 되고 있었다(to have been becoming)

•믿다(to believe): 믿고 있었다(to have been believing)

•부수다(to break): 부수고 있었다(to have been breaking)

•가져오다(to bring): 가져오고 있었다(to have been bringing)

•사다(to buy): 사고 있었다(to have been buying)

•부르다(to call): 부르고 있었다(to have been calling)

•씹다(to chew): 씹고 있었다(to have been chewing)

•울다(to cry): 울고 있었다(to have been crying)

•자르다(to cut): 자르고 있었다(to have been cutting)

•출발하다(to depart): 출발하고 있었다(to have been departing)

•하다(to do): 하고 있었다(to have been doing)

[여기에 입력]
Korean Language: Grammar Pattern

•지우다(erase): 지우고 있었다(to have been erasing)

•흐르다(to flow): 흐르고 있었다(to have been flowing)

•접다(to fold): 접고 있었다(to have been folding)

•볶다(to fry): 볶고 있었다(to have been frying)

•가다(to go): 가고 있었다(to have been going)

•갈다(to grind): 갈고 있었다(to have been grinding)

•걸다(to hang): 걸고 있었다(to have been hanging)

•잡다(to hold): 잡고 있었다(to have been holding)

•웃다(to laugh): 웃고 있었다(to have been laughing)

•배우다(to learn): 배우고 있었다(to have been learning)

•살다(to live): 살고 있었다(to have been living)

•싣다(to load): 싣고 있었다(to have been loading)

•만들다(to make): 만들고 있었다(to have been making)

•채굴하다(to mine): 채굴하고 있었다(to have been mining)

•열다(to open): 열고 있었다(to have been opening)

•준비하다(to prepare): 준비하고 있었다(to have been preparing)

•받다(to receive): 받고 있었다(to have been receiving)

•오르다(to rise): 오르고 있었다(to have been rising)

•말다(to roll): 말고 있었다(to have been rolling)

•보다(to see): 보고 있었다(to have been seeing)

•뽑다(to select): 뽑고 있었다(to have been selecting)

•소리치다(to shout): 소리치고 있었다(to have been shouting)

•입다(to wear): 입고 있었다(to have been wearing)

Korean Language: Grammar Pattern

※The verbs of 앉다/서다/눕다 are more like a static verb or condition instead of action.

•앉다(to sit down): 앉아 있었다(to have been sitting)   *앉고 있었다

•서다(to stand up): 서 있었다(to have been standing)   *서고 있었다

•눕다(to lie down) : 누워 있었다(to have been lying down)   *눕고 있었다

6. verb stem in present progressive tense (to be + present particle = am/are/is + present particle): root verb stem + 고 있다

※고 indicates progressive action.   Drop 다 from the root verb stem and add 고 있다 for present progressive tense.

Examples:

•건너다(to cross): 건너고 있다(to be crossing)

•되다(to become): 되고 있다(to be becoming)

•즐기다(to have fun): 즐기고 있다(to be having fun)

•믿다(to believe): 믿고 있다(to be believing)

•부수다(to break): 부수고 있다(to be breaking)

•가져오다(to bring): 가져오고 있다(to be bringing)

•사다(to buy): 사고 있다(to be buying)

•부르다(to call): 부르고 있다(to be calling)

•씹다(to chew): 씹고 있다(to be chewing)

•울다(to cry): 울고 있다(to be crying)

•자르다(to cut): 자르고 있다(to be cutting)

•출발하다(to depart): 출발하고 있다(to be departing)

[여기에 입력]
Korean Language: Grammar Pattern

•하다(to do): 하고 있다(to be doing)

•복사하다(to copy): 복사하고 있다(to be copying)

•흐르다(to flow): 흐르고 있다(to be flowing)

•접다(to fold): 접고 있다(to be folding)

•볶다(to fry): 볶고 있다(to be frying)

•가다(to go): 가고 있다(to be going)

•갈다(to grind): 갈고 있다(to be grinding)

•걸다(to hang): 걸고 있다(to be hanging)

•붙잡다(to hold): 붙잡고 있다(to be holding)

•웃다(to laugh): 웃고 있다(to be laughing)

•배우다(to learn): 배우고 있다(to be learning)

•살다(to live): 살고 있다(to be living)

•싣다(to load): 싣고 있다(to be loading)

•만들다(to make): 만들고 있다(to be making)

•채굴하다/캐다(to mine): 채굴하고 있다/캐고 있다(to be mining)

•열다(to open): 열고 있다(to be opening)

•준비하다(to prepare): 준비하고 있다(to be preparing)

•받다(to receive): 받고 있다(to be receiving)

•오르다(to rise): 오르고 있다(to be rising)

•말다(to roll): 말고 있다(to be rolling)

•보다(to see): 보고 있다(to be seeing)

•뽑다(to select): 뽑고 있다(to be selecting)

•소리치다(to shout): 소리치고 있다(to be shouting)

•입다(to wear): 입고 있다(to be wearing)

•앉다(to sit): 앉아 있다(to be sitting)   *앉고 있다

•서다(to stand): 서 있다(to be standing)   *서고 있다

•눕다(to lie down) : 누워 있다(to be lying down)   *눕고 있었다

7. verb stem in future progressive tense (to be going to be + present particle = will be + present particle): root verb stem ending in consonant/vowel + 고 있겠다 or 고 있을 것이다 or 고 있을 거다

※ 고 indicates progressive action and 겠 indicates future intention and ㄹ or 을 indicates simple future tense.   Drop 다 from the verb stem and add 고 있겠다/고 있을 것이다/고 있을 거다.

Examples:

•붙이다(to paste): 붙이고 있겠다/붙이고 있을 것이다/붙이고 있을 거다(to be going to be pasting)

•되다(to become): 되고 있겠다/되고 있을 것이다/되고 있을 거다(to be going to be becoming)

•믿다(to believe): 믿고 있겠다/믿고 있을 것이다/믿고 있을 거다(to be going to be believing)

•부수다(to break): 부수고 있겠다/부수고 있을 것이다/부수고 있을 거다(to be going to be breaking)

•가져오다(to bring): 가져오고 있겠다/가져오고 있을 것이다/가져오고 있을 거다(to be going to be bringing)

•사다(to buy): 사고 있겠다/사고 있을 것이다/사고 있을 거다(to be going to be buying)

•부르다(to call): 부르고 있겠다/부르고 있을 것이다/부르고 있을 거다(to be going to be calling)

•씹다(to chew): 씹고 있겠다/씹고 있을 것이다/씹고 있을 거다(to be going to be chewing)

Korean Language: Grammar Pattern

•울다(to cry): 울고 있겠다/울고 있을 것이다/울고 있을 거다(to be going to be crying)

•자르다(to cut): 자르고 있겠다/자르고 있을 것이다/자르고 있을 거다(to be going to be cutting)

•출발하다(to depart): 출발하고 있겠다/출발하고 있을 것이다/출발하고 있을 거다(to be going to be departing)

•하다(to do): 하고 있겠다/하고 있을 것이다/하고 있을 거다(to be going to be doing)

•지우다(erase): 지우고 있겠다/지우고 있을 것이다/지우고 있을 거다(to be going to be erasing)

•흐르다(to flow): 흐르고 있겠다/흐르고 있을 것이다/흐르고 있을 거다(to be going to be flowing)

•접다(to fold): 접고 있겠다/접고 있을 것이다/접고 있을 거다(to be going to be folding)

•볶다(to fry): 볶고 있겠다/볶고 있을 것이다/볶고 있을 거다(to be going to be frying)

•가다(to go): 가고 있겠다/가고 있을 것이다/가고 있을 거다(to be going to be going)

•갈다(to grind): 갈고 있겠다/갈고 있을 것이다/갈고 있을 거다(to be going to be grinding)

•걸다(to hang): 걸고 있겠다/걸고 있을 것이다/걸고 있을 거다(to be going to be hanging)

•붙잡다(to hold): 붙잡고 있겠다/붙잡고 있을 것이다/붙잡고 있을 거다(to be going to be holding)

•웃다(to laugh): 웃고 있겠다/웃고 있을 것이다/웃고 있을 거다(to be going to be laughing)

•배우다(to learn): 배우고 있겠다/배우고 있을 것이다/배우고 있을 거다(to be going to be learning)

•살다(to live): 살고 있겠다/살고 있을 것이다/살고 있을 거다(to be going to be living)

[여기에 입력]
Korean Language: Grammar Pattern

•싣다(to load): 싣고 있겠다/싣고 있을 것이다/싣고 있을 거다(to be going to be loading)

•만들다(to make): 만들고 있겠다/만들고 있을 것이다/만들고 있을 거다(to be going to be making)

•채굴하다(to mine): 채굴하고 있겠다/채굴하고 있을 것이다/채굴하고 있을 거다(to be going to be mining)

•열다(to open): 열고 있겠다/열고 있을 것이다/열고 있을 거다(to be going to be opening)

•준비하다(to prepare): 준비하고 있겠다/준비하고 있을 것이다/준비하고 있을 거다 (to be going to be preparing)

•받다(to receive): 받고 있겠다/받고 있을 것이다/받고 있을 거다(to be going to be receiving)

•오르다(to rise): 오르고 있겠다/오르고 있을 것이다/오르고 있을 거다(to be going to be rising)

•말다(to roll): 말고 있겠다/말고 있을 것이다/말고 있을 거다(to be going to be rolling)

•보다(to see): 보고 있겠다/보고 있을 것이다/보고 있을 거다(to be going to be seeing)

•뽑다(to select): 뽑고 있겠다/뽑고 있을 것이다/뽑고 있을 거다(to be going to be selecting)

•소리치다(to shout): 소리치고 있겠다/소리치고 있을 것이다/소리치고 있을 거다(to be going to be shouting)

•입다(to wear): 입고 있겠다/입고 있을 것이다/입고 있을 거다(to be going to be wearing)

•앉다(to sit): 앉아 있겠다/앉아 있을 것이다/앉아 있을 거다(to be going to be sitting)

*앉고 있겠다/앉고 있을 것이다/앉고 있을 거다 is incorrect.

•서다(to stand): 서 있겠다/서 있을 것이다/서 있을 거다(to be going to be standing) This is a kind of irregular change.   *서고 있겠다/서고 있을 것이다/서고 있을 거다 is incorrect.

Korean Language: Grammar Pattern

•눕다(to lie down): 누워 있겠다/누워 있을 것이다/누워 있을 거다(to be going to be lying down)   *눕고 있겠다/눕고 있을 것이다/눕고 있을 거다

※고 implies progressive action in all types of tense.

In the following Table 10, compare the verb stems in past, present and future progressive tense.

Table 10   *Marks in Italic are incorrect.

root verb stem	verb stem in past progressive tense: (to have been + present participle): 고 있었다	verb stem in present progressive tense: (to be + present participle): 고 있다	verb stem in future progressive tense: (to be going to be + present participle): 고 있겠다/고 있을 것이다/고 있을 거다
먹다 *to eat	먹고 있었다 to have been eating	먹고 있다 to be eating	먹고 있겠다/먹고 있을 것이다/먹고 있을 거다 to be going to be eating
보다 *to look	보고 있었다 to have been looking	보고 있다 to be looking	보고 있겠다/보고 있을 것이다/보고 있을 거다 to be going to be looking
씻다 *to wash	씻고 있었다 to have been washing	씻고 있다 to be washing	씻고 있겠다/씻고 있을 것이다/씻고 있을 거다

Korean Language: Grammar Pattern

			to be going to be washing
오다 *to come	오고 있었다 to have been coming	오고 있다 to be coming	오고 있겠다/오고 있을 것이다/오고 있을 거다 to be going to be coming
잡다 *to catch	잡고 있었다 to have been catching	잡고 있다 to be catching	잡고 있겠다/잡고 있을 것이다/잡고 있을 거다 to be going to be catching
깁다 *to sew	깁고 있었다 to have been sewing	깁고 있다 to be sewing	깁고 있겠다/깁고 있을 것이다/깁고 있을 거다 to be going to be sewing
파다 *to dig	파고 있었다 to have been digging	파고 있다 to be digging	파고 있겠다/파고 있을 것이다/파고 있을 거다 to be going to be digging
보내다 *to send	보내고 있었다 to have been sending	보내고 있다 to be sending	보내고 있겠다/보내고 있을 것이다/보내고 있을 거다

Korean Language: Grammar Pattern

			to be going to be sending
날다 *to fly	날고 있었다 to have been flying	날고 있다 to be flying	날고 있겠다/날고 있을 것이다/날고 있을 거다 to be going to be flying
듣다 *to listen	듣고 있었다 to have been listening	듣고 있다 to be listening	듣고 있겠다/듣고 있을 것이다/듣고 있을 거다 to be going to be listening
노리다 *to aim	노리고 있었다 to have been aiming	노리고 있다 to be aiming	노리고 있겠다/노리고 있을 것이다/노리고 있을 거다 to be going to be aiming
닫다 *to close	닫고 있었다 to have been closing	닫고 있다 to be closing	닫고 있겠다/닫고 있을 것이다/닫고 있을 거다 to be going to be closing
굽히다 *to bend	굽히고 있었다 to have been bending	굽히고 있다 to be bending	굽히고 있겠다/굽히고 있을 것이다/굽히고 있을 거다

Korean Language: Grammar Pattern

			to be going to be bending
꿈꾸다 *to dream	꿈꾸고 있었다 to have been dreaming	꿈꾸고 있다 to be dreaming	꿈꾸고 있겠다/꿈꾸고 있을 것이다/꿈꾸고 있을 거다 to be going to be dreaming
놀다 *to play	놀고 있었다 to have been playing	놀고 있다 to be playing	놀고 있겠다/놀고 있을 것이다/놀고 있을 거다 to be going to be playing
기대다 *to lean	기대고 있었다 to have been leaning	기대고 있다 to be leaning	기대고 있겠다/기대고 있을 것이다/기대고 있을 거다 to be going to be leaning
읽다 *to read	읽고 있었다 to have been reading	읽고 있다 to be reading	읽고 있겠다/읽고 있을 것이다/읽고 있을 거다 to be going to be reading
떨어지다 *to fall	떨어지고 있었다 to have been falling	떨어지고 있다 to be falling	떨어지고 있겠다/떨어지고 있을

Korean Language: Grammar Pattern

			것이다/떨어지고 있을 거다 to be going to be falling
굶다 *to starve	굶고 있었다 to have been starving	굶고 있다 to be starving	굶고 있겠다/굶고 있을 것이다/굶고 있을 거다 to be going to be starving
사용하다 *to use	사용하고 있었다 to have been using	사용하고 있다 to be using	사용하고 있겠다/사용하고 있을 것이다/사용하고 있을 거다 to be going to be using
불다 *to blow	불고 있었다 to have been blowing	불고 있다 to be blowing	불고 있겠다/불고 있을 것이다/불고 있을 거다 to be going to be blowing
얻다 *to gain/obtain	얻고 있었다 to have been gaining/obtaining	얻고 있다 to be gaining/obtaining	얻고 있겠다/얻고 있을 것이다/얻고 있을 거다 to be going to be gaining/obtaining
복사하다 *to copy	복사하고 있었다 to have been copying	복사하고 있다 to be copying	복사하고 있겠다/복사하고 있을

Korean Language: Grammar Pattern

			것이다/복사하고 있을 거다 to be going to be copying
부풀다 *to swell	부풀고 있었다 to have been swelling	부풀고 있다 to be swelling	부풀고 있겠다/부풀고 있을 것이다/부풀고 있을 거다 to be going to be swelling

Exercise 19. Fill in the blank with the appropriate verb stem in Korean.

root verb stem	verb stem in past progressive tense: 고 있었다	verb stem in present progressive tense: 고 있다	verb stem in future progressive tense: 고 있겠다/고 있을 것이다/고 있을 거다
춤추다 *to dance	춤추고 있었다 to have been dancing	춤추고 있다 to be dancing	춤추고 있겠다/춤추고 있을 것이다/춤추고 있을 거다 to be going to be dancing
말하다 *to talk	말하고 있었다 to have been talking	말하고 있다 to be talking	말하고 있겠다/말하고 있을 것이다/말하고 있을 거다 to be going to be talking
짖다 *to bark	짖고 있었다	짖고 있다 to be barking	짖고 있겠다/짖고 있을 것이다/고 있을 거다

Korean Language: Grammar Pattern

	to have been barking		to be going to be barking
도착하다 *to arrive	도착하고 있었다 to have been arriving	도착하고 있다 to be arriving	도착하고 있겠다/도착하고 있을 것이다/도착하고 있을 거다 to be going to be arriving
자다 *to sleep	자고 있었다 to have been sleeping	자고 있다 to be sleeping	자고 있겠다/자고 있을 것이다/자고 있을 거다 to be going to be sleeping
걷다 *to walk	걷고 있었다 to have been walking	걷고 있다 to be walking	걷고 있겠다/걷고 있을 것이다/걷고 있을 거다 to be going to be walking
기다리다 *to wait	기다리고 있었다 to have been waiting	기다리고 있다 to be waiting	기다리고 있겠다/기다리고 있을 것이다/기다리고 있을 거다 to be going to be waiting
쓰다 *to write	쓰고 있었다 to have been writing	쓰고 있다 to be writing	쓰고 있겠다/쓰고 있을 것이다/쓰고 있을 거다 to be going to be writing

Korean Language: Grammar Pattern

보다 *to look	보고 있었다 to have been looking	보고 있다 to be looking	보고 있겠다/보고 있을 것이다/보고 있을 거다 to be going to be looking
수영하다 *to swim	수영하고 있었다 to have been swimming	수영하고 있다 to be swimming	수영하고 있겠다/수영하고 있을 것이다/수영하고 있을 거다 to be going to be swimming
열다 *to open	열고 있었다 to have been opening	열고 있다 to be opening	열고 있겠다/열고 있을 것이다/열고 있을 거다 to be going to be opening
먹다 *to eat	먹고 있었다 to have been eating	먹고 있다 to be eating	먹고 있겠다/먹고 있을 것이다/먹고 있을 거다 to be going to be eating
배우다 *to learn	배우고 있었다 to have been learning	배우고 있다 to be learning	배우고 있겠다/배우고 있을 것이다/배우고 있을 거다 to be going to be learning
운전하다 *to drive	운전하고 있었다 to have been driving	운전하고 있다 to be driving	운전하고 있겠다/운전하고 있을

Korean Language: Grammar Pattern

			것이다/운전하고 있을 거다 to be going to be driving
접다 *to fold	접고 있었다 to have been folding	접고 있다 to be folding	접고 있겠다/접고 있을 것이다/접고 있을 거다 to be going to be folding
밀다 *to push	밀고 있었다 to have been pushing	밀고 있다 to be pushing	밀고 있겠다/밀고 있을 것이다/밀고 있을 거다 to be going to be pushing
당기다 *to pull	당기고 있었다 to have been pulling	당기고 있다 to be pulling	당기고 있겠다/당기고 있을 것이다/당기고 있을 거다 to be going to be pulling
부수다 *to break	부수고 있었다 to have been breaking	부수고 있다 to be breaking	부수고 있겠다/부수고 있을 것이다/부수고 있을 거다 to be going to be breaking
짓다 *to build	짓고 있었다 to have been building	짓고 있다 to be building	짓고 있겠다/짓고 있을 것이다/짓고 있을 거다 to be going to be building

Korean Language: Grammar Pattern

잃다 *to lose	잃고 있었다 to have been losing	잃고 있다 to be losing	잃고 있겠다/잃고 있을 것이다/잃고 있을 거다 to be going to be losing
딛다 *to step	딛고 있었다 to have been stepping	딛고 있다 to be stepping	딛고 있겠다/딛고 있을 것이다/딛고 있을 거다 to be going to be stepping
낚시하다 *to fish	낚시하고 있었다 to have been fishing	낚시하고 있다 to be fishing	낚시하고 있겠다/낚시하고 있을 것이다/낚시하고 있을 거다 to be going to be fishing
만나다 *to meet	만나고 있었다 to have been meeting	만나고 있다 to be meeting	만나고 있겠다/만나고 있을 것이다/만나고 있을 거다 to be going to be meeting
삼키다 *to swallow	삼키고 있었다 to have been swallowing	삼키고 있다 to be swallowing	삼키고 있겠다/삼키고 있을 것이다/삼키고 있을 거다 to be going to be swallowing
막다 *to block	막고 있었다	막고 있다 to be blocking	막고 있겠다/막고 있을 것이다/막고 있을 거다

Korean Language: Grammar Pattern

	to have been blocking		to be going to be blocking
올리다 *to raise	올리고 있었다 to have been raising	올리고 있다 to be raising	올리고 있겠다/올리고 있을 것이다/올리고 있을 거다 to be going to be raising
돕다 *to help	돕고 있었다 to have been helping	돕고 있다 to be helping	돕고 있겠다/돕고 있을 것이다/돕고 있을 거다 to be going to be helping

Exercise 20. Fill in the blanks with the appropriate verb stem.

root verb stem	verb stem in past tense: ㅆ/았/었다	verb stem in future tense: 겠다/(ㄹ/을) 것 이다/(ㄹ/을) 거다	verb stem in past progressive tense: 고 있었다	verb stem in present progressive tense: 고 있다	verb stem in future progressive tense: 고 있겠다/고 있을 것이다/고 있을 거다
던지다 *to throw	던졌다=던지었다 to have thrown	던지겠다/던질 것이다/던질 거다 to be going to throw	던지고 있었다 to have been throwing	던지고 있다 to be throwing	던지고 있겠다/던지고 있을 것이다/던지고 있을 거다

Korean Language: Grammar Pattern

					to be going to be throwing
덮다 *to cover	덮었다 to have covered	덮겠다/덮을 것이다/덮을 거다 to be going to cover	덮고 있었다 to have been covering	덮고 있다 to be covering	덮고 있겠다/덮고 있을 것이다/덮고 있을 거다 to be going to be covering
찾다 *to find	찾았다 to have found	찾겠다/찾을 것이다/찾을 거다 to be going to find	찾고 있었다 to have been finding	찾고 있다 to be finding	찾고 있겠다/찾고 있을 것이다/찾고 있을 거다 to be going to be finding
미워하다 *to hate	미워했다 to have hated	미워하겠다/미워할 것이다/미워할 거다 to be going to hate	미워하고 있었다 to have been hating	미워하고 있다 to be hating	미워하고 있겠다/미워하고 있을 것이다/미워하고 있을 거다 to be going to be hating
쓰다듬다 *to pet	쓰다듬었다 to have petted	쓰다듬겠다/쓰다듬을 것이다/쓰다듬을 거다 to be going to pet	쓰다듬고 있었다 to have been petting	쓰다듬고 있다 to be petting	쓰다듬고 있겠다/쓰다듬고 있을 것이다/쓰다듬고

Korean Language: Grammar Pattern

					있을 거다 to be going to be petting
쏘다 *to shoot	쐈다 = 쏘았다 to have shot	쏘겠다/쏠 것이다/쏠 거다 to be going to shoot	쏘고 있었다 to have been shooting	쏘고 있다 to be shooting	쏘고 있겠다/쏘고 있을 것이다/쏘고 있을 거다 to be going to be shooting
지불하다 *to pay	지불했다 to have paid	지불하겠다/지불할 것이다/지불할 거다 to be going to pay	지불하고 있었다 to have been paying	지불하고 있다 to be paying	지불하고 있겠다/지불하고 있을 것이다/지불하고 있을 거다 to be going to be paying
올리다 *to raise	올렸다 = 올리었다 to have raised	올리겠다/올릴 것이다/올릴 거다 to be going to raise	올리고 있었다 to have been raising	올리고 있다 to be raising	올리고 있겠다/올리고 있을 것이다/올리고 있을 거다 to be going to be raising
빌다 *to beg	빌었다 to have begged	빌겠다/빌 것이다/빌 거다 to be going to beg	빌고 있었다 to have been begging	빌고 있다 to be begging	빌고 있겠다/빌고 있을 것이다/빌고 있을 거다 to be

Korean Language: Grammar Pattern

					going to be begging
빗다 *to comb	빗었다 to have combed	빗겠다/빗을 것이다/빗을 거다 to be going to comb	빗고 있었다 to have been combing	빗고 있다 to be combing	빗고 있겠다/빗고 있을 것이다/빗고 있을 거다 to be going to be combing
칠하다 *to paint	칠했다 to have painted	칠하겠다/칠할 것이다/칠할 거다 to be going to paint	칠하고 있었다 to have been painting	칠하고 있다 to be painting	칠하고 있겠다/칠하고 있을 것이다/칠하고 있을 거다 to be going to be painting
벌다 *to earn	벌었다 to have earned	벌겠다/벌 것이다/벌 거다 to be going to earn	벌고 있었다 to have been earning	벌고 있다 to be earning	벌고 있겠다/벌고 있을 것이다/벌고 있을 거다 to be going to be earning
숨다 *to hide	숨었다 to have hidden	숨겠다/숨을 것이다/숨을 거다 to be going to hide	숨고 있었다 to have been hiding	숨고 있다 to be hiding	숨고 있겠다/숨고 있을 것이다/숨고 있을 거다 to be going to be hiding

Korean Language: Grammar Pattern

물다 *to bite	물었다 to have bitten	물겠다/물 것이다/물 거다 to be going to bite	물고 있었다 to have been biting	물고 있다 to be biting	물고 있겠다/물고 있을 것이다/물고 있을 거다 to be going to be biting
만나다 *to meet	만났다 to have met	만나겠다/만날 것이다/만날 거다 to be going to meet	만나고 있었다 to have been meeting	만나고 있다 to be meeting	만나고 있겠다/만나고 있을 것이다/만나고 있을 거다 to be going to be meeting
굽다 *to roast	구웠다 *굽었다 to have roasted	굽겠다/구울 것이다/구울 거다 to be going to roast	굽고 있었다 to have been roasting	굽고 있다 to be roasting	굽고 있겠다/굽고 있을 것이다/굽고 있을 거다 to be going to be roasting
떠나다 *to leave	떠났다 to have left	떠나겠다/떠날 것이다/떠날 거다 to be going to leave	떠나고 있었다 to have been leaving	떠나고 있다 to be leaving	떠나고 있겠다/떠나고 있을 것이다/떠나고 있을 거다 to be going to be leaving
흔들다 *to shake	흔들었다	흔들겠다/흔들	흔들고 있었다	흔들고 있다	흔들고 있겠다/흔들고 있을

Korean Language: Grammar Pattern

	to have shaken	것이다/흔들 거다 to be going to shake	to have been shaking	to be shaking	것이다/흔 들고 있을 거다 to be going to be shaking
이기다 *to win	이겼다 = 이기었다 to have won	이기겠다/이 길 것이다/이길 거다 to be going to win	이기고 있었다 to have been winning	이기고 있다 to be winning	이기고 있겠다/이 기고 있을 것이다/이 기고 있을 거다 to be going to be winning
잃다 *to lose	잃었다 to have lost	잃겠다/잃을 것이다/잃을 거다 to be going to lose	잃고 있었다 to have been losing	잃고 있다 to be losing	잃고 있겠다/잃 고 있을 것이다/잃 고 있을 거다 to be going to be losing
움직이다 *to move	움직였다 = 움직이었다 to have moved	움직이겠다/ 움직일 것이다/움직 일 거다 to be going to move	움직이고 있었다 to have been moving	움직이고 있다 to be moving	움직이고 있겠다/움 직이고 있을 것이다/움 직이고 있을 거다 to be going to be moving
얼다 *to freeze	얼었다 to have frozen	얼겠다/얼 것이다/얼 거다	얼고 있었다 to have been freezing	얼고 있다 to be freezing	얼고 있겠다/얼 고 있을 것이다/얼

Korean Language: Grammar Pattern

		to be going to freeze			고 있을 거다 to be going to be freezing
훔치다 *to steal	훔쳤다 = 훔치었다 to have stolen	훔치겠다/훔칠 것이다/훔칠 거다 to be going to steal	훔치고 있었다 to have been stealing	훔치고 있다 to be stealing	훔치고 있겠다/훔치고 있을 것이다/훔치고 있을 거다 to be going to be stealing
세다 *to count	셌다 to have counted	세겠다/셀 것이다/셀 거다 to be going to count	세고 있었다 to have been counting	세고 있다 to be counting	세고 있겠다/세고 있을 것이다/세고 있을 거다 to be going to be counting
옮기다 *to move	옮겼다 = 옮기었다 to have moved	옮기겠다/옮길 것이다/옮길 거다 to be going to move	옮기고 있었다 to have been moving	옮기고 있다 to be moving	옮기고 있겠다/옮기고 있을 것이다/옮기고 있을 거다 to be going to be moving
나누다 *to divide	나눴다 = 나누었다 to have divided	나누겠다/나눌 것이다/나눌 거다	나누고 있었다 to have been dividing	나누고 있다 to be dividing	나누고 있겠다/나누고 있을 것이다/나

Korean Language: Grammar Pattern

		to be going to divide			누고 있을 거다 to be going to be dividing
태우다 *to burn	태웠다 = 태우었다 to have burnt	태우겠다/태울 것이다/태울 거다 to be going to burn	태우고 있었다 to have been burning	태우고 있다 to be burning	태우고 있겠다/태우고 있을 것이다/태우고 있을 거다 to be going to be burning

UNIT 8. ADJECTIVE & ADVERB

1. Adjective(ㄴ or 은 or 운) + noun

1) root verb stem ending in vowel + ㄴ

•목마르다(to be thirsty): 목마른(thirsty)   *르 ends in vowel ㅡ.   Just add ㄴ.

2) root verb stem ending in consonant except for ㄹ/ㅂ/ㅎ + 은

•검다(to be dark): 검은(dark)   *검 ends in consonant ㅁ.   Add just 은.

3) root verb stem ending in ㄹ: Drop ㄹ and add ㄴ

•둥글다(to be round): 둥근(round)   *글 ends in consonant ㄹ. Drop ㄹ and add ㄴ.

4) root verb stem ending in ㅂ: Drop ㅂ and add 운

•춥다(to be cold): 추운(cold)   *춥 ends in consonant ㅂ.   Drop ㅂ and add 운.

5) root verb stem ending in ㅎ: Drop ㅎ and add ㄴ

•하얗다(to be white): 하얀(white)   *얗 ends in ㅎ.   Drop ㅎ and add ㄴ.

Examples:

•예쁘다(to be pretty): 예쁜(pretty)   *쁘 ends in vowel ㅡ.

•작다(to be small): 작은(small)   *작 ends in consonant ㄱ.

•높다(to be high): 높은(high)   *높 ends in consonant ㅍ.

Korean Language: Grammar Pattern

•어지럽다(to be dizzy): 어지러운(dizzy)   *럽 ends in ㅂ. Drop ㅂ and add 운.

•배고프다(to be hungry): 배고픈   *프 ends in vowel ㅡ.

•낮다(to be low): 낮은(low)   *낮 ends in consonant ㅈ.

•둥글다(to be round): 둥근(round)

*글 ends in ㄹ. Drop ㄹ and add ㄴ. 둥글은 is not correct.

•파랗다(to be blue): 파란(blue)

*The adjective of color has irregular change. Ending ㅎ is not considered to be consonant because it is pronounced silent. *파랗은 is incorrect.

•빨갛다(to be red): 빨간(red)

•노랗다(to be yellow): 노란(yellow)

•서럽다/슬프다(to be sad): 서러운/슬픈(sad)

*럽 ends in ㅂ. Drop 'ㅂ' and add 운.

Adjective + noun	Korean equivalent
<u>scary</u> tiger(호랑이) *to be scary: 무섭다	무서운 호랑이 *무섭은 *섭 ends in ㅂ. Drop ㅂ and add 운.
<u>beautiful</u> dress(드레스) *to be beautiful: 아름답다	아름다운 드레스 *아름답은 *답 ends in ㅂ.
<u>fast</u> car(자동차) *to be fast: 빠르다	빠른 자동차 *르 ends in vowel ㅡ.
<u>noisy</u> sound(소리) *to be noisy: 시끄럽다	시끄러운 소리 *시끄럽은 *럽 ends in ㅂ.
<u>easy</u> test(시험)	쉬운 시험 *쉽은

Korean Language: Grammar Pattern

*to be easy: 쉽다	*to be difficult(어렵다): 어려운 *어렵은 *to be thick (두껍다): 두꺼운 *두껍은
<u>thin</u> ice(얼음) *to be thin: 얇다	얇은 얼음 *얇 ends in combined consonant ㄹㅂ.
<u>brave</u> soldier(군인) *to be brave: 용감하다	용감한 군인 *하 ends in vowel ㅏ.

Exercise 21. Rewrite the underlined English adjectives in Korean.

adjective	adjective in Korean: ㄴ or 운 or 은
<u>cold</u> coffee(커피) *to be cold: 차갑다 or 차다	차가운 or 찬 *차갑은
<u>hot</u> tea(차) *to be hot: 뜨겁다	뜨거운 *뜨겁은
<u>slow</u> train(기차) *to be slow: 느리다	느린
<u>bright</u> sunlight(햇빛) *to be bright: 밝다	밝은
<u>grateful</u> friend(친구) *to be grateful: 고맙다	고마운 *고맙은
<u>deep</u> river(강) *to be deep: 깊다	깊은
<u>warm</u> room(방)	따뜻한

Korean Language: Grammar Pattern

*to be warm: 따뜻하다	
<u>late</u> night(밤) *to be late: 늦다	늦은
<u>soft</u> milk(우유) *to be soft: 부드럽다	부드러운 *부드럽은
<u>hateful</u> song(노래) *to be hateful: 싫다	싫은
<u>itchy</u> back(등) *to be itchy: 가렵다	가려운 *가렵은
<u>expensive</u> clothes(옷) *to be expensive: 비싸다	비싼
<u>quiet</u> room(방) *to be quiet: 조용하다	조용한
<u>exciting</u> game(경기) *to be exciting: 흥미롭다	흥미로운 *흥미롭은
<u>sweet</u> tea(차) *to be sweet: 달다	단 *달은
<u>thick</u> make-up(화장) *to be thick: 두껍다	두꺼운 *두껍은
<u>steep</u> hill(언덕) *to be steep: 가파르다	가파른
<u>heavy</u> weight(무게) *to be heavy: 무겁다	무거운 *무겁은

Korean Language: Grammar Pattern

<u>light</u> chair(의자) *to be light: 가볍다	가벼운 *가볍은
<u>dead</u> mouse(생쥐) *to be dead: 죽다	죽은
<u>rare</u> case(경우) *to be rare: 드물다	드문 *드물은
<u>shy</u> girl(소녀) *to be shy: 부끄럽다	부끄러운 부끄럽은
<u>strange</u> road(도로) *to be strange: 낯설다/이상하다	낯선/이상한 *낯설은
<u>familiar</u> music(음악) *to be familiar: 낯익다/익숙하다	낯익은/익숙한
<u>funny</u> face(얼굴) *to be funny: 재미있다/우습다	재미있는/우스운 *우습은
<u>narrow</u> road(도로) *to be narrow: 좁다	좁은 *조운
<u>clean</u> floor(바닥) *to be clean: 깨끗하다	깨끗한
<u>small</u> house(집) *to be small: 작다	작은
<u>hard</u> assignment(과제) *to be hard: 힘들다/어렵다	힘든/어려운 *힘들은
<u>smart</u> student(학생)	똑똑한

Korean Language: Grammar Pattern

*to be smart: 똑똑하다	
excessive cost(비용) *to be excessive: 지나치다/과도하다	지나친/과도한
successful businessman(사업가) *to be successful: 성공하다	성공한
dirty trick(속임수) *to be dirty: 더럽다	더러운 *더럽은
unbelievable story(이야기) *to be unbelievable: 믿을 수 없다	믿을 수 없는
new semester(학기) *to be new: 새롭다	새로운 *새롭은
red ocean(바다) *to be red: 빨갛다	빨간 *빨갗은
tired person(사람) *to be tired: 피곤하다	피곤한

2. Adverb

1) root verb stem ending in consonant or vowel + 게

*This rule applies when a verb has a root verb stem. This rule is the most general form of adverb.   This form of adverb sounds more formal than the other forms of adverbs.

•바르다(to be correct): 바르게(correctly)   *르 ends in vowel ㅡ. Drop 다 and add 게.

Korean Language: Grammar Pattern

•밝다(to be bright): 밝게(brightly)　*밝 ends in consonant ㄹㄱ.　Drop 다 and add 게.

2) a word without root verb stem ending in consonant + 이

※Adverbs have so many various forms and no consistent rule of formation.　They will form on case-by-case basis.　Especially for adverbs which don't have root verb stem, they don't have grammatical rules of formation.　They sometimes end in 히 or 으로, etc. such as 대단히(much), 열심히(diligently), 지역적으로(locally), or 무작위로(randomly), etc.

Examples:

•to run(달리다) <u>fast</u>: 빠르게 달리다　*to be fast: 빠르다

*Drop 다 from the verb stem and add 게.　Or 빨리 달리다 is also acceptable. 빨리 sounds a little bit more informal than 빠르게.

•to fly(날다) <u>highly</u>: <u>높게</u> or <u>높이</u> 날다　*to be high: 높다

*Drop 다 and add 게.　높이 날다 is informal and fully acceptable.

•to kick(차다) <u>hard</u>: <u>강하게</u> or <u>세게</u> 차다　* 'hard' as adverb: 강하다 or 세다

*Drop 다 and add 게.

•to drink(마시다) <u>much</u>: <u>많이</u> 마시다　*to be much: 많다

*Grammatically 많게 is not wrong.　However, 많게 means 'a lot in number' while 많이 sounds like 'a lot in amount'.

•to talk(말하다) <u>shortly</u>: <u>짧게</u> 말하다　*to be short: 짧다

verb + adverb	Korean equivalent
to drive(운전하다) <u>slowly</u>	<u>느리게</u> 운전하다

Korean Language: Grammar Pattern

*to be slow: 느리다	
to walk(걷다) <u>beautifully</u> *to be beautiful: 아름답다	<u>아름답게</u> 걷다
to hit(때리다) <u>strongly</u> *to be strong: 강하다	<u>강하게</u> 때리다
to live(살다) <u>happily</u> *to be happy: 행복하다	<u>행복하게</u> 살다
to write(쓰다) <u>wrongly</u> *to be wrong: 틀리다	<u>틀리게</u> 쓰다
to say(말하다) <u>kindly</u> *to be kind: 친절하다	<u>친절하게</u> 말하다
to move(움직이다) <u>quickly</u> *to be quick: 빠르다	<u>빠르게 or 빨리</u> 움직이다

Exercise 22. Rewrite the underlined English adverbs in Korean.

adverb	adverb in Korean: mostly 게 or other equivalents
to finish(끝내다) <u>completely</u> *to be complete: 완전하다	완전하게/완전히 ※In most cases, 히 is interchangeable with 하게.
to refuse(거절하다) <u>coldly</u> *to be cold: 차갑다	차갑게
to act(행동하다) <u>naturally</u> *to be natural: 자연스럽다	자연스럽게

Korean Language: Grammar Pattern

to visit(방문하다) <u>frequently</u> *to be frequent: 빈번하다	빈번하게/빈번히
to talk(말하다) <u>loudly</u> *to be loud: 시끄럽다	시끄럽게
to confirm(확인하다) <u>surely</u> *to be sure: 확실하다	확실하게/확실히
to come(오다) <u>secretly</u> *to be secret: 비밀스럽다	비밀스럽게
to drink(마시다) <u>much</u> *to be much: 많다	많이　※많게 is a lot in number.
to sing(노래하다) <u>cheerfully</u> *to be cheerful: 즐겁다	즐겁게
to say(말하다) <u>briefly</u> *to be brief: 간단하다	간단하게/간단히
to call(전화하다) <u>regularly</u> *to be regular: 규칙적이다	정기적으로
to see(보다) <u>sadly</u> *to be sad: 슬프다	슬프게
to drive(운전하다) <u>carefully</u> *to be careful: 조심스럽다	조심스럽게
to come(오다) <u>late</u> *to be late: 늦다	늦게
to live(살다) <u>eternally</u>	영원하게/영원히

Korean Language: Grammar Pattern

*to be eternal: 영원하다	
to choose(고르다) <u>easily</u> *to be easy: 쉽다	쉽게
to eat(먹다) <u>enough</u> *to be enough: 충분하다	충분하게/충분히
to believe(믿다) <u>absolutely</u> *to be absolute: 절대적이다	절대적으로
to catch(잡다) <u>nicely</u> *to be nice: 근사하다/멋지다	근사하게/멋지게

A. Interrogative adverb: WH-Questions

1) WHEN: 언제

2) WHERE: 어디

-어디<u>에서</u>+ active verb such as run, sleep, eat, study, etc.

*에서 is a location marker.

-어디<u>로</u> + verbs such as 'go', 'come', 'arrive', 'depart', 'leave', 'visit', etc.

*로 is a direction marker.

-어디<u>에</u> + static verb such as am, are, is, was, were, etc.

*에 is a location marker combined with static verbs.

3) WHY: 왜 + all types of verbs

Korean Language: Grammar Pattern

4) HOW: 어떻게 + all types of verbs

B. Adverbs of frequency:

항상(always) 절대로 or 결코(never) 가끔 or 종종(often) 수시로(constantly)
자주(frequently) 가끔(sometimes) 늘(usually) 드물게(rarely) 매일(daily)
매주(weekly) 매달(monthly) 매년(yearly), etc.

C. Adverbs of degree:

아주(very) 극히(extremely) 상당히(quite) 너무(too) 정말로(really)/믿을 수
없이(incredibly) 겨우(barely) 깊이(deeply) 꽤(fairly) 대단히(greatly)
심하게(intensely) 다소(somewhat) 전적으로(totally) 조금(little) 덜(less) 더(more),
etc.

D. Adverbs of manner:

빨리(quickly) 천천히 or 느리게(slowly) 조심스럽게(carefully) 화나게(angrily) 주의
깊게(cautiously) 배고프게(hungrily)/조용히 or 조용하게(quietly) 시끄럽게(loudly)
모르게(unknowingly) 용감하게(bravely) 현명하게(wisely) 은밀하게(secretly), etc.

E. Adverbs of place:

여기(here) 거기(there) 어디에나(everywhere) 어디에도(nowhere)
어딘가(somewhere) 안에(inside) 밖에(outside) 어디든지(wherever) 위에(over)
밑에(under) 왼쪽에(left) 오른쪽에(right) 북쪽에(north) 남쪽에(south) 동쪽에(east)
서쪽에(west), etc.

F. Adverbs of time:

지금(now) 그때(then) 곧(soon) 일찍(early) 늦게(late) 오늘(today) 어제(yesterday)
내일(tomorrow) 오늘밤(tonight) 나중에(later) 마침내(eventually) 결국 or
마침내(finally) 영원히(forever) 여전히(still) 최근에(recently), etc.

UNIT 9. PASSIVE VOICE: 이/히/리/기

1. root verb stem ending in vowel or ㄲ or ㅎ + 이

•섞다(to mix): 섞이다(to be mixed)   *섞 ends in ㄲ.

•보다(to see): 보이다(to be seen)   *보 ends in the vowel ㅗ.

•쓰다(to write): 쓰이다(to be written)   *쓰 ends in vowel ㅡ.

•베다(to cut): 베이다(to be cut)   *베 ends in vowel ㅔ.

•파다(to dig): 파이다(to be dug)   *파 ends in vowel ㅏ.

•차다(to kick): 차이다(to be kicked)   *차 ends in vowel ㅏ.

•바꾸다(to change): 바꾸이다→바뀌다(to be changed)   *꾸 ends in vowel ㅜ.

•꺾다(to bend): 꺾이다(to be bent).

*꺾 ends in ㄲ and the passive voice should be 꺾이다.

•놓다(to place): 놓이다(to be placed)

*놓 ends in ㅎ and the passive voice should be 놓이다. Ending ㅎ is silent.

•닿다(to touch/to reach): 닿이다(to be touched/to be reached).

2. root verb stem ending in consonant + 히

•먹다(to eat): 먹히다(to be eaten)   *먹 ends in a consonant ㄱ. Add 히.

•잡다(to catch): 잡히다(to be caught)   *잡 ends in a consonant ㅂ.

•닫다(to close): 닫히다(to be closed)   *닫 ends in a consonant ㄷ.

•읽다(to read()): 읽히다(to be read)   *읽 ends in a consonant ㄺ.

3. root verb stem ending in ㄹ + 리

Korean Language: Grammar Pattern

•갈다(to grind): 갈리다(to be ground)　　*갈 ends in ㄹ. Add just 리.

•뚫다(to penetrate): 뚫리다(to be penetrated)　　*Since the ending consonant ㅎ is silent, the final consonant is ㄹ.

•열다(to open): 열리다(to be opened)

•걸다(to hang): 걸리다(to be hung)

•밀다(to push): 밀리다(to be pushed)

•털다(to shake off): 털리다(to be shaken off)

4.root verb stem ending in ㅅ or ㅁ or ㅈ or ㅊ + 기

•감다(to wind): 감기다(to be wound)　　*감 ends in ㅁ.

•삶다(to boil): 삶기다(to be boiled)

*삶 ends in combined consonant of ㄹㅁ. However, the left consonant ㄹ is silent.

•심다(to plant): 심기다(to be planted)

•쫓다(to chase): 쫓기다(to be chased)　　*쫓 ends in the consonant of ㅊ.

•빼앗다(to rob): 빼앗기다(to be robbed)　　*앗 ends in the consonant of ㅅ.

•찢다(to rip): 찢기다(to be ripped)　　*찢 ends in the consonant of ㅈ.

5. root verb stem ending in ㄷ:

*Out of verbs ending in ㄷ, only 듣다(to hear)/싣다(to load)/걷다(to walk) have a different form of passive voice.　In this case, ㄷ is dropped and ㄹ리다 is added.

•듣다(to hear): 들리다(to be heard)　　*ㄷ is dropped and ㄹ리다 is added.

•걷다(to walk): 걸리다(to be walked=to be forced to walk)

•싣다(to load): 실리다(to be loaded)

*The other verbs have the following forms of passive voice.

•믿다(to believe): 믿기다(to be believed)

Korean Language: Grammar Pattern

•걷다(to collect): 걷<u>히</u>다(to be collected)

•닫다(to close): 닫<u>히</u>다(to be closed)

•묻다(to bury): 묻<u>히</u>다(to be buried)

※Passive voice can be expressed in so many other ways including but not limited to 지다 or 되다 or 당하다, etc. Expressions of passive voice have lots of irregular changes.

•잊다(to forget): 잊<u>히</u>다(to be forgotten)　　*잊기다 is not correct.

•허락하다(to allow): 허락<u>되다</u>(to be allowed)

*허락하이다 is incorrect.   In many cases, the passive voice of '하다-verb' is 되다.

•주다(to give): 주어<u>지다</u>(to be given)　　*주이다 is incorrect.

•접수하다(to receive): 접수<u>되다</u>(to be received)

*The passive voice of '하다-verb' is 되다 or 지다.

•부수다(to break): 부숴<u>지다</u>(to be broken)

*부숴지다 is the short form of 부수<u>어</u>지다. *부수이다 is incorrect.

•끝내다(to finish): 끝내<u>지다</u>(to be finished)

•언급하다(to mention): 언급<u>되다</u>(to be mentioned)

•말하다(to speak): 말해<u>지다</u>(to be spoken)　　*말해지다 is a short form of 말하여 지다.

UNIT 10. AUXILIARY VERB: can & could/would/used to/must & had to/may & might

1. CAN/COULD implies ability or probability

1) root verb stem ending in consonant + 을 수 있다(can)/을 수 있었다(could)

•찾다(to find): 찾을 수 있다(can find)/찾을 수 있었다(could find)

*찾 ends in consonant ㅊ. Drop 다 and add 을 수 있다 or 을 수 있었다.

2) root verb stem ending in vowel + ㄹ 수 있다(can)/ㄹ 수 있었다(could)

•자르다(to cut): 자를 수 있다(can cut)/자를 수 있었다(could cut)

*르 ends in vowel ㅡ. Drop 다 and add ㄹ 수 있다 or ㄹ 수 있었다.

3) root verb stem ending in ㄹ + 수 있다(can)/수 있었다(could)

•살다(to live): 살 수 있다(can live)/살 수 있었다(could live)

*살 ends in ㄹ. Simply add 수 있다/수 있었다.

4) root verb stem ending in ㄷ: ㄷ is dropped and replaced with ㄹ을 수 있다(can)/ㄹ을 수 있었다(could).   The application of this rule is limited to 듣다(to listen)/싣다(to load)/걷다(to walk)/묻다(to ask).   Regular change rule applies to 받다(to receive)/믿다(to believe)/얻다(to gain)/딛다(to step)/걷다(to collect)/닫다(to close)/묻다(to bury).   See the following Table 11 for more details.

Table 11   *Marks in Italic is incorrect.

root verb stem ending in ㄷ	verb stem in present/past tense(can/could): -ㄹ을 수 있다(can)

Korean Language: Grammar Pattern

	-ㄹ을 수 있었다(could) ※었 implies past tense.
듣다 *to listen	들을 수 있다(can listen) *듣을 수 있다 들을 수 있었다(could listen) *듣을 수 있었다
싣다 *to load	실을 수 있다(can load) *싣을 수 있다 실을 수 있었다(could load) *싣을 수 있었다
걷다 *to walk	걸을 수 있다(can walk) *걷을 수 있다 걸을 수 있었다(could walk) *걷을 수 있었다
묻다 *to ask	물을 수 있다(can ask) *묻을 수 있다 물을 수 있었다(could ask) *묻을 수 있었다
받다 *to receive	받을 수 있다(can receive) 받을 수 있었다(could receive)
믿다 *to believe	믿을 수 있다(can believe) 믿을 수 있었다(could believe)
얻다 *to gain	얻을 수 있다(can gain) 얻을 수 있었다(could gain)
딛다 *to step	딛을 수 있다(can step) 딛을 수 있었다(could step)
걷다 *to collect	걷을 수 있다(can collect) 걷을 수 있었다(could collect)
닫다 *to close	닫을 수 있다(can close) 닫을 수 있었다(could close)
묻다	묻을 수 있다(can bury)

*to bury	묻을 수 있었다(could bury)

5) root verb stem ending in ㅂ: Regular change rule applies to most action verbs ending in ㅂ.   Irregular change rule applies to mostly static verbs (to be + adjective).   In this case, ㅂ is dropped and 울 수 있다/울 수 있었다 is added. 눕다(to lie down) and 돕다(to help) and 깁다(to sew) are action verbs but irregular change rule exceptionally applies.   See the following Table 12 for more information.

Table 12   *Marks in Italic* are wrong.

root verb stem ending in ㅂ	verb stem in present/past tense -regular change: 을 수 있다(can)/을 수 있었다(could) -irregular change: 울 수 있다(can)/울 수 있었다(could)
잡다 *to catch	잡을 수 있다(can catch) 잡을 수 있었다(could catch)
업다 *to carry on the back	업을 수 있다(can carry on the back) 업을 수 있었다(could carry on the back)
입다 *to wear	입을 수 있다(can wear) 입을 수 있었다(could wear)
좁다 *to be narrow *This is a static verb but regular change rule applies.	좁을 수 있다(can be narrow) *조울 수 있다 좁을 수 있었다(could be narrow) *조울 수 있었다
접다 *to fold	접을 수 있다(can fold) 접을 수 있었다(could fold)
뽑다	뽑을 수 있다(can select)

Korean Language: Grammar Pattern

*to select	뽑을 수 있었다(could select)
씹다 *to chew	씹을 수 있다(can chew) 씹을 수 있었다(could chew)
맵다 *to be spicy	매울 수 있다(can be spicy)　　*맵을 수 있다 매울 수 있었다(could be spicy)　　*맵을 수 있었다
춥다 *to be cold	추울 수 있다(can be cold)　　*춥을 수 있다 추울 수 있었다(could be cold)　　*춥을 수 있었다
덥다 *to be hot	더울 수 있다(can be hot)　　*덥을 수 있다 더울 수 있었다(could be hot)　　*덥을 수 있었다
깁다 *to sew *This is an action verb.	기울 수 있다(can sew)　　*깁을 수 있다 기울 수 있었다(could sew)　　*깁을 수 있었다
답다 *to be like	다울 수 있다(can be like)　　*답을 수 있다 다울 수 있었다(could be like)　　*답을 수 있었다
무겁다 *to be heavy	무거울 수 있다(can be heavy)　　*무겁을 수 있다 무거울 수 있었다(could be heavy)　　*무겁을 수 있었다
가렵다 *to be itchy	가려울 수 있다(can be itchy)　　*가렵을 수 있다 가려울 수 있었다(could be itchy)　　*가렵을 수 있었다
가엽다 *to be pathetic	가여울 수 있다(can be pathetic)　　*가엽을 수 있다

Korean Language: Grammar Pattern

	가여울 수 있었다(could be pathetic) *가엽을 수 있었다
눕다 *to lie on the back *This is an action verb.	누울 수 있다(can lie on the back) *눕을 수 있다 누울 수 있었다(could lie on the back) *눕을 수 있었다
가소롭다 *to be ridiculous	가소로울 수 있다(can be ridiculous) *가소롭을 수 있다 가소로울 수 있었다(could be ridiculous) *가소롭을 수 있었다
어렵다 *to be difficult	어려울 수 있다(can be difficult) *어렵을 수 있다 어려울 수 있었다(could be difficult) *어렵을 수 있었다
쉽다 *to be easy	쉬울 수 있다(can be easy) *쉽을 수 있다 쉬울 수 있었다(could be easy) *쉽을 수 있었다
돕다 *to help *This is an action verb.	도울 수 있다(can help) *돕을 수 있다 도울 수 있었다(could help) *돕을 수 있었다
더럽다 *to be dirty	더러울 수 있다(can be dirty) *더럽을 수 있다 더러울 수 있었다(could be dirty) *더럽을 수 있었다
우습다 *to be funny	우스울 수 있다(can be funny) *우습을 수 있다 우스울 수 있었다(could be funny) *우습을 수 있었다
고맙다	고마울 수 있다(can be grateful) *고맙을 수 있다

Korean Language: Grammar Pattern

*to be grateful	고마울 수 있었다(could be grateful) *고맙을 수 있었다
밉다 *to be hateful	미울 수 있다(can be hateful) *밉을 수 있다 미울 수 있었다(could be hateful) *밉을 수 있었다
무섭다 *to be scary	무서울 수 있다(can be scary) *무섭을 수 있다 무서울 수 있었다(could be scary) *무섭을 수 있었다
귀엽다 *to be cute	귀여울 수 있다(can be cute) *귀엽을 수 있다 귀여울 수 있었다(could be cute) *귀엽을 수 있었다
즐겁다 *to be happy	즐거울 수 있다(can be happy) *즐겁을 수 있다 즐거울 수 있었다(could be happy) *즐겁을 수 있었다

Examples:

•가다(to go): 갈 수 있다/갈 수 있었다(can/could go)

•먹다(to eat): 먹을 수 있다/먹을 수 있었다(can/could eat)

•보다(to see): 볼 수 있다/볼 수 있었다(can/could see)

•끊다(to cut): 끊을 수 있다/끊을 수 있었다(can/could cut)

•살다(to live): 살 수 있다/살 수 있었다(can/could live)

•울다(to cry): 울 수 있다/울 수 있었다(can/could cry)

•녹다(to melt down): 녹을 수 있다/녹을 수 있었다(can/could melt down)

•서다(to stand): 설 수 있다/설 수 있었다(can/could stand)

•즐기다(to enjoy): 즐길 수 있다/즐길 수 있었다(can/could enjoy)

Korean Language: Grammar Pattern

•복종하다(to obey): 복종할 수 있다/복종할 수 있었다(can/could obey)

•가지다(to have): 가질 수 있다/가질 수 있었다(can/could have)

•오다(to come): 올 수 있다/올 수 있었다(can/could come)

•솟다(to rise): 솟을 수 있다/솟을 수 있었다(can/could rise)

•잡다(to catch): 잡을 수 있다/잡을 수 있었다(can/could catch)

•싸우다(to fight): 싸울 수 있다/싸울 수 있었다(can/could fight)

•이기다(to win): 이길 수 있다/이길 수 있었다(can/could win)

Exercise 23. Rewrite the English CAN/COULD in Korean.

root verb stem	CAN + verb in Korean: (ㄹ/을) 수 있다/울 수 있다	COULD + verb in Korean: (ㄹ/을) 수 있었다/울 수 있었다
바꾸다 *to change	바꿀 수 있다 can change	바꿀 수 있었다 could change
되다 *to become	될 수 있다 can become	될 수 있었다 could become
운전하다 *to drive	운전할 수 있다 can drive	운전할 수 있었다 could drive
사다 *to buy	살 수 있다 can buy	살 수 있었다 could buy
하다 *to do	할 수 있다 can do	할 수 있었다 could do
쓰다 *to write	쓸 수 있다 can write	쓸 수 있었다 could write
벗다 *to take off	벗을 수 있다 can take off	벗을 수 있었다 could take off
입다 *to wear	입을 수 있다 can wear	입을 수 있었다 could wear

Korean Language: Grammar Pattern

마시다 *to drink	마실 수 있다 can drink	마실 수 있었다 could drink
만들다 *to make	만들 수 있다　　*만들을 수 있다 can make	만들 수 있었다　　*만들을 수 있었다 could make
끓이다 *to boil	끓일 수 있다 can boil	끓일 수 있었다 could boil
도착하다 *to arrive	도착할 수 있다 can arrive	도착할 수 있었다 could arrive
춤추다 *to dance	춤출 수 있다 can dance	춤출 수 있었다 could dance
부르다 *to call	부를 수 있다 can call	부를 수 있었다 could call
잡다 *to catch	잡을 수 있다 can catch	잡을 수 있었다 could catch
타다 *to ride	탈 수 있다 can ride	탈 수 있었다 could ride
앉다 *to sit	앉을 수 있다 can sit	앉을 수 있었다 could sit
서다 *to stand	설 수 있다 can stand	설 수 있었다 could stand
갈다 *to grind	갈 수 있다　　*갈을 수 있다 can grind	갈 수 있었다　　*갈을 수 있었다 could grind
찢다 *to tear	찢을 수 있다 can tear	찢을 수 있었다 could tear
속이다 *to deceive	속일 수 있다 can deceive can deceive	속일 수 있었다 could deceive
걷다	걸을 수 있다　　*걷을 수 있다	걸을 수 있었다　　*걷을 수 있었

Korean Language: Grammar Pattern

*to walk	can walk	다 could walk
걷다 *to collect	걸을 수 있다　*걸을 수 있다 can collect	걸을 수 있었다　*걸을 수 있었 다 could collect
맵다 *to be spicy	매울 수 있다　*맵을 수 있다 can be spicy	매울 수 있었다　*맵을 수 있었 다 could be spicy
알다 *to know	알 수 있다　*알을 수 있다 can know	알 수 있었다　*알을 수 있었다 could know
묻다 *to ask	물을 수 있다　*묻을 수 있다 can ask	물을 수 있었다　*묻을 수 있었 다 could ask
닿다 *to reach	닿을 수 있다 can reach	닿을 수 있었다 could reach
돕다 *to help	도울 수 있다　*돕을 수 있다 can help	도울 수 있었다　*돕을 수 있었 다 could help

2. WOULD as intention in past tense: 려고 했다 or 으려고 했다

*would as intention= 'insisted on/intended to/tried to/was(were) determined to/was(were) about to'.

1) root verb stem ending in consonant + 으려고 했다

•먹다(to eat): 먹으려고 했다(intended to eat)

*먹 ends in consonant ㄱ. Drop 다 and add 으려고 했다.

Korean Language: Grammar Pattern

2) root verb stem ending in vowel or consonant ㄹ + 려고 했다

•말다(to roll): 말려고 했다(intended to roll)

*말 ends in ㄹ. Just add 려고 했다

•보다(to see): 보려고 했다(intended to see)

*보 ends in vowel of ㅗ. Add just 려고 했다   *볼려고* is incorrect.

3) root verb stem ending in consonant ㄷ: Irregular change rule applies to 듣다(to listen)/싣다(to load)/걷다(to walk)/묻다(to ask) and regular change rule applies to the others. For irregular change, ㄷ is dropped and ㄹ으려고 했다 is added. See the following Table 13 for the comparison of the verb stems ending in ㄷ.

Table 13   *Marks in Italic are incorrect.

root verb stem ending in ㄷ	would + verb in Korean ㄹ으려고 했다 or 으려고 했다
듣다 *to listen	들으려고 했다 *듣으려고 했다* would listen
싣다 *to load	실으려고 했다 *싣으려고 했다* would load
걷다 *to walk	걸으려고 했다 *걷으려고 했다* would walk
묻다 *to ask	물으려고 했다 *묻으려고 했다* would ask
받다 *to receive	받으려고 했다 would receive
믿다 *to believe	믿으려고 했다 would believe

Korean Language: Grammar Pattern

얻다	얻으려고 했다
*to gain	would gain
딛다	딛으려고 했다
*to step	would step
걷다	걷으려고 했다
*to collect	would collect
닫다	닫으려고 했다
*to close	would close
묻다	묻으려고 했다
*to bury	would bury

4) root verb stem ending in consonant ㅂ: Verbs ending in ㅂ have either regular or irregular endings. For regular endings, 다 is dropped from the verb stem and 으려고 했다 is added. For irregular endings, ㅂ is dropped and 우려고(NOT *으려고) 했다 is added. Mostly irregular change rule applies to static verbs ending in ㅂ.

See the following Table 14 for the comparison of the verb stems ending in ㅂ.

※ In the case of 'would + static verb', 'would' means a prediction or possibility in the near future.

Table 14   *Marks in Italic are incorrect.

root verb stem ending in ㅂ	would + verb in Korean: 으려고 했다 or 우려고 했다
잡다	잡으려고 했다
*to catch	would catch
업다	업으려고 했다
*to carry on the back	would carry on the back

Korean Language: Grammar Pattern

입다 *to wear	입으려고 했다 would wear
접다 *to fold	접으려고 했다 would fold
뽑다 *to select	뽑으려고 했다 would select
씹다 *to chew	씹으려고 했다 would chew
맵다 *to be spicy	매우려고 했다　　*맵으려고 했다 would be spicy
춥다 *to be cold	추우려고 했다　　*춥으려고 했다 would be cold
덥다 *to be hot	더우려고 했다　　*덥으려고 했다 would be hot
무겁다 *to be heavy	무거우려고 했다　　*무겁으려고 했다 would be heavy
가렵다 *to be itchy	가려우려고 했다　　*가렵으려고 했다 would be itchy
가엽다 *to be pathetic	가여우려고 했다　　*가엽으려고 했다 would be pathetic
눕다 *to lie on the back	누우려고 했다　　*눕으려고 했다 would lie on the back
가소롭다 *to be ridiculous	가소로우려고 했다　　*가소롭으려고 했다 would be ridiculous

Korean Language: Grammar Pattern

어렵다	어려우려고 했다 *어렵으려고 했다
*to be difficult	would be difficult
쉽다	쉬우려고 했다 *쉽으려고 했다
*to be easy	would be easy
돕다	도우려고 했다 *돕으려고 했다
*to help	would help
더럽다	더러우려고 했다 *더럽으려고 했다
*to be dirty	would be dirty
우습다	우스우려고 했다 *우습으려고 했다
*to be funny	would be funny
고맙다	고마우려고 했다 *고맙으려고 했다
*to be grateful	would be grateful
밉다	미우려고 했다 *밉으려고 했다
*to be hateful	would be hateful
무섭다	무서우려고 했다 *무섭으려고 했다
*to be scary	would be scary
귀엽다	귀여우려고 했다 *귀엽으려고 했다
*to be cute	would be cute
깁다	기우려고 했다 *깁으려고 했다
*to sew	would sew
즐겁다	즐거우려고 했다 *즐겁으려고 했다
*to be happy	would be happy

Examples:

•가다(to go): 가려고 했다(would go)   *갈려고

Korean Language: Grammar Pattern

•먹다(to eat): 먹으려고 했다(would eat)

•보다(to see): 보려고 했다(would see)   *볼려고

•끊다(to cut): 끊으려고 했다(would cut)

•살다(to live): 살려고 했다(would live)   *살으려고 했다 is incorrect.

•울다(to cry): 울려고 했다(would cry)   *울으려고 했다 is incorrect.

•녹다(to melt down): 녹으려고 했다(would melt down)

•서다(to stand): 서려고 했다(would stand)   *설려고

•즐기다(to enjoy): 즐기려고 했다(would enjoy)   *즐길려고

•복종하다(to obey): 복종하려고 했다(would obey)

•가지다(to have): 가지려고 했다(would have)   *가질려고

•오다(to come): 오려고 했다(would come)   *올려고

•솟다(to rise): 솟으려고 했다(would rise)

•싸우다(to fight): 싸우려고 했다(would fight)   *싸울려고

•이기다(to win): 이기려고 했다(would win)   *이길려고

Exercise 24. Rewrite the 'would + verb' in Korean.

root verb stem	WOULD + verb in Korean: 려고 했다 or (ㄹ)으려고 했다 or 우려고 했다
바꾸다 *to change	바꾸려고 했다 would change
묶다 *to tie	묶으려고 했다 would tie
운전하다 *to drive	운전하려고 했다 would drive

Korean Language: Grammar Pattern

사다 *to buy	사려고 했다 would buy
걷다 *to walk	걸으려고 했다 *걷으려고 했다 would walk
걷다 *to collect	걷으려고 했다 *걸으려고 했다 would collect
하다 *to do	하려고 했다 would do
쓰다 *to write	쓰려고 했다 would write
춥다 *to be cold	추우려고 했다 *춥으려고 했다 would be cold
벗다 *to take off	벗으려고 했다 would take off
쏘다 *to shoot	쏘려고 했다 would shoot
마시다 *to drink	마시려고 했다 would drink
만들다 *to make	만들려고 했다 *만들으려고 했다 would make
잡다 *to catch	잡으려고 했다 would catch
끓이다 *to boil	끓이려고 했다 would boil

Korean Language: Grammar Pattern

도착하다 *to arrive	도착하려고 했다 would arrive
춤추다 *to dance	춤추려고 했다 would dance
부르다 *to call	부르려고 했다 would call
먹다 *to eat	먹으려고 했다 would eat
타다 *to ride	타려고 했다 would ride
앉다 *to sit	앉으려고 했다 would sit
볶다 *to fry	볶으려고 했다 would fry
갈다 *to grind	갈려고 했다　*갈으려고 했다 would grind
돕다 *to help	도우려고 했다　*돕으려고 했다 would help
찢다 *to tear	찢으려고 했다 would tear
속이다 *to deceive	속이려고 했다 would deceive

3. USED TO as 'the habitual or regularly repeated action' in the past: 곤 했다

Korean Language: Grammar Pattern

*root verb stem ending in consonant or vowel + 곤 했다 with NO irregular changes

※Drop 다 from the root verb stem and add 곤 했다.

Examples:

•가다(to go): 가곤 했다(used to go)　　*가 ends in vowel ㅏ.

•먹다(to eat): 먹곤 했다(used to eat)　　*먹 ends in consonant ㄱ.

•보다(to see): 보곤 했다(used to see)

•끊다(to cut): 끊곤 했다(used to cut)

•살다(to live): 살곤 했다(used to live)　　*살 ends in consonant ㄹ.

•울다(to cry): 울곤 했다(used to cry)

•녹다(to melt down): 녹곤 했다(used to melt down)

•서다(to stand): 서곤 했다(used to stand)

•즐기다(to enjoy): 즐기곤 했다(used to enjoy)

•복종하다(to obey): 복종하곤 했다(used to obey)

•가지다(to have): 가지곤 했다(used to have)

•오다(to come): 오곤 했다(used to come)

•솟다(to rise): 솟곤 했다(used to rise)

•잡다(to catch): 잡곤 했다(used to catch)

•싸우다(to fight): 싸우곤 했다(used to fight)

•이기다(to win): 이기곤 했다(used to win)

•입다(to wear): 입곤 했다(used to wear)

•접다(to fold): 접곤 했다(used to fold)

Korean Language: Grammar Pattern

Exercise 25. Rewrite 'used to + verb' in Korean.

root verb stem	USED TO + verb in Korean: 곤 했다
바꾸다 *to change	바꾸곤 했다 used to change
운전하다 *to drive	운전하곤 했다 used to drive
사다 *to buy	사곤 했다 used to buy
하다 *to do	하곤 했다 used to do
쓰다 *to write	쓰곤 했다 used to write
듣다 *to listen	듣곤 했다 used to listen
벗다 *to take off	벗곤 했다 used to take off
놀다 *to play	놀곤 했다 used to play
마시다 *to drink	마시곤 했다 used to drink
만들다 *to make	만들곤 했다 used to make

Korean Language: Grammar Pattern

끓이다 *to boil	끓이곤 했다 used to boil
도착하다 *to arrive	도착하곤 했다 used to arrive
춤추다 *to dance	춤추곤 했다 used to dance
부르다 *to call	부르곤 했다 used to call
눕다 *to lie down	눕곤 했다 used to lie down
노래하다 *to sing a song	노래하곤 했다 used to sing a song
타다 *to ride	타곤 했다 used to ride
앉다 *to sit	앉곤 했다 used to sit
갈다 *to grind	갈곤 했다 used to grind
찢다 *to tear	찢곤 했다 used to tear
속이다 *to deceive	속이곤 했다 used to deceive
바꾸다 *to change	바꾸곤 했다 used to change

Korean Language: Grammar Pattern

덥다	덥곤 했다
*to be hot	used to be hot

4. MUST & HAD TO implies 'obligation or duty': (아/어)야 한다(present tense)/(아/어)야 했다(past tense)

※Linking vowels are critically important in deciding on either 아야 하다 or 어야 하다.

※Since the verb change rule is extremely similar to the verb endings in past tense, it is highly advised to go back to 'UNIT 7. 2. verb stem in past tense' for more details and comparison.

1) root verb stem ending in the linking vowels of ㅗ or ㅛ WITH or WITHOUT ending consonant + 아야 하다(must)/아야 했다(had to)

•볶다(to fry): 볶아야 하다(must fry)/볶아야 했다(had to fry)

*볶 ends in the linking vowel of ㅗ with ending consonant ㄲ. Drop 다 and add 아야 하다/아야 했다

•보다(to see): 봐야(보아야) 하다(must see)/봐야(보아야) 했다(had to see)

*보 ends in vowel ㅗ with no ending consonant. Drop 다 and add 아야 하다/아야 했다.

2-1) root verb stem ending in the linking vowels of ㅏ or ㅑ WITH ending consonant + 아야 하다(must)/아야 했다(had to)

•막다(to block/to stop): 막아야 하다(must block/stop)/막아야 했다(had to block/stop)

*막 ends in the linking vowel of ㅏ with ending consonant ㄱ. Drop 다 and add 아야 하다/아야 했다.

2-2) root verb stem ending in the linking vowels of ㅏ or ㅑ WITHOUT ending consonant + 야 하다(must)/야 했다(had to)

•가다(to go): 가야 하다(must go)/가야 했다(had to go)

*가아야 하다/가아야 했다 is incorrect.

*가 ends in the linking vowel ㅏ with no ending consonant. Drop 다 and add 야 하다/야 했다.

3) root verb stem ending in the linking vowels of ㅜ or ㅠ or ㅡ or ㅣ WITH or WITHOUT ending consonant + 어야 하다(must)/어야 했다(had to)

•묵다(to stay): 묵어야 하다(must stay)/묵어야 했다(had to stay)

*묵 ends in the linking vowel of ㅜ with ending consonant ㄱ. Drop 다 and add 어야 하다/어야 했다.

•이기다(to win): 이겨야(이기어야) 하다(must win)/이겨야(이기어야) 했다(had to win)

*기 ends in vowel ㅣ with no ending consonant.   Drop 다 and add 어야 하다/어야 했다.

4-1) root verb stem ending in the linking vowels of ㅓ or ㅕ WITH ending consonant + 어야 하다(must)/어야 했다(had to)

•벗다(to take off): 벗어야 하다(must take off)/벗어야 했다(had to take off)

*벗 ends in the linking vowel of ㅓ with ending consonant ㅅ. Drop 다 and add 어야 하다/어야 했다.

4-2) root verb stem ending in the linking vowels of ㅓ or ㅕ WITHOUT ending consonant + 야 하다(must)/야 했다(had to)

•서다(to stand up): 서야 하다(must stand up)/서야 했다(had to stand up)

Korean Language: Grammar Pattern

서어야 하다/서어야 했다 is incorrect.

*서 ends in the linking vowel of ㅓ with no ending consonant. Drop 다 and add just 야 하다/야 했다.

5) root verb stem ending in ㄷ: Irregular change rule applies to 듣다(to listen)/싣다(to load)/걷다(to walk)/묻다(to ask). In this case, ㄷ is dropped and replaced with ㄹ어야 하다 or ㄹ아야 하다/ㄹ어야 했다 ㄹ아야 했다(must/had to). Regular change rule applies to the other verbs ending in ㄷ. See the following Table 15 for more information. The type of linking vowel decides on either 어야 하다/했다 or 아야 하다/했다.

Table 15   *Marks in Italic are incorrect.

root verb stem ending in ㄷ	MUST/HAD TO: -regular change: 아(어)야 하다/아(어)야 했다 -irregular change: ㄹ어야 하다/ㄹ어야 했다
듣다 *to listen	들어야 하다 must listen *듣어야 하다 들어야 했다 had to listen *듣어야 했다 *듣 ends in the vowel ㅡ. Add 어야 하다/어야 했다.
싣다 *to load	실어야 하다 must load *싣어야 하다 실어야 했다 had to load *싣어야 했다 *실 ends in the vowel ㅣ. Add 어야 하다/어야 했다.
걷다 *to walk	걸어야 하다 must walk *걷어야 하다 걸어야 했다 had to walk *걷어야 했다 *걷 ends in the vowel ㅓ. Add 어야 하다/어야 했다.
묻다	물어야 하다 must ask *묻어야 하다

Korean Language: Grammar Pattern

to ask	물어야 했다 had to ask *묻어야 했다 *묻 ends in the vowel ㅜ. So add 어야 하다/어야 했다'.
받다 *to receive	받아야 하다 must receive 받아야 했다 had to receive *받 ends in the vowel ㅏ with ending consonant. Add 아야 하다/아야 했다.
믿다 *to believe	믿어야 하다 must receive 믿어야 했다 had to receive *믿 ends in the vowel ㅣ with ending consonant. Add 어야 하다/어야 했다.
얻다 *to gain	얻어야 하다 must gain 얻어야 했다 had to gain *얻 ends in the vowel ㅓ. Add 어야 하다/어야 했다.
딛다 *to step	딛어야 하다 must step 딛어야 했다 had to step *딛 ends in the vowel ㅣ. Add 어야 하다/어야 했다.
걷다 *to collect	걷어야 하다 must collect 걷어야 했다 had to collect *걷 ends in the vowel ㅓ. Add 어야 하다/어야 했다.
닫다 *to close	닫아야 하다 must close 닫아야 했다 had to close

	*닫 ends in the vowel ㅏ. Add 아야 하다/아야 했다.
묻다 *to bury	묻어야 하다 must bury 묻어야 했다 had to bury *묻 ends in the vowel ㅜ. Add 어야 하다/어야 했다.

6) root verb stem ending in ㅂ: Verbs ending in ㅂ have either regular or irregular endings. For regular endings, ㅂ is kept and add 아야 한다/어야 한다(must)/아야 했다/어야 했다(had to) in accordance with the type of linking vowel. Irregular change rule applies to mostly static verbs. For irregular change, ㅂ is dropped from the verb stem and 워야 하다(must)/워야 했다(had to) is added. See the following Table 16 for the comparison of the verb stems ending in ㅂ. Most irregular verbs are static verbs(to be + adjective) except for 눕다(to lie) and 돕다(to help) which are action verbs.

Table 16   *Marks in Italic* are incorrect.

root verb stem ending in ㅂ	MUST: 아야 하다 or 어야 하다 or 워야 하다	HAD TO: 아야 했다 or 어야 했다 or 워야 했다
잡다 *to catch	잡아야 하다 must catch	잡아야 했다 had to catch
입다 *to wear	입어야 하다 must wear	입어야 했다 had to wear
접다 *to fold	접어야 하다 must fold	접어야 했다 had to wear
뽑다 *to select	뽑아야 하다 must select	뽑아야 했다 had to select

Korean Language: Grammar Pattern

씹다 *to chew	씹어야 하다 must chew	씹어야 했다 had to chew
맵다 *to be spicy	매워야 하다　*맵어야 하다 ※ㅂ is dropped and 워야 하다 is added. must be spicy	매워야 했다　*맵어야 했다 had to be spicy
춥다 *to be cold	추워야 하다　*춥어야 하다 must be cold	추워야 했다　*춥어야 했다 had to be cold
덥다 *to be hot	더워야 하다　*덥어야 하다 must be hot	더워야 했다　*덥어야 했다 had to be hot
무겁다 *to be heavy	무거워야 하다　*무겁어야 하다 must be heavy	무거워야 했다　*무겁어야 했다 had to be heavy
가렵다 *to be itchy	가려워야 하다　*가렵어야 하다 must be itchy	가려워야 했다　*가렵어야 했다 had to be itchy
가엽다 *to be pathetic	가여워야 하다　*가엽어야 하다 must be pathetic	가여워야 했다　*가엽어야 했다 had to be pathetic
눕다 *to lie down	누워야 하다　*눕어야 하다 must lie down	누워야 했다　*눕어야 했다 had to lie down
어렵다 *to be difficult	어려워야 하다　*어렵어야 하다 must be difficult	어려워야 했다　*어렵어야 했다 had to be difficult
쉽다	쉬워야 하다　*쉽어야 하다	쉬워야 했다　*쉽어야 했다

Korean Language: Grammar Pattern

*to be easy	must be easy	had to be easy
돕다 *to help	*도와야 하다　　*돕아야 하다 must help	*도와야 했다　　*돕아야 했다 had to help
더럽다 *to be dirty	더러워야 하다　　*더럽어야 하다 must be dirty	더러워야 했다　　*더럽어야 했다 had to be dirty
우습다 *to be funny	우스워야 하다　　*우습어야 하다 must be funny	우스워야 했다　　*우습어야 했다 had to be funny
고맙다 *to be thankful	고마워야 하다　　*고맙아야 하다 must be thankful	고마워야 했다　　*고맙아야 했다 had to be thankful
밉다 to be hateful	미워야 하다　　*밉어야 하다 must be hateful	미워야 했다　　*밉어야 했다 had to be hateful
무섭다 *to be scary	무서워야 하다　　*무섭어야 하다 must be scary	무서워야 했다　　*무섭어야 했다 had to be scary
귀엽다 *to be cute	귀여워야 하다　　*귀엽어야 하다 must be cute	귀여워야 했다　　*귀엽어야 했다 had to be cute
즐겁다 *to be happy	즐거워야 하다 *즐겁어야 하다	즐거워야 했다 *즐겁어야 했다

7) root verb stem ending in 르다:　The ending syllables of 르다 are dropped and combined with ㄹ라야 하다 or ㄹ러야 하다 depending on the linking vowel which is placed right before 르다. The linking vowels of ㅜ or ㅠ or ㅓ or ㅕ or ㅡ or ㅣ will be combined with ㄹ러야 하다.　And the linking vowels of ㅏ or ㅑ or ㅗ or ㅛ will be combined with ㄹ라야 하다.　The linking vowel decides on whether

Korean Language: Grammar Pattern

ㄹ라야 or ㄹ러야.   Refer to 'UNIT 7. 2. verb stem in past tense' for more details. These cases are kind of irregular changes.   See the following Table 17 for more information.

Table 17   *Marks in Italic are incorrect.

root verb stem ending in 르다	MUST: -ㅏ ㅑ ㅗ ㅛ + ㄹ라야 하다 -ㅜ ㅠ ㅓ ㅕ ㅡ ㅣ + ㄹ러야 하다	HAD TO: -ㅏ ㅑ ㅗ ㅛ + ㄹ라야 했다 -ㅜ ㅠ ㅓ ㅕ ㅡ ㅣ + ㄹ러야 했다
바르다 *to apply	발라야 하다 *발러야 하다 *바 ends in vowel ㅏ. ※Drop 르다 and add ㄹ라야 하다.	발라야 했다 *발러야 했다
부르다 *to call	불러야 하다 *불라야 하다 *부 ends in vowel ㅜ. ※Drop 르다 and add ㄹ러야 하다.	불러야 했다 *불라야 했다
자르다 *to cut	잘라야 하다 *잘러야 하다 *자 ends in vowel ㅏ.	잘라야 했다 *잘러야 했다
목마르다 *to be thirsty	목말라야 하다 *목말러야 하다 *마 ends in vowel ㅏ.	목말라야 했다 *목말러야 했다
이르다 *to be early	일러야 하다 *일라야 하다 *이 ends in vowel ㅣ.	일러야 했다 *일라야 했다
흐르다 *to flow	흘러야 하다 *흘라야 하다 *흐 ends in vowel ㅡ.	흘러야 했다 *흘라야 했다

Korean Language: Grammar Pattern

오르다 *to rise	올라야 하다 　*올러야 하다 *오 ends in vowel ㅗ.	올라야 했다 　*올러야 했다
소리지르다 *to shout	소리질러야 하다 *소리질라야 하다 *지 ends in vowel ㅣ.	소리질러야 했다 *소리질라야 했다
고르다 *to choose	골라야 하다 　*골러야 하다 *고 ends in vowel ㅗ.	골라야 했다 　*골러야 했다

Examples:

•가다(to go): 가야 하다(must go)/가야 했다(had to go)

*linking vowel ㅏ with no ending consonant + 야 하다

•먹다(to eat): 먹어야 하다(must eat)/먹어야 했다(had to eat)

*linking vowel ㅓ with ending consonant ㄱ + 어야 하다

•보다(to see): 봐야(보아야) 하다(must see)/봐야(보아야) 했다(had to see)

*linking vowel ㅗ with no ending consonant + 아야 하다　봐야 is a short form of 보아야. A short form is more natural in writing and speaking.

•끊다(to cut): 끊어야 하다(must cut)/끊어야 했다(had to cut)

*linking vowel ― with ending consonant ᄚ + 어야 하다

•살다(to live): 살아야 하다(must live)/살아야 했다(had to live)

*linking vowel ㅏ with ending consonant ㄹ + 아야 하다

•울다(to cry): 울어야 하다(must cry)/울어야 했다(had to cry)

*linking vowel ㅜ with ending consonant ㄹ + 어야 하다

•녹다(to melt down): 녹아야 하다(must melt down)/녹아야 했다(had to melt down)

*linking vowel ㅗ with ending consonant ㄱ + 아야 하다

Korean Language: Grammar Pattern

•서다(to stand): 서야 하다(must stand)/서야 했다(had to stand)

*linking vowel ㅓ with no ending consonant + 야 하다

•즐기다(to enjoy): 즐겨야(즐기어야) 하다(must enjoy)/즐겨야(즐기어야) 했다(had to enjoy)　※Short form of speech is better than regular form.

*linking vowel ㅣ with no ending consonant + 어야 하다

•복종하다(to obey): 복종해야 하다(must obey)/복종해야 했다(had to obey)

*In the case of '하다-verb', the ending should be 해야. *하야* or *하아야* is incorrect. This is an irregular change. This rule applies to all the '하다-verbs'.

•가지다(to have): 가져야 하다(must have)/가져야 했다(had to have)

*linking vowel ㅣ with no ending consonant + 어야 하다　가져야 is a short form of 가지어야.

•오다(to come): 와야 하다(must come)/와야 했다(had to come)

*linking vowel ㅗ with no ending consonant + 아야 하다　와야 is the short form of 오아야.

•솟다(to rise): 솟아야 하다(must rise)/솟아야 했다(had to rise)

*linking vowel ㅗ with ending consonant ㅅ + 아야 하다

•잡다(to catch): 잡아야 하다(must catch)/잡아야 했다(had to catch)

*linking vowel ㅏ with ending consonant ㅂ + 아야 하다

•싸우다(to fight): 싸워야 하다(must fight)/싸워야 했다(had to fight)

*linking vowel ㅜ with no ending consonant + 어야 하다　싸워야 is a short form of 싸우어야.

•이기다(to win): 이겨야 하다(must win)/이겨야 했다(had to win)

*linking vowel ㅣ with no ending consonant + 어야 하다　이겨야 is a short form of 이기어야.

•입다(to wear): 입어야 하다(must wear)/입어야 했다(had to wear)

*linking vowel ㅣ with ending consonant ㅂ + 어야 하다

[여기에 입력]
Korean Language: Grammar Pattern

•접다(to fold): 접어야 하다(must fold)/접어야 했다(had to fold)

*linking vowel ㅓ with ending consonant ㅂ + 어야 하다

Exercise 26. Rewrite the English verbs of 'MUST/HAD TO' in Korean.

root verb stem	MUST in Korean: (어)야 하다 or (아)야 하다 or 워야 하다 or ㄹ라야 하다 or ㄹ러야 하다	HAD TO in Korean: (어)야 했다 or (아)야 했다 or 워야 했다 or ㄹ라야 했다 or ㄹ러야 했다
바꾸다 *to change	바꿔야(바꾸어야) 하다 must change	바꿔야(바꾸어야) 했다 had to change
되다 *to become	돼야(되어야) 하다 must become	돼야(되어야) 했다 had to become
운전하다 *to drive	운전해야 하다 must drive	운전해야 했다 had to drive
흐르다 *to flow	흘러야 하다 *흐러야 하다 must flow	흘러야 했다 *흐러야 했다 had to flow
사다 *to buy	사야 하다 must buy	사야 했다 had to buy
하다 *to do	해야 하다 must do	해야 했다 had to do
쓰다 *to write	써야 하다 must write	써야 했다 had to write
벗다 *to take off	벗어야 하다 must take off	벗어야 했다 had to take off
입다	입어야 하다	입어야 했다

Korean Language: Grammar Pattern

*to wear	must wear	had to wear
마시다 *to drink	마셔야(마시어야) 하다 must drink	마셔야(마시어야) 했다 had to drink
닫다 *to close	닫아야 하다 must close	닫아야 했다 had to close
만들다 *to make	만들어야 하다 must make	만들어야 했다 had to make
끓이다 *to boil	끓여야(끓이어야) 하다 must boil	끓여야(끓이어야) 했다 had to boil
도착하다 *to arrive	도착해야 하다 must arrive	도착해야 했다 had to arrive
춤추다 *to dance	춤춰야(춤추어야) 하다 must dance	춤춰야(춤추어야) 했다 had to dance
잡다 *to catch	잡아야 하다 must catch	잡아야 했다 had to catch
타다 *to ride	타야 하다 must ride	타야 했다 had to ride
앉다 *to sit	앉아야 하다 must sit	앉아야 했다 had to sit
눕다 *to lie down	누워야 하다 *눕어야 하다 must lie down	누워야 했다 *눕어야 했다 had to lie down
갈다 *to grind	갈아야 하다 must grind	갈아야 했다 had to grind
찢다	찢어야 하다	찢어야 했다

Korean Language: Grammar Pattern

*to tear	must tear	had to tear
속이다 *to deceive	속여야(속이어야) 하다 must deceive	속여야(속이어야) 했다 had to deceive
바르다 *to apply	발라야 하다 *바라야 하다 must apply	발라야 했다 *바라야 했다 had to apply
덥다 *to be hot	더워야 하다 *덥어야 하다 must be hot	더워야 했다 *덥어야 했다 had to be hot
걷다 *to walk	걸어야 하다 *걷어야 하다 must walk	걸어야 했다 *걷어야 했다 had to walk
자르다 *to cut	잘라야 하다 *자라야 하다 must cut	잘라야 했다 *자라야 했다 had to cut
돕다 *to help	도와야 하다 *돕아야 하다 must help	도와야 했다 *돕아야 했다 had to help
잊다 *to forget	잊어야 하다 must forget	잊어야 했다 had to forget
오르다 *to climb	올라야 하다 *오라야 하다 must climb	올라야 했다 *오라야 했다 had to climb
빌다 *to beg	빌어야 하다 must beg	빌어야 했다 had to beg
즐겁다 *to be happy	즐거워야 하다 *즐겁어야 하다 must be happy	즐거워야 했다 *즐겁어야 했다 had to be happy

※to be highly recommended or advised/almost required: 지 않으면 안된다

Korean Language: Grammar Pattern

*Drop 다 from root verb stem and add 지 않으면 안 된다(if--not, it is not good=do not fail to + verb = it is almost required to + verb). 않 and 안 imply negative action. Therefore, 지 않으면 안된다 is a kind of double negation.

Examples:

•읽다(to read): 읽지 않으면 안 된다(it is highly recommended or advised to read)

•보다(to see): 보지 않으면 안 된다

•막다(to block): 막지 않으면 안 된다

•달리다(to run): 달리지 않으면 안 된다

•돕다(to help): 돕지 않으면 안 된다

•닫다(to close): 닫지 않으면 안 된다

•열다(to open): 열지 않으면 안 된다

•하다(to do): 하지 않으면 안 된다

Exercise 27. Rewrite English recommendation or advice in Korean.

root verb stem	strong recommendation or advice in Korean: 지 않으면 안된다 =it is highly recommended to =it is almost required to =it is not good if you fail to
쓰다 *to write	쓰지 않으면 안된다 =it is highly recommended to write =it is almost required to write =it is not good if you fail to write

Korean Language: Grammar Pattern

만들다 *to make	만들지 않으면 안된다
걷다 *to walk	걷지 않으면 안된다
바꾸다 *to change	바꾸지 않으면 안된다
밀다 *to push	밀지 않으면 안된다
갚다 *to pay back	갚지 않으면 안된다
벌다 *to earn	벌지 않으면 안된다
수영하다 *to swim	수영하지 않으면 안된다
묻다 *to ask	묻지 않으면 안된다
즐겁다 *to be happy	즐겁지 않으면 안된다
듣다 *to listen	듣지 않으면 안된다
열다 *to open	열지 않으면 안된다
잡다 *to catch	잡지 않으면 안된다

5. MAY/MIGHT as uncertain action or assumption or prediction in the past, in the present or in the near future: 는지 모른다 or ㄴ지 모른다

※It is not quite sure if any action was conducted in the past and if any action or event would take place in the present or in the future.   모른다(to be unknown) implies uncertainty.

1) verb stem in past tense + 는지 모른다

*Verb stem in past tense ends in ㅆ다 or 았다 or 었다.   Drop 다 from verb stem and add 는지 모른다

•갔다(to have gone): 갔는지 모른다(might have gone): Probably (he) went but (I am) not sure.   Drop 다 from verb stem in past tense and add 는지 모른다.

2) verb stem in past progressive tense + 는지 모른다

*※Verb stem in past progressive tense ends in 고 있었다.   Drop 다 from verb stem and add 는지 모른다

•가고 있었다(to have been going): 가고 있었는 지 모른다(might have been going): It is probable that he was going but (I am) not sure.   Drop 다 from verb stem in past progressive tense and add 는지 모른다

3) root verb stem + 는지 모른다 for present tense.

3-1) root verb stem ending in consonant or vowel + 는지 모른다

•가다(to go): 가는지 모른다(may go): It is probable that he goes.   가 ends in the vowel of ㅏ.   Drop 다 from root verb stem and add 는지 모른다.

•먹다(to eat): 먹는지 모른다(may eat)   먹 ends in the consonant of ㄱ.   Drop 다 from root verb stem and add 는지 모른다.

Korean Language: Grammar Pattern

3-2) root verb stem ending in ㄹ: Drop ㄹ and add 는지 모른다

•갈다(to grind): 가는지 모른다(may grind)   갈 ends in ㄹ. Drop ㄹ from the root verb stem and add 는지 모른다. This looks the same as 'may go' (가는지 모른다).

3-3) root verb stem of static verbs ending in ㅂ: Drop ㅂ and add 운지 모른다.

•사납다(to be wild): 사나운지 모른다(may be wild)   납 ends in ㅂ. Drop ㅂ and add 운지 모른다. This change rule applies to static verbs only.

4) verb stem in present progressive tense + 는지 모른다

*Verb stem in present progressive tense ends in 고 있다. Drop 다 from the verb stem and add 는지 모른다.

•가고 있다(to be going): 가고 있는지 모른다(may be going).   (I am) not sure if he is going now. I just guess that he is.

5) verb stem in future tense + 는지 모른다 or ㄹ을 것이다/ㄹ을 거다 + ㄴ지 모른다

*Verb stem in future tense ends in 겠다/ㄹ을 것이다/ㄹ을 거다. Drop 다 from the verb stem and add 는지 모른다. However, ㄹ을 것이다 and ㄹ을 거다 should be added with ㄴ지 모른다.

•가겠다/갈 것이다/갈 거다(to be going to go): 가겠는지 모른다/갈 것인지 모른다/갈 건지 모른다: It is probable that (he) may go in the near future but (I am) not sure.

6) verb stem in future progressive tense + 는지 모른다

*Verb stem in future progressive tense ends in 고 있겠다/고 있을 것이다/고 있을 거다. Drop 다 from the verb stem and add 는지 모른다.

•오고 있겠다/오고 있을 것이다/오고 있을 거다(to be going to be coming=will be coming): 오고 있겠는지 모른다/오고 있을 것인지 모른다/오고 있을 건지 모른다.

Korean Language: Grammar Pattern

Probably (he) will be coming at this time tomorrow but no one knows.　Drop 다 and add 는지 모른다 or ㄴ지 모른다.

Examples:

•먹었다(to have eaten): 먹었는지 모른다(might have eaten)

•긁고 있었다(to have been scratching): 긁고 있었는지 모른다(might have been scratching)

•춥다(to be cold): 추운지 모른다(may be cold)　　*춥는지 is incorrect.

•입고 있다(to be wearing): 입고 있는지 모른다(may be wearing)

•만들겠다/만들 것이다/만들 거다(to be going to make): 만들겠는지 모른다/만들 것인지 모른다/만들 건지 모른다(may be going to make)

•끓이고 있겠다/끓이고 있을 것이다/끓이고 있을 거다(to be going to be boiling): 끓이고 있겠는지 모른다/끓이고 있을 것인지 모른다/끓이고 있을 건지 모른다(may be going to be boiling)

•춤췄다=춤추었다(to have danced): 춤췄는지 모른다(might have danced)

•잡았다(to have been caught): 잡았는지 모른다(might have caught)

•우습다(to be funny): 우스운지 모른다(may be funny)　　*우습은지 is incorrect.

•싸우고 있다(to be fighting): 싸우고 있는지 모른다(may be fighting)

•알겠다/알 것이다/알 거다(to be going to know): 알겠는지 모른다/알고 있을 것인지 모른다/알고 있을 건지 모른다(may be going to know)

•부르고 있겠다/부르고 있을 것이다/부르고 있을 거다(to be going to be calling): 부르고 있겠는지 모른다/부르고 있을 것인지 모른다/부르고 있을 건지 모른다(may be going to be calling)

•잃었다(to have lost): 잃었는지 모른다(might have lost)

•붙이고 있었다(to have been pasting): 붙이고 있었는지 모른다(might have been pasting)

•맵다(to be spicy): 매운지 모른다(may be spicy)　　*맵은지 is incorrect.

Korean Language: Grammar Pattern

•자라고 있다(to be growing): 자라고 있는지 모른다(may be growing)

•배고프겠다/배고플 것이다/배고플 거다(to be going to be hungry): 배고프겠는지 모른다/배고플 것인지 모른다/배고플 건지 모른다(may be hungry)

Exercise 28. Write the uncertainty in appropriate Korean.

root verb stem	uncertainty in various tenses in Korean: 는지 모른다/ㄴ지 모른다 = it is (highly) probable but not sure
사다 *to buy	past tense: 샀는지 모른다 =it is probable that he bought but not sure. past progressive tense: 사고 있었는지 모른다 =it is probable that he was buying but not sure. present tense: 사는지 모른다 =it is probable that he buys but not sure. present progressive tense: 사고 있는지 모른다 =it is probable that he is buying but not sure. future tense: 사겠는지 모른다/살 것인지 모른다/살 건지 모른다 =it is probable that he will buy but not sure. future progressive tense: 사고 있겠는지 모른다/사고 있을 것인지 모른다/사고 있을 건지 모른다 =it is probable that he will buy but not sure
하다 *to do	past tense: 했는지 모른다 past progressive tense: 하고 있었는지 모른다 present tense: 하는지 모른다 present progressive tense: 하고 있는지 모른다

Korean Language: Grammar Pattern

	future tense: 하겠는지 모른다/할 것인지 모른다/할 건지 모른다 future progressive tense: 하고 있겠는지 모른다/하고 있을 것인지 모른다/하고 있을 건지 모른다
지우다 *to erase	past tense: 지웠는지 모른다 past progressive tense: 지우고 있었는지 모른다 present tense: 지우는지 모른다 present progressive tense: 지우고 있는지 모른다 future tense: 지우겠는지 모른다/지울 것인지 모른다/지울 건지 모른다 future progressive tense: 지우고 있겠는지 모른다/지우고 있을 것인지 모른다/지우고 있을 건지 모른다
노래하다 *to sing	past tense: 노래했는지 모른다 past progressive tense: 노래하고 있었는지 모른다 present tense: 노래하는지 모른다 present progressive tense: 노래하고 있는지 모른다 future tense: 노래하겠는지 모른다/노래할 것인지 모른다/노래할 건지 모른다 future progressive tense: 노래하고 있겠는지 모른다/노래하고 있을 것인지 모른다/노래하고 있을 건지 모른다
먹다 *to eat	past tense: 먹었는지 모른다 past progressive tense: 먹고 있었는지 모른다 present tense: 먹는지 모른다 present progressive tense: 먹고 있는지 모른다

Korean Language: Grammar Pattern

	future tense: 먹겠는지 모른다/먹을 것인지 모른다/먹을 건지 모른다 future progressive tense: 먹고 있겠는지 모른다/먹고 있을 것인지 모른다/먹 고 있을 건지 모른다
걷다 *to walk	past tense: 걸었는지 모른다 past progressive tense: 걷고 있었는지 모른다 present tense: 걷는지 모른다 present progressive tense: 걷고 있는지 모른다 future tense: 걷겠는지 모른다/걸을 것인지 모른다/걸을 건지 모른다 future progressive tense: 걷고 있겠는지 모른다/걷고 있을 것인지 모른다/걷고 있을 건지 모른다
덥다 *to be hot ※Static verbs have no progressive tense.	past tense: 더웠는지 모른다 present tense: 더운지 모른다 future tense: 덥겠는지 모른다/더울 것인지 모른다/더울 건지 모른다
돕다 *to help	past tense: 도왔는지 모른다 past progressive tense: 돕고 있었는지 모른다 present tense: 돕는지 모른다 present progressive tense: 돕고 있는지 모른다 future tense: 돕겠는지 모른다/도울 것인지 모른다/도울 건지 모른다 future progressive tense: 돕고 있겠는지 모른다/돕고 있을 것인지 모른다/돕고 있을 건지 모른다
씹다	past tense: 울었는지 모른다

Korean Language: Grammar Pattern

*to chew	past progressive tense: 씹고 있었는지 모른다 present tense: 씹는지 모른다 present progressive tense: 씹고 있는지 모른다 future tense: 씹겠는지 모른다/씹을 것인지 모른다/씹을 건지 모른다 future progressive tense: 씹고 있겠는지 모른다/씹고 있을 것인지 모른다/씹고 있을 건지 모른다
울다 *to cry	past tense: 울었는지 모른다 past progressive tense: 울고 있었는지 모른다 present tense: 우는지 모른다 present progressive tense: 울고 있는지 모른다 future tense: 울겠는지 모른다/울 것인지 모른다/울 건지 모른다 future progressive tense: 울고 있겠는지 모른다/울고 있을 것인지 모른다/울고 있을 건지 모른다
잊다 *to forget	past tense: 잊었는지 모른다 past progressive tense: 잊고 있었는지 모른다 present tense: 잊는지 모른다 present progressive tense: 잊고 있는지 모른다 future tense: 잊겠는지 모른다/잊을 것인지 모른다/잊을 건지 모른다 future progressive tense: 잊고 있겠는지 모른다/잊고 있을 것인지 모른다/잊고 있을 건지 모른다
읽다 *to read	past tense: 읽었는지 모른다 past progressive tense: 읽고 있었는지 모른다

Korean Language: Grammar Pattern

	present tense: 읽는지 모른다 present progressive tense: 읽고 있는지 모른다 future tense: 읽겠는지 모른다/읽을 것인지 모른다/읽을 건지 모른다 future progressive tense: 고 있겠는지 모른다/고 있을 것인지 모른다/고 있을 건지 모른다
이기다 *to win	past tense: 이겼는지(이기었는지) 모른다 past progressive tense: 이기고 있었는지 모른다 present tense: 이기는지 모른다 present progressive tense: 이기고 있는지 모른다 future tense: 이기겠는지 모른다/이길 것인지 모른다/이길 건지 모른다 future progressive tense: 이기고 있겠는지 모른다/이기고 있을 것인지 모른다/이기고 있을 건지 모른다
묻다 *to ask	past tense: 물었는지 모른다 past progressive tense: 묻고 있었는지 모른다 present tense: 묻는지 모른다 present progressive tense: 묻고 있는지 모른다 future tense: 묻겠는지 모른다/물을 것인지 모른다/물을 건지 모른다 future progressive tense: 묻고 있겠는지 모른다/묻고 있을 것인지 모른다/묻고 있을 건지 모른다
오르다 *to rise	past tense: 올랐는지 모른다 past progressive tense: 오르고 있었는지 모른다 present tense: 오르는지 모른다

Korean Language: Grammar Pattern

	present progressive tense: 오르고 있는지 모른다 future tense: 오르겠는지 모른다/오를 것인지 모른다/오를 건지 모른다 future progressive tense: 오르고 있겠는지 모른다/오르고 있을 것인지 모른다/오르고 있을 건지 모른다
목마르다 *to be thirsty	past tense: 목말랐는지 모른다 present tense: 목마르는지 모른다 future tense: 목마르겠는지 모른다/목마를 것인지 모른다/목마를 건지 모른다
미워하다 *to hate	past tense: 미워했는지 모른다 past progressive tense: 미워하고 있었는지 모른다 present tense: 미워하는지 모른다 present progressive tense: 미워하고 있는지 모른다 future tense: 미워하겠는지 모른다/미워할 것인지 모른다/미워할 건지 모른다 future progressive tense: 미워하고 있겠는지 모른다/미워하고 있을 것인지 모른다/미워하고 있을 건지 모른다
밉다 *to be hateful	past tense: 미웠는지 모른다 present tense: 미운지 모른다 future tense: 미워하겠는지 모른다/미워할 것인지 모른다/미워할 건지 모른다
닫다 *to close	past tense: 닫았는지 모른다 past progressive tense: 닫고 있었는지 모른다 present tense: 닫는지 모른다 present progressive tense: 닫고 있는지 모른다

Korean Language: Grammar Pattern

	future tense: 닫겠는지 모른다/닫을 것인지 모른다/닫을 건지 모른다 future progressive tense: 닫고 있겠는지 모른다/닫고 있을 것인지 모른다/닫고 있을 건지 모른다
밀다 *to push	past tense: 밀었는지 모른다 past progressive tense: 밀고 있었는지 모른다 present tense: 미는지 모른다 present progressive tense: 밀고 있는지 모른다 future tense: 밀겠는지 모른다/밀 것인지 모른다/밀 건지 모른다 future progressive tense: 밀고 있겠는지 모른다/밀고 있을 것인지 모른다/밀고 있을 건지 모른다
열다 *to open	past tense: 열었는지 모른다 past progressive tense: 열고 있었는지 모른다 present tense: 여는지 모른다 present progressive tense: 열고 있는지 모른다 future tense: 열겠는지 모른다/열 것인지 모른다/열 건지 모른다 future progressive tense: 열고 있겠는지 모른다/열고 있을 것인지 모른다/열고 있을 건지 모른다
당기다 *to pull	past tense: 당겼는지 모른다 past progressive tense: 당기고 있었는지 모른다 present tense: 당기는지 모른다 present progressive tense: 당기고 있는지 모른다 future tense: 당기겠는지 모른다/당길 것인지 모른다/당길 건지 모른다

Korean Language: Grammar Pattern

	future progressive tense: 당기고 있겠는지 모른다/당기고 있을 것인지 모른다/당기고 있을 건지 모른다
사다 *to buy	past tense: 샀는지 모른다 past progressive tense: 사고 있었는지 모른다 present tense: 사는지 모른다 present progressive tense: 사고 있는지 모른다 future tense: 사겠는지 모른다/살 것인지 모른다/살 건지 모른다 future progressive tense: 사고 있겠는지 모른다/사고 있을 것인지 모른다/사고 있을 건지 모른다
살다 *to live	past tense: 살았는지 모른다 past progressive tense: 살고 있었는지 모른다 present tense: 사는지 모른다 present progressive tense: 살고 있는지 모른다 future tense: 살겠는지 모른다/살 것인지 모른다/살 건지 모른다 future progressive tense: 살고 있겠는지 모른다/살고 있을 것인지 모른다/살고 있을 건지 모른다
믿다 *to believe	past tense: 믿었는지 모른다 past progressive tense: 믿고 있었는지 모른다 present tense: 믿는지 모른다 present progressive tense: 믿고 있는지 모른다 future tense: 믿겠는지 모른다/믿을 것인지 모른다/믿을 건지 모른다 future progressive tense: 믿고 있겠는지 모른다/믿고 있을 것인지 모른다/믿고 있을 건지 모른다

Korean Language: Grammar Pattern

귀엽다 *to be cute	past tense: 귀여웠는지 모른다 present tense: 귀여운지 모른다 future tense: 귀엽겠는지 모른다/귀여울 것인지 모른다/귀여울 건지 모른다

UNIT 11. MODIFYING VERB

There are six major modifying verbs in accordance with tenses.   There are connective verbs in past, present, future, past progressive, present progressive, future progressive tense.

1. modifying verb in past tense: ㄴ or 은

1) root verb stem ending in vowel + ㄴ

•보다(to see): 본(to have seen)

*보 ends in vowel ㅗ.   Add just ㄴ.   The movie(영화) **that** he(그) **saw**: 그가 **본** 영화

2) root verb stem ending in consonant + 은

•잡다(to catch): 잡은(to have caught)

*잡 ends in consonant ㅂ.   Add 은.   The ball(공) **that** he **caught**: 그가 **잡은** 공

3) root verb stem ending in ㄹ: Drop ㄹ and add ㄴ.

•말다(to roll): 만(to have rolled)

*말 ends in ㄹ.   Drop ㄹ and add ㄴ.   Kimbap **that** he **rolled**: 그가 **만** 김밥

※See the following Table 18 for the modifying verb stems ending in ㄹ.   Drop the ending ㄹ and add ㄴ.

Table 18   *Marks in Italics* are incorrect.

root verb stem ending in ㄹ	modifying verb in past tense: ㄴ

Korean Language: Grammar Pattern

팔다 *to sell	판 *팔은 the car(차) **which** he(그) **sold**: 그가 **판** 차
불다 *to blow	분 *불은 the balloon(풍선) **which** he **blew**: 그가 **분** 풍선
밀다 *to push	민 *밀은 the door(문) **which** he **pushed**: 그가 **민** 문
열다 *to open	연 *열은 the window(창문) **which** he **opened**: 그가 **연** 창문
몰다 *to drive	몬 *몰은 the car(차) **which** he **drove**: 그가 **몬** 차
알다 *to know	안 *알은 the fact(사실) **which** he **knew**: 그가 **안** 대답
놀다 *to play/to hang out	논 *놀은 the playground(놀이터) **in which** he **played**: 그가 **논** 놀이터
줄다 *to decrease	준 *줄은 the population(인구) **which decreased**: **준** 인구
머물다 *to stay	머문 *머물은 the house(집) **in which** he **stayed**: 그가 **머문** 집
돌다 *to turn	돈 *돌은 the car (차)**which turned**: **돈** 차
빌다 *to beg	빈 *빌은 the kid(아이) **who begged**: **빈** 아이

Korean Language: Grammar Pattern

만들다 *to make	만든 *만들은 the toy(장난감) **which** he **made**: 그가 **만든** 장난감
끌다 *to drag	끈 *끌은 the cart(수레) **which** he **dragged**: 그가 **끈** 수레
갈다 *to grind/to change	간 *갈은 the coffee bean(커피콩) **which** he **ground**: 그가 **간** 커피콩 the diapers(기저귀) which he **changed**: 그가 **간** 기저귀
들다 *to pick up/to raise	든 *들은 the bag(가방) **which** he **picked up**: 그가 **든** 가방
얼다 *to freeze	언 *얼은 the water(물) **which was frozen**: **언** 물
졸다 *to doze off	존 *졸은 the student(학생) **who dozed off**: **존** 학생
흔들다 *to shake	흔든 *흔들은 the flag(깃발) **which** he **shook**: 그가 **흔든** 깃발
풀다 *to solve/to untie	푼 *풀은 the question(문제) **which** he **solved**: 그가 **푼** 문제 the rope(로프) **which** he **untied**: 그가 **푼** 로프
살다 to live	산 *살은 the house(집) **in which** he **lived**: 그가 **산** 집

Korean Language: Grammar Pattern

※ 사다 *to buy	The house **which** he **bought**: 그가 **산** 집
벌다 *to earn	번 *벌은 the money(돈) **which** he **earned**: 그가 **번** 돈
물다 *to bite	문 *물은 the bullet(총알) **which** he **bit**: 그가 **문** 총알
걸다 *to hang	건 *걸은 the hat(모자) **which** he **hung**: 그가 **건** 모자
말다 *to roll	만 *말은 the Kimbap **which** he **rolled**: 그가 **만** 김밥
날다 *to fly	난 *날은 the bird(새) **which flew**: **난** 새
빨다 *to wash/to suck	빤 *빨은 the pants(바지) **which** he **washed**: 그가 **빤** 바지 the food(음식) **which** the dog(개) **sucked**: 개가 **빤** 음식
늘다 *to increase	는 *늘은 the stress **which increased**(스트레스): **는** 스트레스
부풀다 *to swell	부푼 *부풀은 the balloon(풍선) **which swelled**: 부푼 풍선
기울다 *to incline	기운 *기울은 the ground(운동장) **which inclined**: **기운** 운동장

Korean Language: Grammar Pattern

4) root verb stem ending in ㄷ: In the case of 듣다(to listen), 싣다(to load), 걷다(to walk), 묻다(to ask), irregular change rule applies. In this case, ㄷ is dropped and ㄹ은 is added. For the other ㄷ ending verbs, regular change rule applies.   See the following Table 19 for more information.

Table 19   *Marks in Italic are incorrect.

root verb stem ending in ㄷ	modifying verb in past tense: ㄹ은 or 은
듣다 *to listen	들은 *듣은 the music(음악) **which** he(그)**listened to**: 그가 **들은** 음악 *ㄷ is replaced with ㄹ은.
싣다 *to load	실은 *싣은 the stuffs(물건) **which** he **loaded**: 그가 **실은** 물건
걷다 *to walk	걸은 *걷은 the street(거리) **on which** he **walked**: 그가 **걸은** 거리
묻다 *to ask	물은 *묻은 the question **which** he **asked**: 그가 **물은** 질문
받다 *to receive	받은 the gift(선물) **which** he **received**: 그가 **받은** 선물
믿다 *to believe	믿은 the religion(종교) **in which** he **believed**: 그가 **믿은** 종교
얻다 *to gain	얻은 the popularity(인기) **which** he **gained**: 그가 **얻은** 인기

Korean Language: Grammar Pattern

딛다 *to step	딛은 the stone(돌) **on which** he **stepped**: 그가 **딛은** 돌
걷다 *to collect	걷은 the money(돈) **which** he **collected**: 그가 **걷은** 돈
닫다 *to close	닫은 the door(문) **which** he **closed**: 그가 **닫은** 문
묻다 *to bury	묻은 the secret(비밀) **which** he **buried**: 그가 **묻은** 비밀

Examples:

•the car(차) which he **fixed**: 그가 **수리한** 차   *to fix: 수리하다

•the fish(고기) which he **caught**: 그가 **잡은** 고기   *to catch: 잡다

•the movie(영화) which he **saw:** 그가 **본** 영화   *to see: 보다

•the food(음식) which he **ate**: 그가 **먹은** 음식   *to eat: 먹다

•the coffee(커피) which he **drank**: 그가 **마신** 커피   *to drink: 마시다

•the bus(버스) which he **took on**: 그가 **탄** 버스   *to take on: 타다

•the pencil(연필) which he **found**: 그가 **찾은** 연필   *to find: 찾다

•the picture(사진) which he **took**: 그가 **찍은** 사진   *to take: 찍다

•Korean language(한국어) which he **learned**: 그가 **배운** 한국어   *(to learn: 배우다)

•the garbage(쓰레기) which he **covered**: 그가 **덮은** 쓰레기   *to cover: 덮다

•the problem(문제) he **solved**: 그가 **푼** 문제   *to solve: 풀다

•the ball(공) which he **hit**: 그가 **친** 공   *to hit: 치다

•the song(노래) which he **sang**: 그가 **부른** 노래   *to sing: 부르다

Korean Language: Grammar Pattern

•the name(이름) which he **called**: 그가 **부른** 이름   *to call: 걸다

Exercise 29. Fill in the blanks with appropriate modifying verbs in past tense in Korean. Write the underlined verb parts only.

verb in past tense	modifying verb in past tense in Korean: ㄴ or 은 or ㄹ은
the dress(옷) which he wore *to wear: 입다	입은 *consonant ending + 은
the meat(고기) which he chewed *to chew: 씹다	씹은
the president(대통령) whom he elected *to elect: 뽑다	뽑은
the language(언어) which he learned *to learn: 배우다	배운
the money(돈) which he spent *to spend: 쓰다	쓴 *vowel ending + ㄴ
the car(차) which he drove *to drive: 몰다(pure Korean)/운전하다(Sino Korean)	몬/운전한 *몰은
the tree(나무) that he planted *to plant: 심다	심은
the door(문) that he pushed *to push: 밀다	민 *밀은
the road(길) that he walked	걸은 *걷은

Korean Language: Grammar Pattern

*to walk: 걷다	
the picture(그림) that he hung *to hang: 걸다	건 *걸은
the bus(버스) that he rode *to ride: 타다	탄
the water(물) that he boiled *to boil: 끓이다	끓인
the food(음식) that he ordered *to order: 주문하다	주문한
the house(집) that he lived in *to live: 살다	산 *살은
the house that he bought *to buy: 사다	산
the question that he asked *to ask: 묻다	물은 *묻은 *ㄷ ending + ㄹ은

2. modifying verb in present tense: 는

1) root verb stem ending in consonant or vowel + 는

•닫다(to close): 닫는(closes)

*닫 ends in consonant ㄷ. Drop 다 and add just 는.

The door(문) that he closes: 그가 닫는 문

•쉬다(to relax): 쉬는(relaxes)

*쉬 ends in vowel ㅣ. Drop 다 and add 는.

Korean Language: Grammar Pattern

The room(방) <u>which</u> he <u>relaxes</u> in: 그가 <u>쉬는</u> 방

2) root verb stem ending in the consonant of ㄹ: ㄹ is dropped and 는 is added. See the following Table 20 for the modifying verb stems ending in ㄹ.

Table 20   *Marks in Italics* are incorrect.

root verb stem ending in ㄹ	modifying verb in present tense: 는
팔다 *to sell	파는 *팔는* the car(차) <u>**which**</u> he(그) <u>**sells**</u>: 그가 **파는** 차 ※Drop ㄹ and add 는.
불다 *to blow	부는 *불는* the balloon(풍선) <u>**which**</u> he <u>**blows**</u>: 그가 **부는** 풍선
밀다 *to push	미는 *밀는* the cart(수레) <u>**which**</u> he <u>**pushes**</u>: 그가 **미는** 문
열다 *to open	여는 *열는* the door <u>**which**</u> he <u>**opens**</u>: 그가 **여는** 문
몰다 *to drive	모는 *몰는* the car(차) <u>**which**</u> he <u>**drives**</u>: 그가 **모는** 차
알다 *to know	아는 *알는* the answer(대답) <u>**which**</u> he <u>**knows**</u>: 그가 **아는** 대답
놀다 *to play/to hang out	노는 *놀는* the playground(놀이터) <u>**in which**</u> he <u>**plays**</u>: 그가 <u>노는</u> 놀이터

Korean Language: Grammar Pattern

줄다 *to decrease	주는 *줄는 the population(인구) **which** decreases: 주는 인구
머물다 *to stay	머무는 *머물는 the house(집) **in which** he **stays**: 그가 **머무는** 집
돌다 *to turn	도는 *돌는 the car **which** **turns**: **도는** 차
빌다 *to beg	비는 *빌는 the kid(아이) **who** **begs**: **비는** 아이
만들다 *to make	만드는 *만들는 the toy(장난감) **which** he **makes**: 그가 **만드는** 장난감
끌다 *to drag	끄는 *끌는 the cart(수레) **which** he **drags**: 그가 **끄는** 수레
갈다 *to grind/to change	가는 *갈는 -the coffee bean(커피콩) **which** he **grinds**: 그가 **가는** 커피콩 -the diaper(기저귀) **which** he **changes**: 그가 **가는** 기저귀
들다 *to pick up/to raise	드는 *들는 the bag(가방) **which** he **picks up**: 그가 **드는** 가방
얼다 *to freeze	어는 *얼는 the water(물) **which** **freezes**: **어는** 물
졸다 *to doze off	조는 *졸는 the chicken(닭) **which** **dozes off**: **조는** 닭

Korean Language: Grammar Pattern

흔들다 *to shake	흔드는 *흔들는 the flag(깃발) **which** he **shakes**: 그가 **흔드는** 깃발
풀다 *to solve/to untie	푸는 *풀는 -the question(문제) **which** he **solves**: 그가 **푸는** 문제 -the rope **which** he **unties**: 그가 푸는 로프
살다 *to live	사는 *살는 the house(집) **in which** he **lives**: 그가 **사는** 집
사다 *to buy	the house **which** he **buys**: 그가 **사는** 집
벌다 *to earn	버는 *벌는 the money(돈) **which** he **earns**: 그가 **버는** 돈
물다 *to bite	무는 *물는 the bullet(총알) **which** he **bites**: 그가 **무는** 총알
걸다 *to hang/to call	거는 *걸는 -the hat(모자) **which** he **hangs**: 그가 **거는** 모자 -the phone(전화) **which** he **calls**: 그가 **거는** 전화
말다 *to roll	마는 *말는 -Kimbap **which** he **rolls**: 그가 **마는** 김밥
날다 *to fly	나는 *날는 the bird(새) **which flies**: **나는** 새
빨다 *to wash/to suck	빠는 *빨는

	-the pants(바지) **which** he **washes**: 그가 **빠는** 바지 -the liquid(액체) **which** he **sucks** through a straw: 빨대로 액체를 **빠는**
늘다 *to increase	느는 *늘는 the stress which **increases**: **느는** 스트레스
부풀다 *to swell	부푸는 *부풀는 the swellfish(복어) **which swells**: **부푸는** 복어
기울다 *to incline	기우는 *기울는 the ground(운동장) **which inclines**: **기우는** 운동장

3) root verb stem ending in consonant ㅂ: These verbs are mostly static verbs(to be + adjective).   In this case, ㅂ is dropped and 운 is added.   This looks exactly like an adjective form.   This is <u>hot</u>(뜨거운) water. = This is water <u>which is hot</u>(뜨거운).   See UNIT 7 for the comparison.   The following Table 21 has more details.

Table 21   *Marks in Italic are incorrect.*

root verb stem ending in ㅂ	modifying verb in present tense: 운
맵다 *to be spicy	매운(=which is spicy) *맵는 ※Drop ㅂ and add 운.
춥다 *to be cold	추운(=which is cold) *춥는
덥다/뜨겁다 *to be hot	더운/뜨거운(=which is hot) *덥는
무겁다	무거운(=which is heavy) *무겁는

Korean Language: Grammar Pattern

*to be heavy	
가렵다 *to be itchy	가려운(=which is itchy)　　*가렵는
가엽다 *to be pathetic	가여운(=which is pathetic)　　*가엽는
가소롭다 *to be ridiculous	가소로운(=which is ridiculous) *가소롭는
어렵다 *to be difficult	어려운(=which is difficult)　　*어렵는
쉽다 *to be easy	쉬운(=which is easy)　　*쉽는
더럽다 *to be dirty	더러운(=which is dirty)　　*더럽는
우습다 *to be funny	우스운(=which is funny)　　*우습는
고맙다 *to be thankful	고마운(=which is thankful)　　*고맙는
밉다 *to be hateful	미운(=which is hateful)　　*밉는
무섭다 *to be scary	무서운(=which is scary)　　*무섭는
귀엽다 *to be cute	귀여운(=which is cute)　　*귀엽는
즐겁다	즐거운(=which is happy)　　*즐겁는

Korean Language: Grammar Pattern

*to be happy	

Examples:

•the car(차) **which** he **fixes**: 그가 **수리하는** 차   *to fix: 수리하다

•the fish(고기) **which** he **catches**: 그가 **잡는** 고기   *to catch: 잡다

•the movie(영화) **which** he **sees**: 그가 **보는** 영화   *to see: 보다

•the food(음식) **which** he **eats**: 그가 **먹는** 음식   *to eat: 먹다

•the coffee(커피) **which** he **drinks**: 그가 **마시는** 커피   *to drink: 마시다

•the house in **which** he **lives**: 그가 **사는** 집   *to live: 살다   *살는* is incorrect.

•the song(노래) **to which** he **listens to**: 그가 **듣는** 노래   *to listen to: 듣다

•the bus(버스) **which** he **ride**: 그가 **타는** 버스   *to ride: 타다

•the pencil(연필) **which** he **finds**: 그가 **찾는** 연필   *to find: 찾다

•the picture(사진) **which** he **takes**: 그가 **찍는** 사진   *to take: 찍다

•Korean language(한국어) **which** he **learns**: 그가 **배우는** 한국어   *to learn: 배우다

•the problem(문제) **which** he **covers**: 그가 **덮는** 문제   *to cover: 덮다

Exercise 30. Write the appropriate modifying verb in present tense in Korean. Write the underlined verb parts only.

verb in present tense	modifier in present tense in Korean: 는 or 은 for static verb
the dress(옷) which he wears *to wear: 입다	입는
the meat(고기) which he chews	씹는

Korean Language: Grammar Pattern

*to chew: 씹다	
the president(대통령) <u>whom</u> he <u>elects</u> *to elect: 뽑다(pure Korean)/선택하다(Sino Korean)	뽑는/선택하는
the language(언어) <u>which</u> he <u>learns</u> *to learn: 배우다	배우는
the hours(시간) <u>for which</u> <u>are enjoyable</u> *to be enjoyable: 즐겁다	즐거운　　*즐겁는 *static verb ending in ㅂ + 운
the car(차) <u>which</u> he <u>drives</u> *to drive: 몰다(pure Korean)/운전하다(Sino Korean)	모는/운전하는
the street(거리) <u>on which</u> he <u>walks</u> *to walk: 걷다	걷는
the letter(편지) <u>which</u> he <u>writes</u> *to write: 쓰다	쓰는
the coffee(커피) <u>which</u> he <u>grinds</u> *to grind: 갈다	가는　　*갈는
my friends <u>who</u> <u>help</u> me *to help: 돕다	돕는
the question(질문) <u>which</u> he <u>asks</u> *to ask: 묻다	묻는
the bottle(병) <u>which</u> he <u>buries</u> *to bury: 묻다	묻는
the paper(종이) <u>which</u> he <u>tears</u>	찢는

*to tear: 찢다	
the movie(영화) <u>which</u> he <u>sees</u> *to see: 보다	보는
the phone(전화) <u>which</u> he <u>calls</u> *to call: 걸다	거는 *걸는
the car(차) <u>which</u> he <u>buys</u> *to buy: 사다	사는
the dream(꿈) <u>which</u> he <u>dreams</u> *to dream: 꾸다	꾸는
the house(집) <u>which</u> he <u>lives in</u> *to live: 살다	사는
the water(물) <u>which</u> he <u>drinks</u> *to drink: 마시다	마시는
Kimchi(김치) <u>which</u> <u>is spicy</u> *to be spicy: 맵다	매운 *맵는

3. modifying verb in future tense: ㄹ or 을 or ㄹ을

1) root verb stem ending in consonant + 을

•벗다(to take off): 벗을(to be going to take off)

*벗 ends in consonant ㅅ. Drop 다 and add 을. The shoes(신발) <u>**which**</u> he <u>**will**</u> <u>**take off**</u>: 그가 **벗을** 신발

2) root verb stem ending in vowel + ㄹ

Korean Language: Grammar Pattern

•붙이다(to attach): 붙일(to be going to attach)

*이 ends in vowel. Drop 다 and add just ㄹ. The file(파일) **which** he **will attach**: 그가 **붙일** 파일

3) root verb stem ending in the consonant of ㄹ: Just drop 다 from the root verb stem. See the following Table 22 for more details.

Table 22   *Marks in Italics* are incorrect.

root verb stem ending in ㄹ	modifying verb in future tense: ㄹ
팔다 *to sell	팔 *팔을 the car(차) **which** he(그) **will sell**: 그가 **팔** 차
불다 *to blow	불 *불을 the balloon(풍선) **which** he **will blow**: 그가 **불** 풍선
밀다 *to push	밀 *밀을 the door(문) **which** he **will push**: 그가 **밀** 문
열다 *to open	열 *열을 the door **which** he **will open**: 그가 **열** 문
몰다/운전하다 *to drive	몰 *몰을 the car(차) **which** he **will drive**: 그가 **몰/운전할** 차
알다 *to know	알 *알을 the truth(진실) **which** he **will know**: 그가 **알** 진실
놀다 *to play/to hang out	놀 *놀을

Korean Language: Grammar Pattern

	the place(장소) <u>**in which**</u> he <u>**will play**</u>: 그가 놀 장소
줄다 *to decrease	줄 *줄을 the accidents(사고) <u>**which will decrease**</u>: **줄** 사고
머물다 *to stay	머물 *머물을 the house(집) <u>**in which**</u> he <u>**will stay**</u>: 그가 **머물** 집
돌다 *to turn	돌 *돌을 the car <u>**which will turn**</u>: **돌** 차
빌다 *to beg	비는 *빌을 the kid(아이) <u>**who will beg**</u>: **빌** 아이
만들다 *to make	만들 *만들을 the toy(장난감) <u>**which**</u> he <u>**will make**</u>: 그가 **만들** 장난감
끌다 *to drag	끌 *끌을 the cart(수레) <u>**which**</u> he <u>**will drag**</u>: 그가 **끌** 수레
갈다 *to grind/to change	갈 *갈을 the coffee bean(커피콩) <u>**which**</u> he <u>**will grind**</u>: 그가 **갈** 커피콩 the ink toner <u>**which**</u> he <u>**will change**</u>: 그가 갈 잉크 토너
들다 *to pick up/to raise	들 *들을 the bag(가방) <u>**which**</u> he <u>**will pick up**</u>: 그가 **들** 가방
얼다	얼 *얼을

Korean Language: Grammar Pattern

*to freeze	the water(물) **which will freeze**: **얼** 물
졸다 *to doze off	졸 *졸을 the student(학생) **who will doze off**: **졸** 학생
흔들다 *to shake	흔들 *흔들을 the milkshake **which** he **will shake**: 그가 **흔들** 밀크셰이크
풀다 *to solve/to untie	풀 *풀을 the question(문제) **which** he **will solve**: 그가 **풀** 문제 the seatbelt **which** he **will untie**: 그가 **풀** 시트벨트
살다 *to live *사다 *to buy	살 *살을 the house(집) **in which** he **will live**: 그가 **살** 집 the house which he **will buy**: 그가 **살** 집
벌다 *to earn	벌 *벌을 the money(돈) **which** he **will earn**: 그가 **벌** 돈
물다 *to bite	물 *물을 the bullet(총알) **which** he **will bite**: 그가 **물** 총알
걸다 *to hang *걸다 *to call (a phone)	걸 *걸을 -the hat(모자) **which** he will hang: 그가 걸 모자 -the phone(전화) **which** he **will call**: 그가 **걸** 전화
말다 *to roll	말 *말을 Kimbap **which** he **will roll**: 그가 **말** 김밥

Korean Language: Grammar Pattern

날다	날 *날을
*to fly	the plane(비행기) **which will fly**: 날 비행기
빨다	빨 *빨을
*to wash/to suck	-the pants(바지) **which** he **will wash**: 그가 **빨** 바지
	-the chocolate syrup **which** he **will suck**: 그가 **빨** 초콜릿 시럽
늘다	늘 *늘을
*to increase	the stress **which will increase**: **늘** 스트레스
부풀다	부풀 *부풀을
*to swell	the wound(상처) **which will swell**: **부풀** 상처
기울다	기울 *기울을
*to incline	the building(건물) **which will incline**: **기울** 건물

4) root verb stem ending in consonant ㄷ: Irregular change rule applies to 듣다(to listen)/싣다(to load)/걷다(to walk)/묻다(to ask). In this case, ㄷ is dropped and ㄹ을 is added. Regular change rule will apply to the other verbs ending in ㄷ. For the regular change, drop 다 from the root verb stem and add just 을. See the following Table 23 for the details.

Table 23   *Marks in Italic are incorrect.

root verb stem ending in ㄷ	modifying verb in future tense: ㄹ을 or 을
듣다	들을 *듣을
*to listen	The music(음악) **which** he **will listen to**: 그가 **들을** 음악

Korean Language: Grammar Pattern

	※Drop the ending consonant ㄷ and replace it with ㄹ을.
싣다 *to load	실을　*싣을 the truck(트럭) **in which** he **will load**: 그가 **실을** 트럭
걷다 *to walk	걸을　*걷을 the road(길) **on which** he **will walk**: 그가 **걸을** 길
묻다 *to ask	물을　*묻을 the question(질문) **which** he **will ask**: 그가 **물을** 이름
받다 *to receive	받을　*받을 the prize(상) **which** he **will receive**: 그가 **받을** 상
믿다 *to believe	믿을　*믿을 the religion(종교) **in which** he **will believe**: 그가 **믿을** 종교
얻다 *to gain	얻을　*얻을 the fortune(행운) **which** he **will gain**: 그가 **얻을** 행운
딛다 *to step	딛을　*딛을 the step stone(디딤돌) **on which** he **will step**: 그가 **딛을** 디딤돌
걷다 *to collect	걷을　*걷을 the tax(세금) **which** he **will collect**: 그가 **걷을** 세금
닫다	닫을　*닫을

*to close	the store(가게) **which** he **will close**: 그가 **닫을** 가게
묻다 *to bury	묻을 *물을 the garbage(쓰레기) **which** he **will bury**: 그가 **묻을** 쓰레기

5) root verb stem ending in consonant ㅂ: These verbs are mostly static verbs(to be + adjective).   In this case, ㅂ is dropped and 울 is added.   See the following Table 24 for more details.

Table 24   *Marks in Italic* are incorrect.

root verb stem ending in ㅂ	modifying verb in future tense: Drop ㅂ and add 울.
맵다 *to be spicy	매울 *맵을 which will be spicy
춥다 *to be cold	추울 *춥을 which will be cold
덥다 *to be hot	더울 *덥을 which will be hot
무겁다 *to be heavy	무거울 *무겁을 which will be heavy
가렵다 *to be itchy	가려울 *가렵을 which will be itchy
가엽다 *to be pathetic	가여울 *가엽을 which be pathetic
눕다	누울 *눕을

Korean Language: Grammar Pattern

*to lie down *This is an action verb but irregular change rule applies.	which will lie down
가소롭다 *to be ridiculous	가소로울 *가소롭을 which will be ridiculous
어렵다 *to be difficult	어려울 *어렵을 which will be difficult
쉽다 *to be easy	쉬울 *쉽을 which will be easy
돕다 *to help *This is an action verb but irregular change rule applies.	도울 *돕을 which will help
더럽다 *to be dirty	더러울 *더럽을 which will be dirty
우습다 *to be funny	우스울 *우습을 which will be funny
고맙다 *to be thankful	고마울 *고맙을 which will be thankful
밉다 *to be hateful	미울 *밉을 which will be hateful
무섭다 *to be scary	무서울 *무섭을 which will be scary
귀엽다 *to be cute	귀여울 *귀엽을 which will be cute

Korean Language: Grammar Pattern

즐겁다 *to be happy	즐거울 *즐겁을 which will be happy

Examples:

•the car(차) **which** he **will fix**: 그가 **수리할** 차   *to fix: 수리하다

•the fish(물고기) **which** he **will catch**: 그가 **잡을** 고기   *to catch: 잡다

•the movie(영화) **which** he **will see**: 그가 **볼** 영화   *to see: 보다

•the food(음식) **which** he **will eat**: 그가 **먹을** 음식   *to eat: 먹다

•the coffee(커피) **which** he **will drink**: 그가 **마실** 커피   *to drink: 마시다

•the pencil(연필) **which** he **will find**: 그가 **찾을** 연필   *to find: 찾다

•the photo(사진) **which** he **will take**: 그가 **찍을** 사진   *to take: 찍다

•Korean language(한국어) **which** he **will learn**: 그가 **배울** 한국어   *to learn: 배우다

Exercise 31. Fill in the blanks with appropriate modifier in future tense in Korean. Write the underlined verb parts only.

modifying verb in future tense	modifier in future tense in Korean: ㄹ or 을 or ㄹ을
the dress(옷) <u>which</u> he <u>will wear</u> *to wear: 입다	입을 *consonant ending + 을
the meat(고기) <u>which</u> he <u>will chew</u> *to chew: 씹다	씹을
the president(대통령) <u>whom</u> he <u>will elect</u> *to elect: 뽑다/선택하다	뽑을/선택할
the language(언어) <u>which</u> he <u>will teach</u>	가르칠

Korean Language: Grammar Pattern

*to teach: 가르치다	*vowel ending + ㄹ
the noise(소음) <u>which</u> he <u>will hear</u> *to hear: 듣다	들을 *듣을 *verbs ending in ㄷ + ㄹ을
the money(돈) <u>which</u> he <u>will spend</u> *to spend: 쓰다	쓸
the car(차) <u>which</u> he <u>will wash</u> *to wash: 씻다	씻을
the street <u>on which</u> he <u>will run</u> *to run: 달리다/뛰다	달릴/뛸
the desk(책상) <u>which</u> he <u>will make</u> *to make: 만들다	만들 *만들을
the street <u>which</u> he <u>will walk on</u> *to walk: 걷다	걸을 *걷을
the weather(날씨) <u>which will be cold</u> *to be cold: 춥다	추울 *춥을
the clothes(옷) <u>which</u> he <u>will buy</u> *to buy: 사다	살
the game(경기) <u>which</u> he <u>will see</u> *to see: 보다	볼
the water(물) <u>which</u> he <u>will boil</u> *to boil: 끓이다	끓일
the bike(자전거) <u>which</u> he <u>will ride</u> *to ride: 타다	탈

Korean Language: Grammar Pattern

the house(집) <u>in which</u> he <u>will live</u> *to live: 살다	살 *살을 *verbs ending in ㄹ + no modifier
the door(문) <u>which</u> he <u>will open</u> *to open: 열다	열 *열을
the window(창문) <u>which</u> he <u>will close</u> *to close: 닫다	닫을
the food(음식) <u>which</u> <u>will be spicy</u> *to be spicy: 맵다	매울 *맵을
the friend(친구) <u>who</u> <u>will help</u> *to help: 돕다	도울 *돕을

※Compare the following modifying verbs in past, present and future tense.

modifying verbs in past, present and future tense	Korean expression
the dream(꿈) **which** he(그) **wished** *to wish: 바라다	그가 **바란** 꿈
the dream **which** he **wishes**	그가 **바라는** 꿈
the dream **which** he **will wish**	그가 **바랄** 꿈
the piano(피아노) **which** he(그) **played** *to play + instrument: 연주하다	그가 **연주한** 피아노
the piano **which** he(그) **plays**	그가 **연주하는** 피아노
the piano **which** he(그) **will play**	그가 **연주할** 피아노
the song(노래) **which** he **sang**	그가 **부른** 노래

Korean Language: Grammar Pattern

*to sing: 부르다	
the song **which** he **sings**	그가 **부르는** 노래
the song **which** he **will sing**	그가 **부를** 노래
the story(이야기) **which** he **heard** *to hear: 듣다	그가 **들은** 이야기
the story **which** he **hears**	그가 **듣는** 이야기
the story **which** he **will hear**	그가 **들은** 이야기
the ground(땅) **which** he **dug** *to dig: 파다	그가 **판** 땅
the ground(땅) **which** he **digs**	그가 **파는** 땅
the ground(땅) **which** he **will dig**	그가 **팔** 땅
the hair(머리카락)**which** he **cut** *to cut: 자르다	그가 **자른** 머리카락
the hair **which** he **cuts**	그가 **자르는** 머리카락
the hair **which** he **will cut**	그가 **자를** 머리카락
the face(얼굴) **which** he **remembered** *to remember: 기억하다	그가 **기억한** 얼굴
the face **which** he **remembers**	그가 **기억하는** 얼굴
the face **which** he **will remember**	그가 **기억할** 얼굴
the bed(침대) **on which** he **lied down** *to lie down: 눕다	그가 **누운** 침대
the bed **on which** he **lies down**	그가 **눕는** 침대
the bed **on which** he **will lie down**	그가 **누울** 침대

the school(학교) **to which** he **went** *to go: 가다	그가 **간** 학교
the school **to which** he **goes**	그가 **가는** 학교
the school **to which** he **will go**	그가 **갈** 학교
the dog(개) **which** he **cared for** *to care for: 돌보다	그가 **돌본** 개
the dog **which** he **cares for**	그가 **돌보는** 개
the dog **which** he **will care for**	그가 **돌볼** 개
the mountain(산) **which** he **climbed** *to climb: 오르다	그가 **오른** 산
the mountain **which** he **climbs**	그가 **오르는** 산
the mountain **which** he **will climb**	그가 **오를** 산
the fish(물고기) **which** he **fished** *to fish: 낚시하다	그가 **낚시한** 물고기
the fish **which** he **fishes**	그가 **낚시하는** 물고기
the fish **which** he **will fish**	그가 **낚시할** 물고기
the coffee bean(커피콩) **which** he **ground** *to grind: 갈다	그가 **간** 커피콩
the coffee bean **which** he **grinds**	그가 **가는** 커피콩
the coffee bean **which** he **will grind**	그가 **갈** 커피콩

4. modifying verb in past progressive tense: 고 있었던 or 고 있던

Korean Language: Grammar Pattern

* Root verb stem + 고 있었던: 고 means a progressive action in all tenses. ㅆ or 았 or 었 means any action which happened in the past.   Past progressive tense ends in 고 있었다.   Drop 다 from the verb stem and add 던.   It sounds more natural to say simply 고 있던 than 고 있었던.   Either one is perfect to use.

Examples:

•the car(차) **which** he **was fixing**: 그가 고치**고**/수리하**고 있(었)던** 차

*to fix: 고치다(pure Korean)/수리하다(Sino Korean)

•the fish(고기) **which** he **was catching**: 그가 잡**고 있(었)던** 고기   *to catch: 잡다

•the movie(영화) **which** he **was seeing**: 그가 보**고 있(었)던** 영화   *to see: 보다

•the food(음식) **which** he **was eating**: 그가 먹**고 있(었)던** 음식   *to eat: 먹다

•the coffee(커피) **which** he **was drinking**: 그가 마시**고 있(었)던** 커피

*to drink: 마시다

•the house **in which** he **was living**: 그가 살**고 있(었)던** 집   *to live: 살다

•the house(집) **which** he **was buying**: 그가 사**고 있(었)던** 집   *to buy: 사다

•the song(노래) **to which** he **was listening**: 그가 듣**고 있(었)던**/청취하**고 있(었)던** 노래   *to listen: 듣다(pure Korean)/청취하다(Sino Korean)

•money(돈) **which** he **was earning**: 그가 벌**고 있(었)던** 돈   *to earn: 벌다

•coffee beans(커피콩) **which** he **was grinding**: 그가 갈**고 있(었)던** 커피콩

*to grind: 갈다

•the bus(버스) **which** he **was riding**: 그가 타**고 있(었)던** 버스   *to ride: 타다

•the pencil(연필) **which** he **was finding**: 그가 찾**고 있(었)던** 연필   *to find: 찾다

•the picture(사진) **which** he **was taking**: 그가 찍**고 있(었)던** 사진   *to take: 찍다

•Korean language(한국어) **which** he **was studying**: 그가 공부하**고 있(었)던** 한국어

*to study: 공부하다

[여기에 입력]

Korean Language: Grammar Pattern

•the problem(문제) **which** he **was covering up**: 그가 덮**고 있(었)던** 문제

*to cover up: 덮다

Exercise 32. Fill in the blanks with appropriate modifying verbs in past progressive tense in Korean. Write the underlined verb parts only.

modifying verb in past progressive tense	modifier in past progressive tense in Korean: 고 있(었)던
the dress(옷) <u>which</u> he <u>was wearing</u> *to wear: 입다	입고 있(었)던
the meat(고기) <u>which</u> he <u>was chewing</u> *to chew: 씹다	씹고 있(었)던
the president(대통령) <u>whom</u> he <u>was electing</u> *to elect: 뽑다(pure Korean)/선출하다(Sino Korean)	뽑고 있(었)던/선출하고 있(었)던
the language(언어) <u>which</u> he <u>was learning</u> *to learn: 배우다	배우고 있(었)던
the money(돈) <u>which</u> he <u>was spending</u> *to spend: 쓰다	쓰고 있(었)던
the car(차) <u>which</u> he <u>was driving</u> *to drive: 몰다(pure Korean)/운전하다(Sino Korean)	몰고 있(었)던/운전하고 있(었)던
the street <u>on which</u> he <u>was walking</u> *to walk: 걷다	걷고 있(었)던

5. modifying verb in present progressive tense: 고 있는

Korean Language: Grammar Pattern

* Root verb stem + 고 있는: 고 means progressive actions in all tenses. 는 implies an action which happens in the present.   Present progressive tense ends in 고 있다.   Drop 다 from the verb stem and add 는.

Examples:

•the car(차) **which** he **is fixing**: 그가 수리하**고 있는** 차   *to fix: 수리하다

•the fish(고기) **which** he **is catching**: 그가 잡**고 있는** 고기   *to catch: 잡다

•the movie(영화) **which** he **is seeing**: 그가 보**고 있는** 영화   *to see: 보다

•the food(음식) **which** he **is eating**: 그가 먹**고 있는** 음식   *to eat: 먹다

•the coffee(커피) **which** he **is drinking**: 그가 마시**고 있는** 커피   *to drink: 마시다

•the house(집) **in which** he **is living**: 그가 살**고 있는** 집   *to live: 살다

•the house(집) **which** he **is buying**: 그가 사**고 있는** 집   *to buy: 사다

•the song(노래) **to which** he **is listening**: 그가 듣**고 있는** 노래   *to listen: 듣다

•money(돈) **which** he **is earning**: 그가 벌**고 있는** 돈   *to earn: 벌다

•coffee beans(커피콩) **which** he **is grinding**: 그가 갈**고 있는** 커피콩   *to grind: 갈다

•the bus(버스) **which** he **is riding**: 그가 타**고 있는** 버스   *to ride: 타다

•the pencil(연필) **which** he **is finding**: 그가 찾**고 있는** 연필   *to find: 찾다

•the photo(사진) **which** he **is taking**: 그가 찍**고 있는** 사진   *to take: 찍다

•Korean language(한국어) **which** he **is learning**: 그가 배우**고 있는** 한국어

*to learn: 배우다

•the problem(문제) **which** he **is covering up**: 그가 덮**고 있는** 문제

*to cover up: 덮다

•the ball(공) **which** he(그) **is hitting**: 그가 치**고 있는** 공   *to hit: 치다

Korean Language: Grammar Pattern

•the door(문) **which** he(그) **is closing**: 그가 닫**고 있는** 문   *to close: 닫다

•the song(노래) **which** he **is singing**: 그가 부르**고 있는** 노래   *to sing: 부르다

•the hat(모자) **which** he **is hanging**: 그가 걸**고 있는** 모자   *to hang: 걸다

Exercise 33.   Fill in the blanks with the appropriate modifier in present progressive tense in Korean. Write the underlined verb parts only.

modifying verb in present progressive tense	modifier in present progressive tense in Korean: 고 있는
the dress(옷) <u>which</u> he <u>is wearing</u> *to wear: 입다	입고 있는
the meat(고기) <u>which</u> he <u>is chewing</u> *to chew: 씹다	씹고 있는
the president(대통령) <u>whom</u> he <u>is electing</u> *to elect: 뽑다/선택하다	뽑고 있는/선택하고 있는
the language(언어) <u>which</u> he <u>is learning</u> *to learn: 배우다	배우고 있는
the money(돈) <u>which</u> he <u>is spending</u> *to spend: 쓰다	쓰고 있는
the car(차) <u>which</u> he <u>is driving</u> *to drive: 몰다/운전하다	몰고 있는/운전하고 있는
the street <u>on which</u> he <u>is walking</u> *walk: 걷다	걷고 있는

6. modifying verb in future progressive tense: 고 있을

Korean Language: Grammar Pattern

*Verb stem in present progressive tense ends in 고 있다. Drop 다 from the verb stem in present progressive tense and add 을.

※Modifying verbs in progressive tense are as follows:

*modifying verb in past progressive tense: 고 있던

*modifying verb in present progressive tense: 고 있는

*modifying verb in future progressive tense: 고 있을

Examples:

•the car(차) **which** he **will be fixing**: 그가 수리하**고 있을** 차   *to fix: 수리하다

•the fish(고기) **which** he **will be catching**: 그가 잡**고 있을** 고기   *to catch: 잡다

•the movie(영화) **which** he **will be seeing**: 그가 보**고 있을** 영화   *to see: 보다

•the food(음식) **which** he **will be eating**: 그가 먹**고 있을** 음식   *to eat: 먹다

•the coffee(커피) **which** he **will be drinking**: 그가 마시**고 있을** 커피

*to drink: 마시다

•the house in **which** he **will be living**: 그가 살**고 있을** 집   *to live: 살다

•the house(집) **which** he **will be buying**: 그가 사**고 있을** 집   *to buy: 사다

•the song(노래) to **which** he **will be listening**: 그가 듣**고 있을**/청취하**고 있을** 노래
*to listen: 듣다(pure Korean)/청취하다(Sino Korean)

•money(돈) **which** he **will be earning**: 그가 벌**고 있을** 돈   *to earn: 벌다

•the coffee beans(커피콩) **which** he **will be grinding**: 그가 갈**고 있을** 커피콩

*to grind: 갈다

•the bus(버스) **which** he **will be riding**: 그가 타**고 있을** 버스   *to ride: 타다

•the pencil(연필) **which** he **will be finding**: 그가 찾**고 있을** 연필   *to find: 찾다

[여기에 입력]
Korean Language: Grammar Pattern

•the picture(사진) **which** he **will be taking**: 그가 찍**고 있을** 사진   *to take: 찍다

•Korean language(한국어) **which** he **will be learning**: 그가 배우**고 있을** 한국어

*to learn: 배우다

•the problem(문제) **which** he **will be solving**: 그가 풀**고 있을** 문제   *to solve: 풀다

Exercise 34. Fill in the blanks with the appropriate modifying verb in future progressive tense in Korean. Rewrite the underlined parts in only.

modifying verb in future progressive tense	modifier in future progressive tense in Korean: 고 있을
the dress(옷) <u>which</u> he <u>will be wearing</u> *to wear: 입다	입고 있을
the meat(고기) <u>which</u> he <u>will be chewing</u> *to chew: 씹다	씹고 있을
the president(대통령) <u>whom</u> he <u>will be electing</u> *to elect: 뽑다	뽑고 있을
the language(언어) <u>which</u> he <u>will be learning</u> *to learn: 배우다	배우고 있을
the money(돈) <u>which</u> he <u>will be spending</u> *to spend: 쓰다	쓰고 있을
the car(차) <u>which</u> he <u>will be driving</u> *to drive: 몰다/운전하다	몰고 있을/운전하고 있을
the street <u>on which</u> he <u>will be walking</u>	걷고 있을

Korean Language: Grammar Pattern

*to walk: 걷다	
the ball(공) <u>which</u> he(그) <u>will be hitting</u> *to hit: 치다	치고 있을
the door(문) <u>which</u> he(그) <u>will be closing</u> *to close: 닫다	닫고 있을
the song(노래) <u>which</u> he <u>will be singing</u> *to sing: 부르다	부르고 있을
the food(음식) call <u>which</u> he <u>will be making</u> *to make: 만들다	만들고 있을
the hat(모자) <u>which</u> he <u>will be hanging</u> *to hang: 걸다	걸고 있을

※Compare the following modifying verbs in various progressive tenses.

modifying verbs in various progressive tenses	Korean expression: 고 있(었)던 or 고 있는 or 고 있을
the dream(꿈) **which** he(그) **was dreaming** *to dream: 꾸다	그가 꾸**고 있(었)던** 꿈 ※있던 sounds more natural than 있었던.
the dream **which** he **is dreaming**	그가 꾸**고 있는** 꿈
the dream **which** he **will be dreaming**	그가 꾸**고 있을** 꿈
the piano(피아노) **which** he **was playing** *to play: 연주하다	그가 연주하**고 있(었)던** 피아노

Korean Language: Grammar Pattern

the piano **which** he **is playing**	그가 연주하**고 있는** 피아노
the piano **which** he **will be playing**	그가 연주하**고 있을** 피아노
the song(노래) **which** he **was singing** *to sing: 부르다	그가 부르고 있(었)던 노래
the song **which** he **is singing**	그가 부르**고 있는** 노래
the song **which** he **will be singing**	그가 부르**고 있을** 노래
the ground(땅) **which** he **was digging** *to dig: 파다	그가 파**고 있(었)던** 땅
the ground **which** he **is digging**	그가 파**고 있는** 땅
the ground **which** he **will be digging**	그가 파**고 있을** 땅
the hair(머리카락) **which** he **was cutting** *to cut: 자르다	그가 자르**고 있(었)던** 머리
the hair **which** he **is cutting**	그가 자르**고 있는** 머리
the hair **which** he **will be cutting**	그가 자르**고 있을** 머리

Exercise 35. Fill in the blanks with the appropriate modifying verb in progressive tense in Korean. Rewrite the underlined parts only.

modifying verbs in various progressive tenses	Korean equivalent: 고 있(었)던 or 고 있는 or 고 있을
the perfume(향수) which he was spraying *to spray: 뿌리다	뿌리고 있던 ※있던 sounds more informal than 있었던 and it is to my personal preference.

Korean Language: Grammar Pattern

the perfume <u>which</u> he <u>is spraying</u>	뿌리고 있는
the perfume <u>which</u> he <u>will be spraying</u>	뿌리고 있을
the wine(포도주) <u>which</u> he <u>was tasting</u> *to taste: 맛보다	맛보고 있던
the wine <u>which</u> he <u>is tasting</u>	맛보고 있는
the wine <u>which</u> he <u>will be tasting</u>	맛보고 있을
the river(강) <u>which</u> <u>was flowing</u> *to flow: 흐르다	흐르고 있던
the river <u>which</u> <u>is flowing</u>	흐르고 있는
the river <u>which</u> <u>will be flowing</u>	흐르고 있을
the food(음식) <u>which</u> he <u>was ordering</u> *to order: 주문하다	주문하고 있던
the food <u>which</u> he <u>is ordering</u>	주문하고 있는
the food <u>which</u> he <u>will be ordering</u>	주문하고 있을
the knowledge(지식) <u>which</u> he <u>was knowing</u> *to know: 알다	알고 있던
the knowledge <u>which</u> he <u>is knowing</u>	알고 있는
the knowledge <u>which</u> he <u>will be knowing</u>	알고 있을
the horse <u>which</u> <u>was running</u> *to run: 뛰다/달리다	뛰고 있던/달리고 있던
the horse <u>which</u> <u>is running</u>	뛰고 있는/달리고 있는
the horse <u>which</u> <u>will be running</u>	뛰고 있을/달리고 있을

Korean Language: Grammar Pattern

the street(거리) <u>on which</u> he <u>was walking</u> *to walk: 걷다	걷고 있던
the street <u>on which</u> he <u>is walking</u>	걷고 있는
the street <u>on which</u> he <u>will be walking</u>	걷고 있을
the park(공원) <u>in which</u> he <u>was playing</u> *to play: 놀다	놀고 있던
the park(공원) <u>in which</u> he <u>is playing</u>	놀고 있는
the park(공원) <u>in which</u> he <u>will be playing</u>	놀고 있을
rain(비) <u>which</u> <u>was falling</u> *to fall: 내리다	내리고 있던
rain <u>which</u> <u>is falling</u>	내리고 있는
rain <u>which</u> <u>will be falling</u>	내리고 있을
the house(집) <u>which</u> he <u>was building</u> *to build: 짓다	짓고 있던
the house <u>which</u> he <u>is building</u>	짓고 있는
the house <u>which</u> he <u>will be building</u>	짓고 있을
the river(강) <u>which</u> he <u>was crossing</u> *to cross: 건너다	건너고 있던
the river <u>which</u> he <u>is crossing</u>	건너고 있는
the river <u>which</u> he <u>will be crossing</u>	건너고 있을
the cell phone(휴대폰) <u>which</u> he <u>was wanting</u> *to want: 원하다	원하고 있던

Korean Language: Grammar Pattern

the cell phone <u>which</u> he <u>is wanting</u>	원하고 있는
the cell phone <u>which</u> he <u>will be wanting</u>	원하고 있을

UNIT 12. CONJUNCTION

1. verb + AND(고) + verb

1) root verb stem + 고 for present tense:

*Drop 다 from the root verb stem and add 고.

•come **and**: 오**고**   *to come: 오다

•catch **and**: 잡**고**   *to catch: 잡다

2) verb stem in past tense + 고

*Drop 다 from the verb stem in past tense and add 고.

•came **and**: 왔**고**   *to have come: 왔다

•caught **and**: 잡았**고**   *to have caught: 잡았다

3) verb stem in future tense + 고

*Drop 다 from the verb stem in future tense and add 고.

•will come **and**: 오겠**고**/올 것이**고**/올 거**고**

*to be going to come: 오겠다/올 것이다/올 거다

•will catch **and**: 잡겠**고**/잡을 것이**고**/잡을 거**고**

*to be going to catch: 잡겠다/잡을 것이다/잡을 거다

4) verb stem in past progressive tense + 고

*Past progressive tense ends in 고 있었다. Drop 다 from the verb stem and add 고.

Korean Language: Grammar Pattern

•was/were coming **and**: 오고 있었**고**   *to have been coming: 오고 있었다

•was/were catching **and**: 잡고 있었**고**   *to have been catching: 잡고 있었다

5) verb stem in present progressive tense + 고

*Present progressive tense ends in 고 있다. Drop 다 from the verb stem and add 고.

•am/are/is coming **and**: 오고 있**고**   *to be coming: 오고 있다

•am/are/is catching **and**: 잡고 있**고**   *to be catching: 잡고 있다

6) verb stem in future progressive tense + 고

*Future progressive tense ends in 고 있겠다/고 있을 것이다/고 있을 거다. Drop 다 from the verb stem and add 고.

•will be coming **and**: 오고 있겠**고**/오고 있을 것이**고**/오고 있을 거**고**

*to be going to be coming: 오고 있겠다/오고 있을 것이다/오고 있을 거다

•will be catching **and**: 잡고 있겠**고**/잡고 있을 것이**고**/잡고 있을 거**고**

*to be going to be catching: 잡고 있겠다/잡고 있을 것이다/잡고 있을 거다

※In the case of 'NOUN + <u>AND</u>', 'and' will be <u>와/과/(이)랑/하고</u>. Avoid the confusion with 'VERB + <u>AND</u>'.

Examples:

•worked and: 일했고   *to have worked: 일했다

•will sing and: 노래하겠고/노래할 것이고/노래할 거고

*to be going to sing: 노래하겠다/노래할 것이다/노래할거다

•is fast and: 빠르고   *to be fast: 빠르다

Korean Language: Grammar Pattern

•could run and: 뛸 수 있었고　*to have been able to run: 뛸 수 있었다

•did and: 했고　*to have done: 했다

•is a teacher(교사) and: 교사이고　*to be: 이다

•was a teacher and: 교사였고　*to have been: 이었다=였다

※였고 is the short form of 이었고.　A short form sounds more natural.

•must see and: 봐야 하고　*to have to see: 봐야 하다=보아야 하다

•had to see and: 봐야 했고　*to have had to: 봐야 했다

•chose and: 선택했고　*to have chosen: 선택했다

•will look and: 보겠고/볼 것이고/볼 거고　*to be going to look: 보겠다/볼 것이다/볼 거다

※보겠다 is formal and 볼 거다 is informal.　Either one is perfect to write and speak.

•was teaching and: 가르치고 있었고　*to have been teaching: 가르치고 있었다

•will be breaking and: 부수고 있겠고/부수고 있을 것이다/부수고 있을 거고

*to be going to be breaking: 부수고 있겠다/부수고 있을 것이다/부수고 있을 거다

•helped and: 도왔고　*to have helped: 도왔다

•forget and: 잊고　*to forget: 잊다

•lost and: 잃었고　*to have lost: 잃었다

•will open and: 열겠고/열 것이고/열 거고

*to be going to open: 열겠다/열 것이다/열 거다

•was swimming and: 수영하고 있었고　*to have been swimming: 수영하고 있었다

•is eating and: 먹고 있고　*to be eating: 먹고 있다

•will be hiking and: 등산하고 있겠고/등산하고 있을 것이고/등산하고 있을 거고

Korean Language: Grammar Pattern

*to be going to be hiking: 등산하고 있겠다/등산하고 있을 것이다/등산하고 있을 거다

•cleaned up and: 청소했고   *to have cleaned up: 청소했다

•dance and: 춤추고   *to dance: 춤추다

•will walk and: 걷겠고/걸을 것이고/걸을 거고

*to be going to walk: 걷겠다/걸을 것이다/걸을 거다

•was sleeping and: 자고 있었고   *to have been sleeping: 자고 있었다

•am leaving and: 떠나고 있고   *to be leaving: 떠나고 있다

•will be arriving and: 도착하고 있겠고/도착하고 있을 것이고/도착하고 있을 거고
*to be going to be arriving: 도착하고 있겠다/도착하고 있을 것이다/도착하고 있을
거다

•reads and: 읽고/독서하고   *to read: 읽다(pure Korean)/독서하다(Sino Korean)

•wore and: 입었고   *to have worn: 입었다

•will cook and: 요리하겠고/요리할 것이고/요리할 거고

*to be going to cook: 요리하겠다/요리할 것이다/요리할 거다

•must drink and: 마셔야(마시어야) 하고   *to have to drink: 마셔야 하다

•can open and: 열 수 있고   *to be able to open: 열 수 있다

•could correct and: 고칠 수 있었고   *to have been able to correct: 고칠 수
있었다

•make a phone call and: 전화하고   *to make a phone call: 전화하다

Exercise 36. Rewrite the English conjunction 'AND' in Korean.

verb + conjunction AND	conjunction AND in Korean: 고
stood up <u>and</u>	섰고

Korean Language: Grammar Pattern

*to stand: 서다	*to have sat: 섰다.
sit down <u>and</u> *to sit down: 앉다	앉고
will begin <u>and</u> *to begin: 시작하다	시작하겠고/시작할 것이고/시작할 거고 *to be going to begin: 시작하겠다/시작할 것이다/시작할 거다
can make <u>and</u> *to make: 만들다	만들 수 있고 *to be able to make: 만들 수 있다
could wait <u>and</u> *to wait: 기다리다	기다릴 수 있었고 *to have been able to wait: 기다릴 수 있었다
must finish <u>and</u> *to finish: 끝내다	끝내야 하고 *to have to finish: 끝내야 하다
had to keep <u>and</u> *to keep: 지키다	지켜야(지키어야) 했고 *to have had to keep: 지켜야 했다
is sad <u>and</u> *to be sad: 슬프다	슬프고
was counting <u>and</u> *to count: 세다	세고 있었고 *to have been counting: 세고 있었다
will be departing <u>and</u> *to depart: 출발하다	출발하고 있겠고/출발하고 있을 것이고/출발하고 있을 거고 *to be going to be departing: 출발하고 있겠다/출발하고 있을 것이다/출발하고 있을 거다
is rising <u>and</u>	오르고 있고

Korean Language: Grammar Pattern

*to rise: 오르다	*to be rising: 오르고 있다
will be tired <u>and</u> *to be tired: 지치다	지치겠고/지칠 것이고/지칠 거고 *to be going to be tired: 지치겠다/지칠 것이다/지칠 거다
must tear <u>and</u> *to tear: 찢다	찢어야 하고 *to have to tear: 찢어야 하다
can order <u>and</u> *to order: 주문하다	주문할 수 있고 *to be able to order: 주문할 수 있다
was boarding <u>and</u> *to board: 탑승하다	탑승하고 있었고 *to have been boarding: 탑승하고 있었다
turned on <u>and</u> *to turn on: 켜다	켰고 *to have turned on: 켰다
go out <u>and</u> *to go out: 나가다	나가고
had to invite <u>and</u> *to invite: 초대하다	초대해야 했고 *to have had to invite: 초대해야 했다
is blocking <u>and</u> *to block: 막다	막고 있고 *to be blocking: 막고 있다

2. verb + BUT(지만) + verb

1) root verb stem ending in consonant or vowel + 지만 for present tense

*Drop 다 from the root verb stem and add 지만.

Korean Language: Grammar Pattern

•buy **but**: 사**지만**   *to buy: 사다

*지 ends in vowel ㅣ. Drop 다 and add 지만.

•mix **but**: 섞**지만**   *to mix: 섞다

*섞 ends in consonant ㄲ. Drop 다 and add 지만.

2) verb stem in past tense + 지만

*Past tense ends in ㅆ다 or 었다 or 았다. Drop 다 from the verb stem and add 지만.

•bought **but**: 샀**지만**   *to have bought: 샀다

•mixed **but**: 섞었**지만**   *to have mixed: 섞었다

3) verb stem future tense + 지만

*Future tense ends in 겠다 or ㄹ을 것이다 or ㄹ을 거다. Drop 다 from the verb stem and add 지만.

•will buy **but**: 사겠**지만**/살 것이**지만**/살 거**지만**

*to be going to buy: 사겠다/살 것이다/살 거다

•will mix **but**: 섞겠**지만**/섞을 것이**지만**/섞을 거**지만**

*to be going to mix: 섞겠다/섞을 것이다/섞을 거다

4) verb stem in past progressive tense + 지만

*Past progressive tense ends in 고 있었다. Drop 다 from the verb stem and add 지만.

•was/were buying **but**: 사고 있었**지만**   *to have been buying: 사고 있었다

•was/were mixing **but**: 섞고 있었**지만**   *to have been mixing: 섞고 있었다

Korean Language: Grammar Pattern

5) verb stem in present progressive tense + 지만

*Present progressive tense ends in 고 있다. Drop 다 from the verb stem and add 지만.

•am/are/is buying **but**: 사고 있**지만**   *to be buying: 사고 있다

•am/are/is mixing **but**: 섞고 있**지만**   *to be mixing: 섞고 있다

6) verb stem in future progressive tense + 지만

*Future progressive tense ends in 고 있겠다 or 고 있을 것이다 or 고 있을 거다. Drop 다 from the verb stem and add 지만

•will be buying **but**: 사고 있겠**지만**/사고 있을 것이**지만**/사고 있을 거**지만**

*to be going to be buying: 사고 있겠다/사고 있을 것이다/사고 있을 거다

•will be mixing **but**: 섞고 있겠**지만**/섞고 있을 것이**지만**/섞고 있을 거**지만**

*to be going to be mixing: 섞고 있겠다/섞고 있을 것이다/섞고 있을 거다

Examples:

•went but: 갔지만   *to have gone: 갔다

•dislikes but: 싫어하지만   *to dislike: 싫어하다

•will love but: 사랑하겠지만/사랑할 것이지만/사랑할 거지만

*to be going to love: 사랑하겠다/사랑할 것이다/사랑할 거다

•can work out but: 운동할 수 있지만   *to be able to work out: 운동할 수 있다

•could break but: 깰 수 있었지만   *to have been able to break: 깰 수 있었다

•must help but: 도와야 하지만   *to have to help: 도와야 하다

•had to forget but: 잊어야 했지만   *to have had to: 잊어야 했다

•chose but: 골랐지만   *to have chosen: 골랐다

•go but: 가지만   *to go: 가다

Korean Language: Grammar Pattern

•will look but: 보겠지만/볼 것이지만/볼 거지만   *to be going to look: 보겠다/볼 것이다/볼 거다

•was working but: 일하고 있었지만   *to have been working: 일하고 있었다

•is singing but: 노래하고 있지만   *to be singing: 노래하고 있다

•will be running but: 달리고 있겠지만/달리고 있을 것이지만/달리고 있을 거지만

*to be going to be running: 달리고 있겠다/달리고 있을 것이다/달리고 있을 거다

•can do but: 할 수 있지만   *to be able to do: 할 수 있다

•could see but: 볼 수 있었지만   *to have been able to see: 볼 수 있었다

•must catch but: 잡아야 하지만   *to have to catch: 잡아야 하다

•had to fish but: 낚시해야 했지만   *to have had to fish: 낚시해야 했다

•swam but: 수영했지만   *to have swum: 수영했다

•clean up but: 청소하지만   *to clean up: 청소하다

•will do the dishes but: 설거지하겠지만/설거지할 것이지만/설거지할 거지만

*to be going to do the dishes: 설거지하겠다/설거지할 것이다/설거지할 거다

•was driving but: 운전하고 있었지만   *to have been driving: 운전하고 있었다

•is dancing but: 춤추고 있지만   *to be dancing: 춤추고 있다

•will be walking but: 걷고 있겠지만/걷고 있을 것이지만/걷고 있을 거지만

*to be going to be walking: 걷고 있겠다/걷고 있을 것이다/걷고 있을 거다

•can sleep but: 잘 수 있지만 *to be able to sleep: 잘 수 있다

•could leave but: 떠날 수 있었지만   *to have been able to leave: 떠날 수 있었다

•must arrive but: 도착해야 하지만   *to have to arrive: 도착해야 하다

•had to depart but: 출발해야 하지만

*to have had to depart: 출발해야 했다

•reads but: 읽지만/독서하지만   *to read: 읽다(pure Korean)/독서하다(Sino Korean)

Korean Language: Grammar Pattern

•wore but: 입었지만   *to have worn: 입었다

•will cook but: 요리하겠지만/요리할 것이지만/요리할 거지만

*to be going to cook: 요리하겠다/요리할 것이다/요리할 거다

•must drink but: 마셔야 하지만   *to have to drink: 마셔야 하다

•had to drive but: 운전해야 했지만   *to have had to drive: 운전해야 했다

•can open but: 열 수 있지만   *to be able to open: 열 수 있다

•could correct but: 수정할 수 있었지만

*to have been able to correct: 수정할 수 있었다

•called but: 불렀지만   *to have called: 불렀다

Exercise 37. Rewrite the English conjunction 'BUT' in Korean.

verb + conjunction 'BUT'	conjunction BUT in Korean: 지만
stood up <u>but</u> *to stand: 서다	섰지만 *to have stood: 섰다
sit down <u>but</u> *to sit down: 앉다	앉지만
will begin <u>but</u> *to begin: 시작하다	시작하겠지만/시작할 것이지만/시작할 거지만 *to be going to begin: 시작하겠다/시작할 것이다/시작할 거다
can finish <u>but</u> *to finish: 끝내다	끝낼 수 있지만 *to be able to finish: 끝낼 수 있다
will make <u>but</u> *to make: 만들다	만들겠지만/만들 것이지만/만들 거지만

Korean Language: Grammar Pattern

	*to be going to make: 만들겠다/만들 것이다/만들 거다
could wait <u>but</u> *to wait: 기다리다	기다릴 수 있었지만 *to have been able to wait: 기다릴 수 있었다
must write <u>but</u> *to write: 쓰다	쓰야 하지만 *to have to write: 쓰야 하다
had to keep <u>but</u> *to keep: 지키다	지켜야 했지만 *to have had to keep: 지켜야 했다
is reading <u>but</u> *to read: 읽다/독서하다	읽고 있지만/독서하고 있지만 *to be reading: 읽고 있다/독서하고 있다
kicked <u>but</u> *to kick: 차다	찼지만 *to have kicked: 찼다
will be listening <u>but</u> *to listen: 듣다	듣고 있겠지만/듣고 있을 것이지만/듣고 있을 거지만 *to be going to be listening: 듣고 있겠다/듣고 있을 것이다/듣고 있을 거다
could move <u>but</u> *to move: 움직이다	움직일 수 있었지만 *to have been able to move: 움직일 수 있었다
had to fix <u>but</u> *to fix: 고치다/수리하다	고쳐야 했지만 *to have had to fix: 고쳐야 했다
use <u>but</u> *to use: 쓰다(pure Korean)/사용하다(Sino Korean)	쓰지만/사용하지만
washed <u>but</u>	씻었지만

Korean Language: Grammar Pattern

*to wash: 씻다	*to have washed: 씻었다
must stop <u>but</u> *to stop: 멈추다	멈춰야(멈추어야) 하지만 *to have to stop: 멈춰야(멈추어야) 하다
can change <u>but</u> *to change: 바꾸다	바꿀 수 있지만 *to be able to change: 바꿀 수 있다
will buy <u>but</u> *to buy: 사다	사겠지만/살 것이지만/살 거지만 *to be going to buy: 사겠다/살 것이다/살 거다
was cutting <u>but</u> *to cut: 자르다	자르고 있었지만 *to have been cutting: 자르고 있었다
covered <u>but</u> *to cover: 덮다	덮었지만 *to have covered: 덮었다

3. verb + OR (거나) + verb

1) root verb stem ending in consonant or vowel + 거나 for present tense

*The verbs are in present tense.   Drop 다 from the root verb stem and add 거나.

•raise <u>or</u>(*to raise: 올리다): 올리**거나**

•bark <u>or</u>(*to bark: 짖다): 짖**거나**

2) verb stem in past tense + 거나

*Past tense ends in 씨다 or 었다 or 았다.   Drop 다 from verb stem and add 거나.

•raised <u>or</u>: 올렸**거나**   *to have raised: 올렸다

•barked <u>or</u>: 짖었**거나**   *to have barked: 짖었다

3) verb stem in future tense + 거나

*Future tense ends in 겠다 or ㄹ을 것이다 or ㄹ을 거다. Drop 다 from verb stem and add 거나.

•will raise <u>or</u>: 올리겠**거나**/올릴 것이**거나**/올릴 거**거나**

*to be going to raise: 올리겠다/올릴 것이다/올릴 거다

•will bark <u>or</u>: 짖겠**거나**/짖을 것이**거나**/짖을 거**거나**

*to be going to bark: 짖겠다/짖을 것이다/짖을 거다

4) verb stem in past progressive tense + 거나

*Past progressive tense ends in 고 있었다. Drop 다 from verb stem and add 거나.

•was/were raising <u>or</u>: 올리고 있었**거나**   *to have been raising: 올리고 있었다

•was/were barking <u>or</u>: 짖고 있었**거나**   *to have been barking: 짖고 있었다

5) verb stem in present progressive tense + 거나

*Present progressive tense ends in 고 있다. Drop 다 from verb stem and add 거나.

•am/are/is raising <u>or</u>: 올리고 있**거나**   *to be raising: 올리고 있다

•am/are/is barking <u>or</u>: 짖고 있**거나**   *to be barking: 짖고 있다

6) verb stem in future progressive tense + 거나

*Future progressive tense ends in 고 있겠다 or 고 있을 것이다 or 고 있을 거다. Drop 다 from verb stem and add 거나.

•will be raising <u>or</u>: 올리고 있겠**거나**/올리고 있을 것이**거나**/올리고 있을 거**거나**

*to be going to be raising: 올리고 있겠다/올리고 있을 것이다/올리고 있을 거다

Korean Language: Grammar Pattern

•will be barking <u>or</u>: 짖고 있겠**거나**/짖고 있을 것이**거나**/짖고 있을 거**거나**

*to be going to be barking: 짖고 있겠다/짖고 있을 것이다/짖고 있을 거다

Examples:

•come or: 오거나   *to come: 오다 *온다 is verb stem in present tense.

•chose or: 골랐거나/선택했거나   *to have chosen: 골랐다/선택했다

*to choose: 고르다(pure Korean)/선택하다(Sino Korean)

•will catch or: 잡겠거나/잡을 것이거나/잡을 거거나

*to be going to catch: 잡겠다/잡을 것이다/잡을 거다

•can go hiking or: 등산할 수 있거나 *to be able to go hiking: 등산할 수 있다

•could swim or: 수영할 수 있었거나   *to have been able to swim: 수영할 수 있었다

•must clean up or: 청소해야 하거나   *to have to clean up: 청소해야 하다

•had to eat or: 먹어야 했거나   *to have had to eat: 먹어야 했다

•went or: 갔거나   *to have gone: 갔다

•look or: 보거나   *to look/see: 보다   *본다 is verb stem in present tense.

•will teach or: 가르치겠거나/가르칠 것이거나/가르칠 거거나

*to be going to teach: 가르치겠다/가르칠 것이다/가르칠 거다

•was working or: 일하고 있었거나   *to have been working: 일하고 있었다

•is singing or: 노래하고 있거나   *to be singing: 노래하고 있다

•will be running or: 달리고 있겠거나/달리고 있을 것이거나/달리고 있을 거거나

*to be going to be running: 달리고 있겠다/달리고 있을 것이다/달리고 있을 거다

•can do or: 할 수 있거나   *to be able to do: 할 수 있다

•could see or: 볼 수 있었거나   *to have been able to see: 볼 수 있었다

Korean Language: Grammar Pattern

•must dislike or: 싫어해야 하거나   *to have to dislike: 싫어해야 하다

•had to love or: 사랑해야 했거나   *to have had to love: 사랑해야 했다

•broke or: 깼거나   *to have broken: 깼다

•help or: 돕거나   *to help: 돕다   *돕는다* is verb stem in present tense.

•will forget or: 잊겠거나/잊을 것이거나/잊을 거거나

*to be going to forget: 잊겠다/잊을 것이다/잊을 거다

•can eat or: 먹을 수 있거나   *to be able to eat: 먹을 수 있다

•could drive or: 운전할 수 있었거나   *to have been able to: 운전할 수 있었다

•must dance or: 춤춰야 하거나   *to have to dance: 춤춰야 하다

•had to walk or: 걸어야 했거나   *to have had to walk: 걸어야 했다

•slept or: 잤거나   *to have slept: 잤다

•leaves or: 떠나거나   *to leave: 떠나다.   *떠난다* is verb stem in present tense.

•will arrive or: 도착하겠거나/도착할 것이거나/도착할 거거나

*to be going to arrive: 도착하겠다/도착할 것이다/도착할 거다

•reads or: 읽거나   *to read: 읽다   *읽는다* is verb stem in present tense.

•wore or: 입었거나   *to have worn: 입었다

•will cook or: 요리하겠거나/요리할 것이거나/요리할 거거나

*to be going to cook: 요리하겠다/요리할 것이다/요리할 거다

•must drink or: 마셔야 하거나   *to have to drink: 마셔야 하다

•can open or: 열 수 있거나   *to be able to open: 열 수 있다

•could correct or: 고칠 수 있었거나/수정할 수 있었거나

*to have been able to correct: 고칠 수 있었다/수정할 수 있었다

Exercise 38. Rewrite the English conjunction 'OR' in Korean.

Korean Language: Grammar Pattern

verb + conjunction OR	conjunction OR in Korean: 거나
will dream <u>or</u> *to dream: 꿈꾸다	꿈꾸겠거나/꿈꿀 것이거나/꿈꿀 거거나 *to be going to dream: 꿈꾸겠다/꿈꿀 것이다/꿈꿀 거다
stood up <u>or</u> *to stand: 서다	섰거나 *to have stood: 섰다
sit down <u>or</u> *to sit down: 앉다	앉거나
will begin <u>or</u> *to begin: 시작하다	시작하겠거나/시작할 것이거나/시작할 거거나 *to be going to begin: 시작하겠다/시작할 것이다/시작할 거다
can make <u>or</u> *to make: 만들다	만들 수 있거나 *to be able to make: 만들 수 있다
could wait <u>or</u> *to wait: 기다리다	기다릴 수 있었거나 *to have been able to wait: 기다릴 수 있었다
must finish <u>or</u> *to finish: 끝내다	끝내야 하거나 *to have to finish: 끝내야 하다
had to keep <u>or</u> *to keep: 지키다	지켜야 했거나 *to have had to keep: 지켜야 했다
will be dreaming <u>or</u> *to dream: 꿈꾸다	꿈꾸고 있겠거나/꿈꾸고 있을 것이거나/꿈꾸고 있을 거거나 *to be going to be dreaming: 꿈꾸고 있겠다/꿈꾸고 있을 것이다/꿈꾸고 있을 거다
gain <u>or</u>	얻거나

Korean Language: Grammar Pattern

*to gain: 얻다	
was losing or *to lose: 잃다	잃고 있었거나 *to have been losing: 잃고 있었다
shot or *to shoot: 쏘다	쐈거나(쏘았거나) *to have shot: 쐈다(쏘았다)
can ride or *to ride: 타다	탈 수 있거나 *to be able to ride: 탈 수 있다
will play or *to play: 놀다	놀겠거나/놀 것이거나/놀 거거나 *to be going to play: 놀겠다/놀 것이다/놀 거다
must fix or *to fix 고치다/수리하다	고쳐야 하거나/수리해야 하거나 *to have to fix: 고쳐야 하다/수리해야 하다
could deny or *to deny: 거부하다	거부할 수 있었거나 *to have been able to deny: 거부할 수 있었다
had to throw or *to throw: 던지다	던져야 했거나 *to have had to throw: 던져야 했다
kicked or *to kick: 차다	찼거나 *to have kicked: 찼다
is reading or *to read: 읽다/독서하다	읽고 있거나/독서하고 있거나 *to be reading: 읽고 있다/독서하고 있다
was entering or *to enter: 들어오다	들어오고 있었거나 *to have been entering: 들어오고 있었다

4. WHEN as adverb clause: ㄹ 때 or 을 때

Korean Language: Grammar Pattern

※The underlined when-clause is an example sentence of adverb clause: I stop watching TV <u>when I eat.</u>

*The verb tenses to be used with WHEN are limited to past, past progressive, present and present progressive tense.   Even though the action is in present tense, the actual action is not yet conducted. Technically the verb is in the form of present tense but the actual action is something predictable in the future. In short, the present tense reflects a future action.

1-1) root verb stem ending in consonant + 을 때 for present tense

•when--chews: 씹을 때   *to chew: 씹다

*씹 ends in consonant ㅂ. Drop 다 and add 을 때.

1-2) root verb stem ending in vowel + ㄹ 때 for present tense

•When--writes: 쓸 때   *to write: 쓰다

*쓰 ends in vowel ㅡ. Drop 다 and add just ㄹ 때.

2) verb stem in past tense + 을 때

*Past tense ends in 썼다 or 었다 or 았다. Drop 다 from verb stem and add 을 때.

•when--liked: 좋아했을 때   *to have liked: 좋아했다

*했 ends in consonant ㅆ. Drop 다 from verb stem and add 을 때

3) verb stem in past progressive tense + 을 때

*Past progressive tense ends in 고 있었다. Drop 다 from verb stem and add 을 때.

•when--was/were playing: 놀고 있었을 때   *to have been playing: 놀고 있었다

4) verb stem in present progressive tense + 을 때

*Present progressive tense ends in 고 있다. Drop 다 from the verb stem and add 을 때.

•when--am/are/is laughing: 웃고 있을 때   *to be laughing: 웃고 있다

5) root verb stem ending in ㄷ: In the case of 듣다(to listen)/싣다(to load)/걷다(to walk)/묻다(to ask), ㄷ is dropped and ㄹ을 때 is added. For the other verbs ending in ㄷ, 다 is dropped from root verb stem and 을 때 is added. See the following Table 25 for the comparison of the verb stems ending in ㄷ.

Table 25   *Marks in Italic are incorrect.

root verb stem ending in ㄷ	conjunction WHEN in Korean: ㄹ을 때 or 을 때
when--listen *to listen: 듣다	들을 때 *듣을 때 *to have listened: 들었다
when--load *to load: 싣다	실을 때 *싣을 때 *to have loaded: 실었다
when--walk *to walk: 걷다	걸을 때 *걷을 때 *to have walked: 걸었다
when--ask *to ask: 묻다	물을 때 *묻을 때 *to have asked: 물었다
when--receive *to receive: 받다	받을 때 *to have received: 받았다
when--believe *to believe: 믿다	믿을 때 *to have believed: 믿었다

when--gain *to gain: 얻다	얻을 때 *to have gained: 얻었다
when--step *to step: 딛다	딛을 때 *to have stepped: 딛었다
when--collect *to collect: 걷다	걷을 때 *to have collected: 걷었다
when--close *to close: 닫다	닫을 때 *to have closed: 닫았다
when--bury *to bury: 묻다	묻을 때 *to have buried: 묻었다

6) static verbs ending in ㅂ: ㅂ is dropped and 울 때(present tense) and 웠을 때(past tense) is added.   See the following Table 26 for more information.

Table 26   *Marks in Italic* are incorrect.

root verb stem ending in ㅂ	conjunction WHEN in Korean: 울 때
when--is spicy *to be spicy: 맵다	매울 때 *맵을 때* *to have been spicy: 매웠다
when--is cold *to be cold: 춥다	추울 때 *춥을 때* *to have been cold: 추웠다
when--is hot *to be hot: 덥다	더울 때 *덥을 때* *to have been hot: 더웠다
when--is heavy *to be heavy: 무겁다	무거울 때 *무겁을 때* *to have been heavy: 무거웠다

Korean Language: Grammar Pattern

when--is light *to be light: 가볍다	가벼울 때 *가볍을 때 *to have been light: 가벼웠다
when--is difficult *to be difficult: 어렵다	어려울 때 *어렵을 때 *to have been difficult: 어려웠다
when--is easy *to be easy: 쉽다	쉬울 때 *쉽을 때 *to have been easy: 쉬웠다

7) root verb stem ending in ㄹ: Drop 다 and add just 때   See the following Table 27 for more.

Table 27   *Marks in Italic* are incorrect.

root verb stem ending in ㄹ	conjunction WHEN in Korean: 때
when--sell *to sell: 팔다	팔 때 *팔을 때 ※ Drop 다 and add just 때. *to have sold: 팔았다
when--blow *to blow: 불다	불 때 *불을 때 *to have blown: 불었다
when--push *to push: 밀다	밀 때 *밀을 때 *to have pushed: 밀었다
when--open *to open: 열다	열 때 *열을 때 *to have opened: 열었다
when--drive *to drive: 몰다	몰 때 *몰을 때 *to have driven: 몰았다
when--know	알 때 *알을 때

Korean Language: Grammar Pattern

*to know: 알다	*to have known: 알았다
when--play *to play: 놀다	놀 때　　*놀을 때 *to have played: 놀았다
when--decrease *to decrease: 줄다	줄 때　　*줄을 때 *to have decreased: 줄었다
when--stay *to stay: 머물다	머물 때　　*머물을 때 *to have stayed: 머물렀다
when--turn *to turn: 돌다	돌 때　　*돌을 때 *to have turned: 돌았다
when--pray *to pray/to beg: 빌다	빌 때　　*별을 때 *to have prayed/to have begged: 빌었다
when--make *to make: 만들다	만들 때　　*만들을 때 *to have made: 만들었다
when--drag *to drag: 끌다	끌 때　　*끌을 때 *to have dragged: 끌었다
when--freeze *to freeze: 얼다	얼 때　　*얼을 때 *to have frozen: 얼었다
when--doze off *to doze off: 졸다	졸 때　　*졸을 때 *to have dozed off: 졸았다
when--shake *to shake: 흔들다	흔들 때　　*흔들을 때 *to have shaken: 흔들었다
when--solve *to solve/to untie: 풀다	풀 때　　*풀을 때 *to have solved/to have untied: 풀었다

Korean Language: Grammar Pattern

when--live *to live: 살다	살 때 *살을 때 *to have lived: 살았다
when--earn *to earn: 벌다	벌 때 *벌을 때 *to have earned: 벌었다
when--bite *to bite: 물다	물 때 *물을 때 *to have bitten: 물었다
when--hang *to hang: 걸다	걸 때 *걸을 때 *to have hanged: 걸었다
when--roll *to roll: 말다	말 때 *말을 때 *to have rolled: 말았다
when--fly *to fly: 날다	날 때 *날을 때 *to have flown: 날았다
when--wash *to wash/to suck: 빨다	빨 때 *빨을 때 *to have washed/to have sucked: 빨았다
when--increase *to increase: 늘다	늘 때 *늘을 때 *to have increased: 늘었다
when--swell *to swell: 부풀다	부풀 때 *부풀을 때 *to have swollen: 부풀었다
when--incline *to incline: 기울다	기울 때 *기울을 때 *to have inclined: 기울었다
when--grind *to grind/to change: 갈다	갈 때 *갈을 때 *to have ground/to have changed: 갈았다

[여기에 입력]
Korean Language: Grammar Pattern

Examples:

•when--came: 왔을 때   *to have come: 왔다

•when--chooses: 고를 때   *to choose: 고르다

•when--is going: 가고 있을 때   *to be going: 가고 있다

•when--was looking: 보고 있었을 때   *to have been looking: 보고 있었다

•when--am teaching: 가르치고 있을 때   *to be teaching: 가르치고 있다

•when--did: 했을 때   *to have done: 했다

•when--raises: 올릴 때   *to raise: 올리다

•when--ran: 뛰었을 때/달렸을 때(달리었을 때)

*to have run: 뛰었다/달렸다(달리었다)

•when--was cooking: 요리하고 있었을 때   *to have been cooking: 요리하고 있었다

•when--am working: 일하고 있을 때   *to be working: 일하고 있다

•when--dances: 춤출 때   *to dance: 춤추다

•when--sang: 노래했을 때   *to have sung: 노래했다

•when--rides: 탈 때   *to ride: 타다

•when--dislikes: 싫어할 때   *to dislike: 싫어하다

•when--is breaking: 부수고 있을 때   *to be breaking: 부수고 있다

•when--was helping: 돕고 있었을 때   *to have been helping: 돕고 있었다

•when--helps: 도울 때   *to help: 돕다   *돕을 때* is incorrect.

•when--lie down: 누울 때   *to lie down: 눕다   *눕을 때* is incorrect.

※돕다 and 눕다 have irregular changes.   ㅂ is dropped and 울 때 is added.

•when--helped: 도왔을 때   *to have helped: 도왔다

•when--lied down: 누웠을 때   *to have lied down: 누웠다   *눕었다* is incorrect.

Korean Language: Grammar Pattern

※In the case of 돕다 and 눕다, ㅂ is dropped and 왔 or 웠 is added respectively.

•when--: 잊을 때   *to forget: 잊다

•when--: 잃을 때   *to lose: 잃다

•when--is hiking: 등산하고 있을 때   *to be hiking: 등산하고 있다

•when--was swimming: 수영하고 있었을 때

*to have been swimming: 수영하고 있었다

•when--cleans up: 청소할 때   *to clean up: 청소하다

•when--flies: 날 때   *to fly: 날다   *날을 때* is incorrect.

•when--drank: 마셨을 때(마시었을 때)   *to have drunk: 마셨다(마시었다)

•when--shoots: 쏠 때   *to shoot: 쏘다

•when--was turning: 돌고 있었을 때   *to have been turning: 돌고 있었다

•when--is asking: 묻고 있을 때   *to be asking: 묻고 있다

•when--walks: 걸을 때   *to walk: 걷다

Exercise 39. Rewrite the English conjunction 'WHEN' as adverb clause in Korean.

conjunction 'WHEN' as adverb clause	WHEN as adverb clause in Korean: 때 or ㄹ 때 or 을 때 or 울 때
when--played piano *to play piano: 피아노를 치다	피아노를 쳤을 때 *to have played piano: 피아노를 쳤다 *consonant ending + 을 때
when--touches *to touch: 만지다	만질 때 *vowel ending + ㄹ 때
when--likes	좋아할 때

Korean Language: Grammar Pattern

*to like: 좋아하다	
when--is fishing *to fish: 낚시하다	낚시하고 있을 때 *to be fishing: 낚시하고 있다
when--sends *to send: 보내다	보낼 때
when--is cold *to be cold: 춥다	추울 때 *춥을 때 *static verbs ending in ㅂ + 울 때
when--was receiving *to receive: 받다	받고 있었을 때 *to have been receiving: 받고 있었다
when--opens *to open: 열다	열 때 *열을 때 *verbs ending in ㄹ + 때
when--hits *to hit: 때리다/치다	때릴 때/칠 때
when--walks *to walk: 걷다	걸을 때 *걷을 때 *verbs ending in ㄷ + ㄹ을 때 for irregular change.
when--collects *to collect: 걷다	걷을 때 *걷을 때 *Regular change rule applies to this verb.
when--was using *to use: 쓰다(pure Korean)/사용하다(Sino Korean)	쓰고 있었을 때/사용하고 있었을 때 *to have been using: 쓰고 있었다/사용하고 있었다
when--is shopping *to shop: 쇼핑하다	쇼핑하고 있을 때 *to be shopping: 쇼핑하고 있다
when--was shouting	소리치고 있었을 때

Korean Language: Grammar Pattern

*to shout: 소리치다	*to have been shopping: 소리치고 있었다
when--waits *to wait: 기다리다	기다릴 때
when--taught *to teach: 가르치다	가르쳤을 때(가르치었을 때) *to have taught: 가르쳤다
when--is tasting *to taste: 맛보다	맛보고 있을 때 *to be tasting: 맛보고 있다
when--lives *to live: 살다	살 때 *살을 때
when--buys *to buy: 사다	살 때
when--was throwing *to throw: 던지다	던지고 있었을 때 *to have been throwing: 던지고 있었다
when--is wearing *to wear: 입다	입고 있을 때 *to be wearing: 입고 있다
when--gave *to give: 주다	줬을 때(주었을 때) *to have given: 주었다
when--paints *to paint: 칠하다	칠할 때
when--traveled *to travel: 여행하다	여행했을 때 *to have travelled: 여행했다
when--was sending *to send: 보내다	보내고 있었을 때 *to have been sending: 보내고 있었다

when--is counting *to count: 세다	세고 있을 때 *to be counting: 세고 있다
when--wrote *to write: 쓰다	썼을 때 *to have written: 썼다
when--was hot *to be hot: 덥다	더웠을 때 *덥었을 때 *to have been hot: 더웠다
when--is easy *to be easy: 쉽다	쉬울 때 *쉽을 때
when--sold *to sell: 팔다	팔았을 때 *to have sold: 팔았다
when--kicks *to kick: 차다	찰 때
when--blows *to blow: 불다	불 때 *불을 때
when--was dead *to be dead: 죽다	죽었을 때 *to have been dead: 죽었다
when--smelled *to smell: 냄새 맡다	냄새 맡았을 때 *to have smelled: 냄새 맡았다
when--helps *to help: 돕다	도울 때 *돕을 때 *Irregular change rule applies to this verb.

5. WHEN as noun clause: 언제--는지

Korean Language: Grammar Pattern

※The following underlined part is a sample sentence of 'WHEN' as a noun clause: I know <u>when you go</u>.

1-1) root verb stem ending in vowel or consonant + 언제--는지 for present tense

•when--boils: 언제 끓이는지   *to boil: 끓이다

*이 ends in vowel ㅣ. Drop 다 and add 는지.

•when—cuts: 언제 끊는지   *to cut: 끊다

*끊 ends in combined consonant ㄶ. Drop 다 and add 는지.

1-2) root verb stem ending in ㄹ for present tense: ㄹ is dropped and 는지 is added.

•when--hangs: 언제 거는지   *to hang: 걸다

*걸 ends in consonant ㄹ. Drop ㄹ and add just 는지

2) verb stem in past tense + 는지

*Past tense ends in ㅆ다 or 었다 or 았다. Drop 다 from verb stem and add 는지.

•when--kicked: 언제 찼는지   *to have kicked: 찼다

3) verb stem in future tense + 는지

*Future tense ends in 겠다 or ㄹ/을 것이다 or ㄹ/을 거다. Drop 다 from verb stem and add 는지.

•when--will leave: 언제 떠나겠는지/언제 떠날 것 *인지*/언제 떠날 *건지*

*to be going to leave: 떠나겠다/떠날 것이다/떠날 거다   In the case of 것이다 and 거다, drop 다 from the verb stem and add ㄴ지 instead of 는지. This is a kind of irregular change.

4) verb stem in past progressive tense + 는지

*Past progressive tense ends in 고 있었다. Drop 다 from verb stem and add 는지.

•when--was/were calling: 언제 부르고 있었는지

*to have been calling: 부르고 있었다

5) verb stem in present progressive tense + 는지

*Present progressive tense ends in 고 있다. Drop 다 from verb stem and add 는지.

•when--am/are/is crying: 언제 울고 있는지   *to be crying: 울고 있다

6) verb stem in future progressive tense + 는지

*Future progressive tense ends in 고 있겠다/고 있을 것이다/고 있을 거다. Drop 다 from verb stem and add 는지. in the case of 것이다 and 거다, add ㄴ지.

•when--will be making: 언제 말들고 있겠는지/언제 말들고 있을 것 *인지*/언제 만들고 있을 *건지*   *to be going to be making: 만들고 있겠다/만들고 있을 것이다/만들고 있을 거다

7) root verb stem of static verbs ending in ㅂ: ㅂ is dropped and 운지 is added.

•when--is cold: 언제 추운지   *to be cold: 춥다

*춥다 is a static verb ending in ㅂ. Drop ㅂ and add 운지

•when--is happy: 언제 즐거운지   *to be happy: 즐겁다

Examples:

•when--listened: 언제 들었는지   *to have listened: 들었다

[여기에 입력]
Korean Language: Grammar Pattern

•when--live: 언제 사는지   *살는지/   *to live: 살다

•when--will buy: 언제 사겠는지/언제 살 것인지/언제 살 건지/

*to be going to buy: 사겠다/살 것이다/살 거다

•when--was/were eating: 언제 먹고 있었는지   *to have been eating: 먹고 있었다

•when--am/are/is singing: 언제 노래하고 있는지   *to be singing: 노래하고 있다

•when--will be drawing: 그리고 있겠는지/그리고 있을 것인지/그리고 있을 건지/

*to be going to be drawing: 그리고 있겠다/그리고 있을 것이다/그리고 있을 거다

Exercise 40.   Rewrite the underlined WHEN as noun clause in Korean.

WHEN as noun clause such as He knows <u>when + verb in various tenses</u>	WHEN as noun clause in Korean: 언제--는지/언제--운지/언제--ㄴ지
when--<u>did</u> *to do: 하다	언제 했는지 *to have done: 했다
when--<u>makes</u> *to make: 만들다	언제 만드는지 *만들는지/ *Irregular change rule applies to the verbs ending in ㄹ.
when--<u>will be hot</u> *to be hot: 덥다	언제 덥겠는지/언제 더울 것인지/언제 더울 건지 *to be going to be hot: 덥겠다/더울 것이다/더울 거다
when--<u>was deleting</u> *to delete: 삭제하다(Sino Korean)	언제 삭제하고 있었는지 *to have been deleting: 삭제하고 있었다
when--<u>is fighting</u> *to fight: 싸우다	언제 싸우고 있는지 *to be fighting: 싸우고 있다

Korean Language: Grammar Pattern

when--<u>was cold</u> *to be cold: 춥다	언제 추웠는지 *춥었는지/ *to have been cold: 추웠다
when--<u>helps</u> *to help: 돕다	언제 돕는지
when--<u>will ask</u> *to ask: 묻다(pure Korean)	언제 묻겠는지/언제 물을 것인지/언제 물을 건지 *to be going to ask: 묻겠다/물을 것이다/물을 거다
when--<u>was dancing</u> *to dance: 춤추다	언제 춤추고 있었는지 *to have been dancing: 춤추고 있었다
when--<u>is changing</u> *to change: 바꾸다/갈다	언제 바꾸고 있는지/언제 갈고 있는지 *to be changing: 바꾸고 있다/갈고 있다
when--<u>hated</u> *to hate: 미워하다	언제 미워했는지 *to have hated: 미워했다
when--<u>is thirsty</u> *to be thirsty: 목마르다	언제 목마르는지
when--<u>will sit down</u> *to sit down: 앉다	언제 앉겠는지/언제 앉을 것인지/언제 앉을 건지 *to be going to sit down: 앉겠다/앉을 것이다/앉을 거다
when--<u>is happy</u> *to be happy: 즐겁다	언제 즐거운지 *즐겁은지/ *Static verbs ending in ㅂ + 운지

6. BEFORE + 기 전에

※before =earlier than the time that

*root verb stem + 기 전에   The change of verb ending of 'BEFORE' is in accordance with the ROOT VERB STEM.   Drop 다 from ROOT VERB STEM and add 기 전에.

Examples:

•before--came: 오기 전에   *왔기 전에   *to come: 오다

•before--eats: 먹기 전에   *to eat: 먹다

•before--will leave: 떠나기 전에   *떠나겠기 전에   *to leave: 떠나다

•before--choses: 고르기 전에/선택하기 전에   *골랐기 전에/선택했기 전에

*to choose: 고르다/선택하다

•before--goes: 가기 전에   *to go: 가다

•before--will look: 보기 전에   *보겠기 전에   *to look: 보다

•before--taught: 가르치기 전에   *가르쳤기 전에   *to teach: 가르치다

•before--works: 일하기 전에   *to work: 일하다

•before--will sing: 노래하기 전에   *노래하겠기 전에   *to sing: 노래하다

•before--ran: 달리기 전에/뛰기 전에   *달렸기 전에/뛰었기 전에

*to run: 달리다/뛰다

•before--does: 하기 전에   *to do: 하다

•before--will see: 보기 전에   *보겠기 전에   *to see: 보다

•before--disliked: 싫어하기 전에   *싫어했기 전에   *to dislike: 싫어하다

•before--loves: 사랑하기 전에   *to love: 사랑하다

Korean Language: Grammar Pattern

•before--will break: 부수기 전에/깨기 전에   *부수겠기 전에/깨겠기 전에

*to break: 부수다/깨다

•before--helped: 돕기 전에   *도왔기 전에   *to help: 돕다

•before--forgets: 잊기 전에   *to forget: 잊다

•before--will catch: 잡기 전에   *잡겠기 전에   *to catch: 잡다

•before--went hiking: 등산가기 전에   *등산갔기 전에   *to hike: 등산가다

•before--swims: 수영하기 전에   *to swim: 수영하다

•before--will clean up: 청소하기 전에   *청소하겠기 전에   *to clean up: 청소하다

•before--drove: 운전하기 전에   *운전했기 전에   *to drive: 운전하다

•before--dances: 춤추기 전에   *to dance: 춤추다

•before--will walk: 걷기 전에   *걷겠기 전에   *to walk: 걷다

※The change of verb ending of 'BEFORE(기 전에)' is in accordance with the ROOT VERB STEM.

Exercise 41. Rewrite the English conjunction 'BEFORE' in Korean.

conjunction 'BEFORE'	conjunction BEFORE in Korean: 기 전에
before--<u>played guitar</u> *to play: 기타치다	기타치기 전에 *기타쳤기 전에
before--<u>touches</u> *to touch: 만지다	만지기 전에
before--<u>will like</u> *to like: 좋아하다	좋아하기 전에 *좋아하겠기 전에

Korean Language: Grammar Pattern

before--<u>threw away</u> *to throw away: 버리다	버리기 전에 *버렸기 전에
before--<u>fished</u> *to fish: 낚시하다	낚시하기 전에 *낚시했기 전에
before--<u>is thirsty</u> *to be thirsty: 목마르다	목마르기 전에
before--<u>went home</u> *to go home: 집에 가다	집에 가기 전에 *집에 갔기 전에
before--<u>sends</u> *to send: 보내다	보내기 전에
before--<u>will receive</u> *to receive: 받다	받기 전에 *받겠기 전에
before--<u>changed</u> *to change: 바꾸다	바꾸기 전에 *바꿨기 전에
before--<u>will win</u> *to win: 이기다	이기기 전에 *이기겠기 전에
before--<u>hits</u> *to hit: 때리다/치다	때리기 전에/치기 전에
before--<u>will use</u> *to use: 쓰다(pure Korean)/사용하다(Sino Korean)	쓰기 전에/사용하기 전에 *쓰겠기 전에/사용하겠기 전에
before--<u>wrote</u> *to write: 쓰다	쓰기 전에 *썼기 전에
before--<u>shopped</u>	쇼핑하기 전에 *쇼핑했기 전에

Korean Language: Grammar Pattern

*to shop: 쇼핑하다	
before--<u>shouts</u> *to shout: 소리치다	소리치기 전에
before--<u>will wait</u> *to wait: 기다리다	기다리기 전에 *기다리겠기 전에
before--<u>pushed</u> *to push: 밀다	밀기 전에 *밀었기 전에
before--<u>pulls</u> *to pull: 당기다	당기기 전에
before--<u>are hungry</u> *to be hungry: 배고프다	배고프기 전에
before--<u>lived</u> *to live: 살다	살기 전에 *살았기 전에
before--<u>buys</u> *to buy: 사다	사기 전에
before--<u>exchanged</u> *to exchange: 바꾸다(pure Korean)/교환하다(Sino Korean)	바꾸기 전에/교환하기 전에 *바꿨기 전에/교환했기 전에
before--<u>will open</u> *to open: 열다	열기 전에 *열겠기 전에
before--<u>believed</u> *to believe: 믿다	믿기 전에 *믿었기 전에
before--<u>returns</u> *to return: 돌아가다	돌아가기 전에

before--<u>will decide</u> *to decked: 결정하다	결정하기 전에 *결정하겠기 전에
before--<u>listens</u> *to listen: 듣다	듣기 전에
before--<u>will breathe</u> *to breathe: 숨쉬다	숨쉬기 전에 *숨쉬겠기 전에
before--<u>reads</u> *to read: 읽다	읽기 전에
before--<u>are tired</u> *to be tired: 피곤하다	피곤하기 전에
before--<u>loses</u> *to lose: 잃다	잃기 전에
before--<u>will make</u> *to make: 만들다	만들기 전에 *만들겠기 전에
before--<u>is cold</u> *to be cold: 춥다	춥기 전에

7. AFTER + ㄴ 후에 or 은 후에

※after = subsequently to the time when

*root verb stem + ㄴ 후에 or 은 후에   The change of verb ending of 'AFTER' is in accordance with the ROOT VERB STEM.   Drop 다 from root verb stem and add ㄴ 후에 or 은 후에.

1) root verb stem ending in consonant + 은 후에

•after--chewed: 씹은 후에   *씹었은 후에   *to chew: 씹다

Korean Language: Grammar Pattern

*씹 ends in consonant ㅂ. Drop 다 and add 은 후에

2) root verb stem ending in vowel + ㄴ 후에

•after--drank: 마신 후에   *마셨은 후에   *to drink: 마시다

*시 ends in vowel ㅣ. Drop 다 and add ㄴ 후에.

3) root verb stem ending in ㄹ: Drop ㄹ and add ㄴ 후에.

•after--knew: 안 후에   *알았은 후에   *to know: 알다

*알 ends in ㄹ. Drop ㄹ 다 and add ㄴ 후에.

4) root verb stem ending in ㄷ: In the case of 듣다(to listen)/싣다(to load)/걷다(to walk)/묻다(to ask), ㄷ is dropped and ㄹ은 후에 is added. For the other verbs ending in ㄷ, regular change rule applies, in which ㄷ is dropped and 은 후에 is added. See the following Table 28 for the comparison of the verb stems ending in ㄷ.

Table 28   *Marks in Italic are incorrect.

conjunction 'AFTER'	Korean equivalent for the verbs ending in ㄷ: 은 후에 or ㄹ은 후에
after--listen(듣다)	들은 후에 *듣은 후에 ※The final ㄷ is dropped and ㄹ은 후에 is added.
after--load(싣다)	실은 후에 *싣은 후에
after--walk(걷다)	걸은 후에 *걷은 후에
after--ask(묻다)	물은 후에 *묻은 후에
after--receive(받다)	받은 후에

Korean Language: Grammar Pattern

after--believe(믿다)	믿은 후에
after--gain(얻다)	얻은 후에
after--step(딛다)	딛은 후에
after--collect(걷다)	걷은 후에
after--close(닫다)	닫은 후에
after--bury(묻다)	묻은 후에

5) root verb stem ending in ㅂ: 운 후에

*Irregular verb change rule applies to mostly static verbs.   In this case, ㅂ is dropped and 운 후에 is added.   Out of action verbs ending in ㅂ, very limited number of verbs like 깁다(to sew), 눕다(to lie down) and 돕다(to help) fall in this case.   See the following Table 29 for more information.

Table 29   *Marks in Italic are incorrect.

verb stem ending in ㅂ	conjunction AFTER ending in ㅂ in Korean: 운 후에
맵다 *to be spicy	매운 후에 *맵은 후에 after---is spicy
춥다 *to be cold	추운 후에 *춥은 후에 after—was cold
덥다 *to be hot	더운 후에 *덥은 후에 after---is hot
무겁다 *to be heavy	무거운 후에 *무겁은 후에 after---will be heavy
가렵다 *to be itchy	가려운 후에 *가렵은 후에 after---is itchy

Korean Language: Grammar Pattern

가엽다 *to be pathetic	가여운 후에 *가엽은 후에 after---is pathetic
눕다 *action verb *to lie down	누운 후에 *눕은 후에 after---will lie down
가소롭다 *to be ridiculous	가소로운 후에 *가소롭은 후에 after---was ridiculous
어렵다 *to be difficult	어려운 후에 *어렵은 후에 after---is difficult
쉽다 *to be easy	쉬운 후에 *쉽은 후에 after---will be easy
돕다 *action verb *to help	도운 후에 *돕은 후에 after---help
더럽다 *to be dirty	더러운 후에 *더럽은 후에 after---is dirty
우습다 *to be funny	우스운 후에 *우습은 후에 after---was funny
고맙다 *to be thankful	고마운 후에 *고맙은 후에 after---will be thankful
밉다 *to be hateful	미운 후에 *밉은 후에 after---is hateful
무섭다 *to be scary	무서운 후에 *무섭은 후에 after---was scary
귀엽다 *to be cute	귀여운 후에 *귀엽은 후에 after---is cut

[여기에 입력]
Korean Language: Grammar Pattern

즐겁다 *to be happy	즐거운 후에 *즐겁은 후에 after---will be happy
깁다 *action verb *to sew	기운 후에 *깁은 후에 after--sew

Examples:

•after--arrived: 도착한 후에   *도착했은 후에   *to arrive: 도착하다

•after--eat: 먹은 후에   *to eat: 먹다

•after--left: 떠난 후에   *떠났은 후에   *to leave: 떠나다

•after--will choose: 고른 후에/선택한 후에   *고르겠은 후에/선택했은 후에

*to choose: 고르다(pure Korean)/선택하다(Sino Korean)

•after--went: 간 후에   *갔은 후에   *to go: 가다

•after--looks: 본 후에   *to look: 보다

•after--will teach: 가르친 후에   *가르치겠은 후에   *to teach: 가르치다

•after--worked: 일한 후에   *일했은 후에   *to work: 일하다

•after--sings: 노래한 후에   *to sing: 노래하다

•after--will run: 달린 후에/뛴 후에   *달리겠은 후에   *to run: 달리다/뛰다

•after--did: 한 후에   *했은 후에   *to do: 하다

※ 'to do' is a typical '하다-verb'.

•after--sees: 본 후에   *to see: 보다

•after--pushed: 민 후에   *밀었은 후에   *to push: 밀다

•after--will break: 부순 후에/깬 후에   *부수겠은 후에/깼은 후에

*to break: 부수다/깨다

Korean Language: Grammar Pattern

•after--hated: 미워한 후에　*미워했은 후에　*to hate: 미워하다

•after--loves: 사랑한 후에　*to love: 사랑하다

•after--got married: 결혼한 후에　*결혼했은 후에　*to get married: 결혼하다

•after--lied down: 누운 후에　*누웠은 후에　*to lie down: 눕다

•after--forgot: 잊은 후에　*잊었은 후에　*to forget: 잊다

•after--catches: 잡은 후에　*to catch: 잡다

•after--swam: 수영한 후에　*수영했은 후에　*to swim: 수영하다

•after--cleans up: 청소한 후에　*to clean up: 청소하다

•after--will dance: 춤춘 후에　*춤추겠은 후에　*to dance: 춤추다

•after--open: 연 후에　*to open: 열다

Exercise 42. Rewrite the English conjunction 'AFTER' in Korean.

conjunction 'AFTER'	conjunction AFTER in Korean: ㄴ 후에 or 은 후에 or ㄹ은 후에
after--<u>played golf</u> *to play golf: 골프치다	골프 친 후에 *vowel ending + ㄴ 후에
after--<u>touches</u> *to touch: 만지다	만진 후에
after--<u>finished</u> *to finish: 끝내다	끝낸 후에
after--<u>will like</u> *to like: 좋아하다	좋아한 후에
after--<u>listened</u> *to listen: 듣다	들은 후에　*듣은 후에 *Irregular change rule applies to this verb.

Korean Language: Grammar Pattern

after--<u>fished</u> *to fish: 낚시하다	낚시한 후에
after--<u>sends</u> *to send: 보내다	보낸 후에
after--<u>will hang</u> *to hang: 걸다	건 후에　　*걸은 후에 *verbs ending in ㄹ + ㄴ 후에
after--<u>woke up</u> *to wake up: 일어나다	일어난 후에
after--<u>changed</u> *to change: 갈다/바꾸다	간 후에/바꾼 후에　　*갈은 후에
after--<u>hits</u> *to hit: 때리다/치다	때린 후에/친 후에
after--<u>will use</u> *to use: 쓰다(pure Korean)/사용하다(Sino Korean)	쓴 후에/사용한 후에
after--<u>walks</u> *to walk: 걷다	걸은 후에　　*걷은 후에
after--<u>collected</u> *to collect: 걷다	걷은 후에　　*걸은 후에
after--<u>shopped</u> *to shop: 쇼핑하다	쇼핑한 후에
after--<u>is cold</u> *to be cold: 춥다	추운 후에　　*춥은 후에 *static verbs ending in ㅂ + 운 후에
after--<u>shouts</u>	소리친 후에

Korean Language: Grammar Pattern

*to shout: 소리치다	
after--<u>will wait</u> *to wait: 기다리다(pure Korean)/대기하다(Sino Korean)	기다린 후에/대기한 후에
after--<u>flies</u> *to fly: 날다	난 후에　*날은 후에
after--<u>knew</u> *to know: 알다	안 후에　*알은 후에
after--<u>rolled</u> *to roll: 말다	만 후에　*말은 후에
after--<u>grinds</u> *to grind: 갈다	간 후에　*갈은 후에
after--<u>will push</u> *to push: 밀다	민 후에　*밀은 후에
after--<u>got drunk</u> *to get drunk: 취하다	취한 후에
after--<u>pulled</u> *to pull: 당기다	당긴 후에
after--<u>catches</u> *to catch: 잡다	잡은 후에 *consonant ending + 은 후에
after--<u>studies</u> *to study: 공부하다	공부한 후에
after--<u>closed</u> *to close: 닫다	닫은 후에

Korean Language: Grammar Pattern

after--<u>will live</u> *to live: 살다	산 후에 *살은 후에 *verbs ending in ㄹ + ㄴ 후에
after--<u>bought</u> *to buy: 사다	산 후에 *vowel ending + ㄴ 후에
after--<u>opens</u> *to open: 열다	연 후에 *열은 후에
after--<u>will tie</u> *to tie: 묶다	묶은 후에
after--<u>crashed</u> *to crash: 충돌하다	충돌한 후에
after--<u>broke</u> *to break: 깨다/부수다	깬 후에/부순 후에
after--<u>happens</u> *to happen: 일어나다(pure Korean)/발생하다(Sino Korean)	일어난 후에/발생한 후에
after--<u>shoots</u> *to shoot: 쏘다(pure Korean)/발사하다(Sino Korean)	쏜 후에/발사한 후에
after--<u>will travel</u> *to travel: 여행하다	여행한 후에
after--<u>bit</u> *to bite: 물다	문 후에 *물은 후에
after--<u>hunts</u>	사냥한 후에

Korean Language: Grammar Pattern

*to hunt: 사냥하다	
after--<u>will read</u> *to read: 읽다(pure Korean)/독서하다(Sino Korean)	읽은 후에/독서한 후에
after--<u>lost</u> *to lose: 잃다(pure Korean)/분실하다(Sino Korean)	잃은 후에/분실한 후에

8. AS SOON AS + 자마자

※as soon as = immediately after the time that

*root verb stem + 자마자   The change of verb ending of 'AS SOON AS' is in accordance with the ROOT VERB STEM.   Drop 다 from ROOT VERB STEM ending in consonant or vowel and add 자마자

•as soon as-- listen: 듣자마자   *to listen: 듣다

•as soon as--saw: 보자마자   *보았자 마자 is incorrect.   *to see: 보다

Examples:

•as soon as--arrived: 도착하자마자   *도착했자마자   *to arrive: 도착하다

•as soon as--eats: 먹자마자   *to eat: 먹다

•as soon as--will catch: 잡자마자   *잡겠자마자   *to catch: 잡다

•as soon as--came: 오자마자   *왔자마자   *to come: 오다

•as soon as--leaves: 떠나자마자   *to leave: 떠나다

•as soon as--will choose: 고르자마자/선택하자마자
*고르겠자마자/선택하겠자마자

[여기에 입력]
Korean Language: Grammar Pattern

*to choose: 고르다(pure Korean)/선택하다(Sino Korean)

•as soon as--went: 가자마자   *갔자마자   *to go: 가다

•as soon as--looks: 보자마자   *to look: 보다

•as soon as--will teach: 가르치자마자   *가르치겠자마자   *to teach: 가르치다

•as soon as--sang: 노래하자마자   *노래했자마자   *to sing: 노래하다

•as soon as--runs: 달리자마자/뛰자마자   *to run: 달리다/뛰다

•as soon as--will do: 하자마자   *하겠자마자   *to do: 하다

•as soon as--found: 발견하자마자/찾자마자   *발견했자마자/찾았자마자

*to find: 찾다(pure Korean)/발견하다(Sino Korean)

•as soon as--breaks: 깨자마자/부수자마자   *to break: 깨다/부수다

•as soon as--will help: 돕자마자   *돕겠자마자   *to help: 돕다

•as soon as--caught: 잡자마자   *잡았자마자   *to catch: 잡다

•as soon as--will swim: 수영하자마자   *수영하겠자마자   *to swim: 수영하다

•as soon as--cleaned up: 청소하자마자   *청소했자마자   *to clean up: 청소하다

•as soon as--dances: 춤추자마자   *to dance: 춤추다

•as soon as--will walk: 걷자마자   *걸었자마자   *to walk: 걷다

Exercise 43. Rewrite the English conjunction 'AS SOON AS' in Korean.

conjunction 'AS SOON AS'	conjunction AS SOON AS in Korean: 자마자
as soon as--<u>worked</u> *to work: 일하다	일하자마자 *일했자마자
as soon as--<u>gets up</u> *to get up: 일어나다	일어나자마자

Korean Language: Grammar Pattern

as soon as--<u>works out</u> *to work out: 운동하다	운동하자마자
as soon as--<u>fixed</u> *to fix: 고치다(pure Korean)/수리하다(Sino Korean)	고치자마자/수리하자마자 *고쳤다마자/수리했자마자
as soon as--<u>collects</u> *to collect: 걷다/모으다	걷자마자
as soon as--<u>will write</u> *to write: 쓰다	쓰자마자 *쓰겠자마자
as soon as--<u>changes</u> *to change: 갈다/바꾸다	갈자마자/바꾸자마자
as soon as--<u>comes out</u> *to come out: 나오다	나오자마자
as soon as--<u>will ride</u> *to ride: 타다	타자마자 *타겠자마자
as soon as--<u>cooked</u> *to cook: 요리하다	요리하자마자 *요리했자마자
as soon as--<u>knows</u> *to know: 알다	알자마자
as soon as--<u>will save</u> *to save: 저장하다	저장하자마자 *저장하겠자마자
as soon as--<u>saw</u> *to see: 보다	보자마자 *봤자마자(보았자마자)
as soon as--<u>closes</u>	닫자마자

*to close: 닫다	
as soon as--<u>will push</u> *to push: 밀다	밀자마자　　*밀겠자마자
as soon as--<u>believed</u> *to believe: 믿다	믿자마자　　*믿었자마자
as soon as--<u>lives</u> *to live: 살다	살자마자
as soon as--<u>will buy</u> *to buy: 사다	사자마자　　*사겠자마자

9. UNTIL + 때까지 or ㄹ 때까지 or (ㄹ)을 때까지 or 울 때까지

※until = up to the time that

*root verb stem + 때까지 or ㄹ 때까지 or (ㄹ)을 때까지 or 울 때까지　　The change of verb ending of 'UNTIL' is in accordance with the ROOT VERB STEM. Drop 다 from ROOT VERB STEM and add 때까지/ㄹ 때까지/을 때까지

1) root verb stem ending in consonant + 을 때까지

•until--forget: 잊을 때까지　　*to forget: 잊다

*잊 ends in consonant ㅈ. Drop 다 and add 을 때까지

2) root verb stem ending in vowel + ㄹ 때까지

•until--left: 떠날 때까지　　*떠났을 때까지 is incorrect.　　*to leave: 떠나다

*나 ends in vowel ㅏ. Drop 다 and add ㄹ 때까지

3) root verb stem ending in ㄹ + 때까지

Korean Language: Grammar Pattern

•until--lived: 살 때까지   *살았을 때까지 is incorrect.   *to live: 살다

*살 ends in ㄹ.   Drop 다 and add just 때까지.

4) root verb stem ending in ㅂ: Irregular change rule applies to 깁다(to sew)/눕다(to lie down) and 돕다(to help) and other static verbs(to be + adjective). In the case of irregular change, ㅂ is dropped and 울 때까지 is added.   For the other verbs ending in ㅂ, regular change rule applies.   See the following Table 30 for more details.

Table 30   *Marks in Italic are incorrect.

verb stem ending in ㅂ	conjunction UNTIL in Korean: 울 때까지
맵다 *to be spicy	매울 때까지 *맵을 때까지 until---is spicy
춥다 *to be cold	추울 때까지 *춥을 때까지 until--was cold
덥다 *to be hot	더울 때까지 *덥을 때까지 until---is hot
무겁다 *to be heavy	무거울 때까지 무겁을 때까지 until---will be heavy
가렵다 *to be itchy	가려울 때까지 *가렵을 때까지 until---is itchy
깁다 *action verb *to sew	기울 때까지 *깁을 때까지 until--sew
가엽다 to be pathetic	가여울 때까지 *가엽을 때까지 until---is pathetic
눕다 *action verb	누울 때까지 *눕을 때까지

Korean Language: Grammar Pattern

*to lie down	until---will lie down
가소롭다 *to be ridiculous	가소로울 때까지 *가소롭을 때까지 until---was ridiculous
어렵다 *to be difficult	어려울 때까지 *어렵을 때까지 until---is difficult
쉽다 *to be easy	쉬울 때까지 *쉽을 때까지 until---will be easy
돕다 *action verb *to help	도울 때가지 *돕을 때까지 until---help
더럽다 *to be dirty	더러울 때까지 *더럽을 때까지 until---is dirty
우습다 *to be funny	우스울 때까지 *우습을 때까지 until---was funny
고맙다 *to be grateful	고마울 때까지 *고맙을 때까지 until---will be grateful
밉다 *to be hateful	미울 때까지 *밉을 때까지 until---is hateful
무섭다 *to be scary	무서울 때까지 *무섭을 때까지 until---was scary
귀엽다 *to be cute	귀여울 때까지 *귀엽을 때까지 until---is cut
즐겁다 *to be happy	즐거울 때까지 *즐겁을 때까지 until---will be happy

5) root verb stem ending in ㄷ: In the case of 싣다(to load)/듣다(to listen)/걷다(to walk)/묻다(to ask), ㄷ is dropped and ㄹ을 때까지 is added. For the rest of the verbs ending in ㄷ, the regular rule applies. See the following Table 31 for the comparison of the verb stems ending in ㄷ.

Table 31   *Marks in Italic* are incorrect.

conjunction 'UNTIL' ending in ㄷ	conjunction UNTIL in Korean: ㄹ을 때까지 or 을 때까지
듣다 *to listen	들을 때까지 *들을 때까지 until--listen
싣다 *to load	실을 때까지 *싣을 때까지 until--load
걷다 *to walk	걸을 때까지 *걷을 때까지 until--walk
묻다 *to ask	물을 때까지 *묻을 때까지 until--ask
받다 *to receive	받을 때까지 until--receive
믿다 *to believe	믿을 때까지 until--believe
얻다 *to gain	얻을 때까지 until--gain
딛다 *to step	딛을 때까지 until--step
걷다/모으다 *to collect	걷을 때까지/모을 때까지 until--collect

Korean Language: Grammar Pattern

닫다 *to close	닫을 때까지 until--close
묻다 *to bury	묻을 때까지 until--bury

Examples:

•until--caught: 잡을 때까지   *잡았을 때까지   *to catch: 잡다

•until--go: 갈 때까지   *to go: 가다

•until--will come: 올 때까지   *오겠을 때까지   *to come: 오다

•until--arrived: 도착할 때까지   *도착했을 때까지   *to arrive: 도착하다

• until--eat: 먹을 때까지   *to eat: 먹다

• until--will choose: 고를 때까지/선택할 때까지   *고르겠을 때까지/선택하겠을 때까지   *to choose: 고르다/선택하다

• until--left: 떠날 때까지   *떠났을 때까지   *to leave: 떠나다

• until--looks: 볼 때까지   *to look: 보다

• until--will teach: 가르칠 때까지   *가르치겠을 때까지   *to teach: 가르치다

• until--worked: 일할 때까지   *일했을 때까지   *to work: 일하다

• until--sings: 노래할 때까지   *to sing: 노래하다

• until--will run: 달릴 때까지/뛸 때까지   *달리겠을 때까지/뛰겠을 때까지

*to run: 달리다/뛰다

• until--did: 할 때까지   *했을 때까지   *to do: 하다

• until--burns: 태울 때까지   *to burn: 태우다

• until--will break: 부술 때까지/깰 때까지   *부수겠을 때까지/깨겠을 때까지

*to break: 부수다/깨다

[여기에 입력]
Korean Language: Grammar Pattern

•after--disliked: 싫어할 때까지   *싫어했을 때까지*   *to dislike: 싫어하다

• until--loves: 사랑할 때까지   *to love: 사랑하다

• until--will help: 도울 때까지   *돕겠을 때까지*   *to help: 돕다

• until--forgot: 잊을 때까지   *잊었을 때까지*   *to forget: 잊다

• until--catches: 잡을 때까지   *to catch: 잡다

• until--swam: 수영할 때까지   *수영했을 때까지*   *to swim: 수영하다

• until--cleans up: 청소할 때까지   *to clean up: 청소하다

• until--will go: 갈 때까지   *가겠을 때까지*   *to go: 가다

• until--agreed: 동의할 때까지   *동의했을 때까지*   *to agree: 동의하다

• until--drives: 운전할 때까지   *to drive: 운전하다

• until--will dance: 춤출 때까지   *춤추겠을 때까지*   *to dance: 춤추다

Exercise 44. Rewrite the English conjunction 'UNTIL' in Korean.

conjunction 'UNTIL'	conjunction UNTIL in Korean: 때까지 or ㄹ 때까지 or (ㄹ)을 때까지 or 울 때까지
until--<u>played golf</u> *to play golf: 골프 치다	골프 칠 때까지 *vowel ending + ㄹ 때까지
until--<u>touches</u> *to touch: 만지다	만질 때까지
until--<u>will like</u> *to like: 좋아하다	좋아할 때까지
until--<u>fished</u> *to fish: 낚시하다	낚시할 때까지

Korean Language: Grammar Pattern

until--<u>sends</u> *to send: 보내다	보낼 때까지
until--<u>will hang</u> *to hang: 걸다	걸 때까지 *걸을 때까지 *verbs ending in ㄹ + 때까지
until--<u>changed</u> *to change: 바꾸다/갈다	바꿀 때까지/갈 때까지
until--<u>hits</u> *to hit: 때리다/치다	때릴 때까지/칠 때까지
until--<u>will use</u> *to use: 쓰다/사용하다	쓸 때까지/사용할 때까지
until--<u>shopped</u> *to shop: 쇼핑하다	쇼핑할 때까지
until--<u>shouts</u> *to shout: 소리치다	소리칠 때까지
until--<u>will wait</u> *to wait: 기다리다	기다릴 때까지
until--<u>pushed</u> *to push: 밀다	밀 때까지 *밀을 때까지
until--<u>drags</u> *to drag: 끌다	끌 때까지
until--<u>will shoot</u> *to shoot: 쏘다	쏠 때까지
until--<u>folds</u> *to fold: 접다	접을 때까지 *consonant ending + 을 때까지

Korean Language: Grammar Pattern

until--<u>is hot</u> *to hot: 덥다	더울 때까지 *_덥을 때까지_ *static verbs ending in ㅂ + 울 때까지
until--<u>blocked</u> *to block: 막다	막을 때까지
until--<u>will attack</u> *to attack: 공격하다	공격할 때까지
until--<u>defended</u> *to defend: 방어하다	방어할 때까지
until--<u>grinds</u> *to grind: 갈다	갈 때까지 *_갈을 때까지_
until--<u>will go</u> *to go: 가다	갈 때까지
until--<u>was satisfied</u> *to be satisfied: 만족하다	만족할 때까지
until--<u>will win</u> *to win: 이기다	이길 때까지
until--<u>ended</u> *to end: 끝나다	끝날 때까지
until--<u>started</u> *to start: 시작하다	시작할 때까지
until--<u>is seen</u> *to be seen: 보이다	보일 때까지
until--<u>can eat</u> *to eat: 먹다	먹을 수 있을 때까지 *to be able to eat: 먹을 수 있다

until--<u>must block</u>	막아야할 때까지
*to block: 막다	*to have to block: 막아야 하다

10. WHILE + 는 동안

※while = during the time that

*The tenses which are combined with 'WHILE' are limited to present tense and present progressive tense only.   Drop 다 from verb stem and add 는 동안. 동안 means 'the duration of time'.

1) root verb stem ending in consonant or vowel + 는 동안

•while--sleep: 자는 동안   *to sleep: 자다

*자 ends in vowel ㅏ. Drop 다 and add 는 동안

•while--helped: 돕는 동안   *도왔는 동안   *to help: 돕다

*돕 ends in consonant ㅂ. Drop 다 and add 는 동안.

2) root verb stem ending in ㄹ: Drop ㄹ and add 는 동안

•while--push: 미는 동안   *to push: 밀다

*밀 ends in consonant ㄹ. Drop ㄹ and add 는 동안.

3) root verb stem ending in ㅂ: Irregular change rule applies to STATIC VERBS ONLY. ㅂ is dropped and 운 동안 is added.

•while--was cold: 추운 동안   *추웠는 동안   *to be cold: 춥다

•while--is happy: 즐거운 동안   *즐겁는 동안   *to be happy: 즐겁다

[여기에 입력]
Korean Language: Grammar Pattern

4) verb stem in present progressive tense + 는 동안

*Present progressive tense ends in 고 있다. Drop 다 from the verb stem and add 는 동안.

•while--is looking: 보고 있는 동안   *to be looking: 보고 있다

•while--was/were eating: 먹고 있는 동안   *먹고 있었는 동안

*to be eating: 먹고 있다

•while--will be travelling: 여행하고 있는 동안 *여행하고 있겠는 동안

*to be travelling: 여행하고 있다

※The verb change of any progressive action regarding 'WHILE' should be in accordance with the present progressive tense NOT past or future progressive tense.

Examples:

•while--eat: 먹는 동안   *to eat: 먹다

•while--is running: 달리고 있는 동안   *to be running: 달리고 있다

•while--watches: 지켜보는 동안   *to watch: 지켜보다

•while--opens→여는 동안 *열는 동안 is incorrect.   *to open: 열다

※Drop ㄹ and add 는 동안.

•while--is coming: 오고 있는 동안   *to be coming: 오고 있다

•while--is living: 살고 있는 동안   *to be living: 살고 있다

•while--live: 사는 동안   *to live: 살다

•while--buy: 사는 동안   *to buy: 사다

•while--is buying: 사고 있는 동안   *to be buying: 사고 있다

•while--scratch: 긁는 동안   *to scratch: 긁다

Korean Language: Grammar Pattern

•while--am eating: 먹고 있는 동안   *to be eating: 먹고 있다

•while--are biting: 물고 있는 동안   *to be biting: 물고 있다

•while--bite: 무는 동안   *to bite: 물다

•while--prepare: 준비하는 동안   *to prepare: 준비하다

•while--was choosing: 선택하고 있는 동안/고르고 있는 동안   *선택하고 있었는 동안/고르고 있었는 동안   *to be choosing: 선택하고 있다/고르고 있다

•while--teaches: 가르치는 동안   *to teach: 가르치다

•while--is singing: 노래하고 있는 동안/노래 부르고 있는 동안

*to be singing: 노래하고 있다/노래 부르고 있다

•while--is breaking: 부수고 있는 동안/깨고 있는 동안

*to be breaking: 부수고 있다/깨고 있다

•while--swims: 수영하는 동안   *to swim: 수영하다

•while—will be cleaning up: 청소하고 있는 동안   *청소하고 있겠는 동안

*to be cleaning up: 청소하고 있다

•while--dance: 춤추는 동안   *to dance: 춤추다

•while--am walking: 걷고 있는 동안   *to be walking: 걷고 있다

•while--draw: 그리는 동안   *to draw: 그리다

•while --will be flowing: 흐르고 있는 동안   *흐르고 있겠는 동안

*to be flowing: 흐르고 있다

•while--live: 사는 동안   *to live: 살다

•while--buy: 사는 동안   *to buy: 사다

Exercise 45. Rewrite the English conjunction 'WHILE' in Korean.

conjunction 'WHILE'=during	conjunction WHILE in Korean:

Korean Language: Grammar Pattern

	는 동안 or ㄴ 동안 or 운 동안
while--<u>played golf</u> *to play golf: 골프치다	골프치는 동안 *vowel ending + 는 동안
while--<u>is receiving</u> *to receive: 받다	받는 동안 *consonant ending + 는 동안
while--<u>touches</u> *to touch: 만지다	만지는 동안
while--<u>is selling</u> *to sell: 팔다	파는 동안 *팔는 동안 *verbs ending in ㄹ. ㄹ is dropped and 는 동안 is added.
while--<u>likes</u> *to like: 좋아하다	좋아하는 동안
while--<u>is studying</u> *study: 공부하다	공부하는 동안
while--<u>fishes</u> *to fish: 낚시하다	낚시하는 동안
while--<u>asks</u> *to ask: 묻다(pure Korean)/질문하다(Sino Korean)	묻는 동안/질문하는 동안
while--<u>cries</u> *to cry: 울다	우는 동안 *울는 동안
while--<u>is sending</u> *to send: 보내다	보내는 동안
while--<u>hangs</u>	거는 동안 *걸는 동안

Korean Language: Grammar Pattern

*to hang: 걸다	
while--is buying *to buy: 사다	사는 동안
while--<u>is living</u> *to live: 살다	사는 동안 *살는 동안
while--<u>changes</u> *to change: 바꾸다/갈다	바꾸는 동안/가는 동안 *갈는 동안
while--<u>listens</u> *to listen: 듣다	듣는 동안
while--<u>hits</u> *to hit: 때리다/치다	때리는 동안/치는 동안
while--is warm *to be warm: 따뜻하다	따뜻한 동안 *따뜻하는 동안 *static verb ending in 하다 + ㄴ 동안
while--<u>is thirsty</u> *to be thirsty: 목마르다	목마른 동안 *목마르는 동안 *목마르다 is a static verb ending in 하다.
while--<u>is lonely</u> *to be lonely: 쓸쓸하다	쓸쓸한 동안 *쓸쓸하는 동안 *쓸쓸하다 is a static verb ending in 하다. Add just ㄴ 동안.
while--<u>is sunny</u> *to be sunny: 화창하다	화창한 동안 *화창하는 동안 *화창하다 is a static verb ending in 하다.
while--<u>is believing</u> *to believe: 믿다	믿는 동안
while--<u>will use</u>	쓰는 동안/사용하는 동안

Korean Language: Grammar Pattern

*to use: 쓰다(pure Korean)/사용하다(Sino Korean)	
while--<u>is hot</u> *to be hot: 덥다	더운 동안 *덥는 동안 *static verbs ending in ㅂ ㅂ is dropped and 운 동안 is added.
while--<u>am travelling</u> *to travel: 여행하다	여행하는 동안
while--<u>shops</u> *to shop: 쇼핑하다	쇼핑하는 동안
while--<u>walks</u> *to walk: 걷다	걷는 동안
while--<u>is reading</u> *to read: 읽다(pure Korean)독서하다(Sino Korean)	읽는 동안/독서하는 동안
while--<u>shouts</u> *to shout: 소리치다	소리치는 동안
while--<u>is tearing</u> *to tear: 찢다	찢는 동안
while--<u>am waiting</u> *to wait: 기다리다	기다리는 동안
while--<u>laughs</u> *to laugh: 웃다	웃는 동안
while--<u>am working out</u> *to work out: 운동하다	운동하는 동안
while--<u>pushes</u>	미는 동안 *밀는 동안

Korean Language: Grammar Pattern

*to push: 밀다	
while--<u>tastes</u> *to taste: 맛보다	맛보는 동안
while--<u>drags</u> *to drag: 끌다	끄는 동안　　*끌는 동안
while--<u>is fixing</u> *to fix: 고치다(pure Korean)/수리하다(Sino Korean)	고치는 동안/수리하는 동안
while--<u>shoots</u> *to shoot: 쏘다	쏘는 동안
while--<u>am cooking</u> *to cook: 요리하다	요리하는 동안
while--<u>makes</u> *to make: 만들다	만드는 동안　　*만들는 동안

11. BECAUSE + 기 때문에 or (으)니까 or 우니까

※기 때문에 is formal expression and 으니까 or 우니까 is informal expression.

※For PRESENT TENSE, 기 때문에 or 으니까 or 니까 is combined with ROOT VERB STEM ONLY.

1) root verb stem ending in consonant or vowel + 기 때문에 for present tense

*Drop 다 from root verb stem and add 기 때문에.

•because--forget: 잊기 때문에　　*to forget: 잊다

*잊 ends in consonant ㅈ. Drop 다 and add 기 때문에

[여기에 입력]
Korean Language: Grammar Pattern

•because--do: 하기 때문에   *to do: 하다

*하 ends in vowel ㅏ. Drop 다 and add 기 때문에

2-1) root verb stem ending in consonant + 으니까 for present tense

•because--take off: 벗으니까   *to take off: 벗다

*벗 ends in consonant ㅅ. Drop 다 from root verb stem and add 으니까.

•because--sit down: 앉으니까   *to sit down: 앉다

*앉 ends in consonant ㄵ. Drop 다 from root verb stem and add 으니까.

2-2) root verb stem ending in vowel + 니까 for present tense.

•because--spray: 뿌리니까   *to spray: 뿌리다

*리 ends in vowel ㅣ. Drop 다 from root verb stem and add 니까.

•because--is cheap: 싸니까   *to be cheap: 싸다

*싸 ends in vowel ㅏ. Drop 다 from root verb stem and add 니까.

3) verb stem in past tense + 기 때문에/으니까

*Past tense ends in ㅆ다/었다/았다. Drop 다 from the verb stem and add 기 때문에/으니까.

•because--starved: 굶었기 때문에/굶었으니까   *to have starved: 굶었다

*Drop 다 from verb stem in past tense and add 기 때문에/(으)니까

•because--flew: 날았기 때문에/날았으니까   *to fly: 날다

*Drop 다 from verb stem in past tense and add 기 때문에/(으)니까

3) verb stem in future tense + 기 때문에/(으)니까

[여기에 입력]
Korean Language: Grammar Pattern

*Future tense ends in 겠다/ㄹ(을) 것이다/ㄹ(을) 거다. Drop 다 from the verb stem and add (으)니까   In the case of future tense, 기 때문에 is not used with 겠다. It is because 겠기 때문에 sounds very awkward. However, 겠으니까 is perfect to use.

•because--will win: 이길 것이기 때문에/이길 거기 때문에 or 이기겠*으니까*/이길 것이*니까*/이길 거*니까*   *이기겠기 때문에* is grammatically perfect but sounds awkward.

*to be going to win: 이기겠다/이길 것이다/이길 거다

※consonant ending + 으니까/vowel ending + 니까

•because--will turn off: 끌 것이기 때문에/끌 거기 때문에 or 끄겠으니까/끌 것이니까/끌 거니까   *to be going to turn off: 끄겠다/끌 것이다/끌 거다

4) verb stem in past progressive tense + 기 때문에/으니까

*Past progressive tense ends in 고 있었다. Drop 다 from verb stem and add 기 때문에/으니까

•because--was waiting: 기다리고 있었기 때문에/기다리고 있었으니까

*to have been waiting: 기다리고 있었다

•because--was drinking: 마시고 있었기 때문에/마시고 있었으니까

5) verb stem in present progressive tense + 기 때문에/으니까

*Present progressive tense ends in 고 있다. Drop 다 from verb stem and add 기 때문에/으니까

•because--is helping: 돕고 있기 때문에/돕고 있으니까   *to be helping: 돕고 있다

•because--was sleeping: 자고 있기 때문에/자고 있으니까

*to be sleeping: 자고 있다

6) verb stem in future progressive tense + 기 때문에/으니까

Korean Language: Grammar Pattern

*Future progressive tense ends in 고 있겠다/고 있을 것이다/고 있을 거다   Drop 다 from verb stem and add 기 때문에/으니까. However, 고 있겠기 때문에 is not perfect in writing and speaking.

•because--will be showing: 보여주고 있을 것이기 때문에/보여주고 있을 거기 때문에 or 보여주고 있겠으니까/보여주고 있을 것이니까/보여주고 있을 거니까 *보여주고 있겠기 때문에 sounds awkward.

*to be going to be showing: 보여주고 있겠다/보여주고 있을 것이다/보여주고 있을 거다

•because--will be working out: 운동하고 있을 것이기 때문에/운동하고 있을 거기 때문에 or 운동하고 있겠으니까/운동하고 있을 것이니까/운동하고 있을 거니까

*to be going to be working out: 운동하고 있겠다/운동하고 있을 것이다/운동하고 있을 거다

7) verb stem ending in ㄹ: Drop ㄹ and add 니까. See the following Table 32 for the comparison of the verb stems ending in ㄹ.

Table 32   *Marks in Italic are incorrect.

conjunction 'BECAUSE'	Korean equivalent for informal expression in present tense: 니까	conjunction 'BECAUSE''	Korean equivalent for informal expression in present tense: 니까
because--sells *to sell: 팔다	파니까 *팔으니까	because--drags *to drag: 끌다	끄니까 *끌으니까
because--cries *to cry: 울다	우니까 *울으니까	because--grinds *to grind/change: 갈다	가니까 *갈으니까
because--blows *to blow: 불다	부니까 *불으니까	because--raises *to raise: 들다	드니까 *들으니까

Korean Language: Grammar Pattern

because--pushes *to push: 밀다	미니까 *밀으니까	because--is long *to be long: 길다	기니까 *팔으니까
because--opens *to open: 열다	여니까 *팔으니까	because--freezes *to freeze: 얼다	어니까 *얼으니까
because--drives *to drive: 몰다	모니까 * '몰으니까	because--dozes off *to doze off: 졸다	조니까 *졸으니까
because--is far *to be far: 멀다	머니까 *멀으니까	because--shakes *to shake: 흔들다	흔드니까 *흔들으니까
because--knows *to know: 알다	아니까 *알으니까	because--is tired *to be tired: 힘들다	힘드니까 *힘들으니까
because--plays *to play: 놀다	노니까 *놀으니까	because--solves *to solve: 풀다	푸니까 *풀으니까
because--decreases *to decrease: 줄다	주니까 *줄으니까	because--lives *to live: 살다	사니까 *살으니까
because--stays *to stay: 머물다	머무니까 *머물으니까	because--earns *to earn: 벌다	버니까 *벌으니까
because--turns *to turn: 돌다	도니까 *돌으니까	because--bites *to bite: 물다	무니까 *물으니까
because--begs *to beg: 빌다	비니까 *빌으니까	because--hangs *to hang/call: 걸다	거니까 *걸으니까
because--makes *to make: 만들다	만드니까 *만들으니까	because--rolls *to roll: 말다	마니까 *말으니까

because--flies	나니까	because--swells	부푸니까
*to fly: 날다	*날으니까	*to swell: 부풀다	*부풀으니까
because--sucks *to wash/suck: 빨다	빠니까 *빨으니까	because--inclines *to incline: 기울다	기우니까 *기울으니까
because--increases *to increase: 늘다	느니까 *늘으니까	because--breaks *to break: 헐다	허니까 *헐으니까

8) verb stem ending in ㄷ: Irregular change rule applies to 듣다(to listen)/싣다(to load)/걷다(to walk)/묻다(to ask). In this case, ㄷ is dropped and ㄹ으니까 is added. For the other verbs ending in ㄷ, regular verb change rule applies. See the following Table 33 for the comparison of the verb stems ending in ㄷ.

Table 33   *Marks in Italic are incorrect.

conjunction 'BECAUSE'	Korean equivalent for informal expression in present tense: ㄹ으니까 or 으니까
because--listen *to listen: 듣다	들으니까 *듣으니까 ※ㄷ is dropped and ㄹ으니까 is added.
because--load *to load: 싣다	실으니까 *싣으니까
because--walk *to walk: 걷다	걸으니까 *걷으니까
because--ask *to ask: 묻다	물으니까 *묻으니까
because--receive	받으니까

Korean Language: Grammar Pattern

*to receive: 받다	
because--believe *to believe: 믿다	믿으니까
because--gain *to gain: 얻다	얻으니까
because--step *to step: 딛다	딛으니까
because--collect/gather *to collect: 걷다	걷으니까
because--close *to close: 닫다	닫으니까
because--bury *to bury: 묻다	묻으니까

9) verb stem ending in ㅂ: Irregular change rule applies to 눕다(to lie down)/돕다(to help) and the other STATIC VERBS(to be + adjective).   In this case, ㅂ is dropped and 우니까 is added.   For the other verbs ending in ㅂ, regular change rule applies.   See the following Table 34 for the irregular verb endings.

Table 34   *Marks in Italic* are incorrect.

conjunction 'BECAUSE'	verbs ending in ㅂ with irregular change: 우니까
because--lie down *action verb *to lie down: 눕다	누우니까 *눕으니까* ※Drop 다 and add 우니까
because--help *action verb *to help: 돕다	도우니까 *돕으니까*

Korean Language: Grammar Pattern

because--is spicy *to be spicy: 맵다	매우니까 *맵으니까
because--is cold *to be cold: 춥다	추우니까 *춥으니까
because--is hot *to be hot: 덥다	더우니까 *덥으니까
because--is heavy *to be heavy: 무겁다	무거우니까 *무겁으니까
because--is light *to be light: 가볍다	가벼우니까 *가볍으니까
because--is itchy *to be itchy: 가렵다	가려우니까 *가렵으니까
because--is pathetic *to be pathetic: 가엽다	가여우니까 *가엽으니까
because--ridiculous *to be ridiculous: 가소롭다	가소로우니까 *가소롭으니까
because--is difficult *to be difficult: 어렵다	어려우니까 *어렵으니까
because--easy *to be easy: 쉽다	쉬우니까 *쉽으니까
because--is dirty *to be dirty: 더럽다	더러우니까 *더럽으니까
because--is funny *to be funny: 우습다	우스우니까 *우습으니까

Korean Language: Grammar Pattern

because--is thankful *to be thankful/grateful: 고맙다	고마우니까 *고맙으니까
because--is hateful *to be hateful: 밉다	미우니까 *밉으니까
because--is scary *to be scary: 무섭다	무서우니까 *무섭으니까
because--is cute *to be cure: 귀엽다	귀여우니까 *귀엽으니까
because--is happy *to be happy: 즐겁다	즐거우니까 *즐겁으니까

Examples:

•because--slept: 잤기 때문에/잤으니까   *to have slept: 잤다

•because--was building: 짓고 있었기 때문에/짓고 있었으니까

*to have been building: 짓고 있었다

•because--is cooking: 요리하고 있기 때문에/요리하고 있으니까

*to be cooking: 요리하고 있다

•because--will receive: 받을 것이기 때문에/받을 거기 때문에 or 받겠으니까/받을 것이니까/받을 거니까   *받겠기 때문에 is awkward.

*to be going to receive: 받겠다/받을 것이다/받을 거다

•because--will be giving: 주고 있을 것이기 때문에/주고 있을 거기 때문에 or 주고 있겠으니까/주고 있을 것이니까/주고 있을   *주고 있겠기 때문에 is awkward.

*to be going to be giving: 주고 있겠다/주고 있을 것이다/주고 있을 거다

•because--came: 왔기 때문에/왔으니까   *to have come: 왔다

•because--was eating 먹고 있었기 때문에/먹고 있었으니까

[여기에 입력]
Korean Language: Grammar Pattern

*to have been eating: 먹고 있었다

•because--leaves: 떠나기 때문에/떠나니까   *to leave: 떠나다

•because--is choosing: 고르고 있기 때문에/선택하고 있기 때문에 or 고르고 있으니까/선택하고 있으니까

*to be choosing: 고르고 있다(pure Korean)/선택하고 있다(Sino Korean)

•because--will go: 갈 것이기 때문에/갈 거기 때문에 or 가겠으니까/갈 것이니까/갈 거니까   ※가겠기 때문에 is awkward.

*to be going to go: 가겠다/갈 것이다/갈 거다

•because--will be looking: 보고 있을 것이기 때문에/보고 있을 거기 때문에 or 보고 있겠으니까/보고 있을 것이니까/보고 있을 거니까   *보고 있겠기 때문에 is awkward.

*to be going to be looking: 보고 있겠다/보고 있을 것이다/보고 있을 거다

•because--taught: 가르쳤기 때문에/가르쳤으니까   *to have taught: 가르쳤다

•because--was working: 일하고 있었기 때문에/일하고 있었으니까

*to have been working: 일하고 있었다

•because--sings: 노래하기 때문에/노래하니까   *to sing: 노래하다

•because--is running: 달리고 있기 때문에/뛰고 있기 때문에 or 달리고 있으니까/뛰고 있으니까

*to be running: 달리고 있다/뛰고 있다

•because--will do: 할 것이기 때문에/할 거기 때문에 or 하겠으니까/할 것이니까/할 거니까

*to be going to do: 하겠다/할 것이다/할 거다

•because--will be breaking: 부수고 있을 것이니까/부수고 있을 거니까 or 부수고 있겠으니까/부수고 있을 것이니까/부수고 있을 거니까   *부수고 있겠기 때문에

*to be going to be breaking: 부수고 있을 것이다/부수고 있을 거다

[여기에 입력]
Korean Language: Grammar Pattern

※In the following gird, compare the formal and informal expression of BECAUSE.

*Marks in Italic sound awkward.

conjunction 'BECAUSE'	conjunction BECAUSE in Korean	
	formal: 기 때문에	informal: 으니까 or 우니까 or 니까
because--disliked *to have disliked: 싫어했다	싫어했기 때문에	싫어했으니까
because--was loving *to have been loving: 사랑하고 있었다	사랑하고 있었기 때문에	사랑하고 있었으니까
because--cleans up *to clean up: 청소하다	청소하기 때문에	청소하니까
because--is catching *to be catching: 잡고 있다	잡고 있기 때문에	잡고 있으니까
because--is happy *to be happy: 즐겁다	즐겁기 때문에	즐거우니까 *즐겁으니까
because--will hike *to be going to hike: 등산하겠다/등산할 것이다/등산할 거다	등산할 것이기 때문에/등산할 거기 때문에 *등산하겠기 때문에	등산하겠으니까/등산할 것이니까/등산할 거니까
because--will be swimming *to be going to be swimming: 수영하고	수영하고 있을 것이기 때문에/수영하고 있을 거기 때문에	수영하고 있겠으니까/수영하고 있을 것이니까/수영하고 있을 거니까

Korean Language: Grammar Pattern

있겠다/수영하고 있을 것이다/수영하고 있을 거다	*수영하고 있겠기 때문에	
because--drove *to have driven: 운전했다	운전했기 때문에	운전했으니까
because--is far *to be far: 멀다	멀기 때문에	머니까 *멀으니까
because--was dancing *to have been dancing: 춤추고 있었다	춤추고 있었기 때문에	춤추고 있었으니까
because--writes *to write: 쓰다	쓰기 때문에	쓰니까
because--is drinking *to be drinking: 마시고 있다	마시고 있기 때문에	마시고 있으니까
because--will tell *to be going to tell: 말하겠다/말할 것이다/말할 거다	말할 것이기 때문에/말할 거기 때문에 *말하겠기 때문에	말하겠으니까/말할 것이니까/말할 거니까
because--will be throwing *to be going to be throwing: 던지고 있겠다/던지고 있을 것이다/던지고 있을 거다	던지고 있을 것이기 때문에/던지고 있을 거기 때문에 *던지고 있겠기 때문에	던지고 있겠으니까/던지고 있을 것이니까/던지고 있을 거니까
because--catch *to catch: 잡다	잡기 때문에	잡으니까

Korean Language: Grammar Pattern

because--kicked *to have kicked: 찼다	찼기 때문에	찼으니까
because--was using *to have been using: 사용하고 있었다	사용하고 있었기 때문에	사용하고 있었으니까
because--makes *to make: 만들다	만들기 때문에	만드니까 *만들으니까
because--is learning *to be learning: 배우고 있다	배우고 있기 때문에	배우고 있으니까
because--will cut *to be going to cut: 자르겠다/자를 것이다/자를 거다	자를 것이기 때문에/자를 거기 때문에 *자르겠기 때문에	자르겠으니까/자를 것이니까/자를 거니까
because--push *to push: 밀다	밀기 때문에	미니까 *밀으니까
because--will be pulling *to be going to be pulling: 당기고 있겠다/당기고 있을 것이다/당기고 있을 거다	당기고 있을 것이기 때문에/당기고 있을 거기 때문에 *당기고 있겠기 때문에	당기고 있겠으니까/당기고 있을 것이니까/당기고 있을 거니까

Exercise 46. Rewrite the English 'BECAUSE' in Korean.

conjunction 'BECAUSE'	conjunction BECAUSE in Korean:	
	formal ending:	informal ending:

Korean Language: Grammar Pattern

	기 때문에	으니까 or 우니까 or 니까
because--<u>played golf</u> *to play gold: 골프 치다	골프 쳤기 때문에 *to have played golf: 골프 쳤다	골프 쳤으니까 *consonant ending + 으니까
because--<u>was receiving</u> *to receive: 받다	받고 있었기 때문에 *to have been receiving: 받고 있었다	받고 있었으니까
because--<u>walks</u> *to walk: 걷다	걷기 때문에	걸으니까 *걷으니까 *verbs ending in ㄷ ㄷ is dropped and ㄹ 으니까 is added.
because--<u>touches</u> *to touch: 만지다	만지기 때문에	만지니까 *vowel ending + 니까
because--<u>is selling</u> *to sell: 팔다	팔고 있기 때문에 *to be selling: 팔고 있다	팔고 있으니까
because--<u>asks</u> *to ask: 묻다	묻기 때문에	물으니까 *묻으니까
because--<u>will like</u> *to like: 좋아하다	좋아할 것이기 때문에/좋아할 거기 때문에 *좋아하겠기 때문에 *to be going to like: 좋아하겠다/좋아할 것이다/좋아할 거다	좋아하겠으니까/좋아할 것이니까/좋아할 거니까
because--<u>was spicy</u> *to be spicy: 맵다	매웠기 때문에 *맵었기 때문에	매웠으니까(매우었으니까)

Korean Language: Grammar Pattern

	*to have been spicy: 매웠다 **맵었다*	
because--<u>will be studying</u> *to study: 공부하다	공부하고 있을 것이기 때문에/공부하고 있을 거기 때문에 **공부하고 있겠기 때문에* *to be going to be studying: 공부하고 있겠다/공부하고 있을 것이다/공부하고 있을 거다	공부하고 있겠으니까/공부하고 있을 것이니까/공부하고 있을 거니까
because--<u>fished</u> *to fish: 낚시하다	낚시했기 때문에 *to have fished: 낚시했다	낚시했으니까
because--<u>was cute</u> *to be cute: 귀엽다	귀여웠기 때문에 **귀엽었기 때문에* *to have been cute: 귀여웠다 **귀엽었다*	귀여웠으니까
because--<u>was asking</u> *to ask: 묻다/질문하다	묻고 있었기 때문에 *to have been asking: 묻고 있었다	묻고 있었으니까/질문하고 있었으니까
because--<u>folds</u> *to fold: 접다	접기 때문에	접으니까
because--<u>is scary</u> *to be scary: 무섭다	무섭기 때문에	무서우니까 **무섭으니까*
because--<u>is sending</u> *to send: 보내다	보내고 있기 때문에 *to be sending: 보내고 있다	보내고 있으니까

Korean Language: Grammar Pattern

because--<u>will hang</u> *to hang: 걸다	걸 것이기 때문에/걸 거기 때문에 *걸겠기 때문에 *to be going to hang: 걸겠다/걸 것이다/걸 거다	걸겠으니까/걸 것이니까/걸 거니까
because--<u>will be buying</u> *to buy: 사다	사고 있을 것이기 때문에/사고 있을 거기 때문에 *사고 있겠기 때문에 *to be going to be buying: 사고 있겠다/사고 있을 것이다/사고 있을 거다	사고 있겠으니까/사고 있을 것이니까/사고 있을 거니까
because--<u>pushes</u> *to push: 밀다	밀기 때문에	미니까 *밀으니까 *verbs ending in ㄹ ㄹ is dropped and 니까 is added.
because--<u>changed</u> *to change: 바꾸다/갈다	바꿨기(바꾸었기) 때문에/갈았기 때문에 *to have changed: 바꿨다/갈았다	바꿨으니까(바꾸었으니까)/갈았으니까
because--<u>was listening</u> *to listen: 듣다	듣고 있었기 때문에 *to have been listening: 듣고 있었다	듣고 있었으니까
because--<u>hits</u> *to hit: 치다/때리다	치기 때문에/때리기 때문에	치니까/때리니까
because--<u>is believing</u> *to believe: 믿다	믿고 있기 때문에	믿고 있으니까

Korean Language: Grammar Pattern

	*to be believing: 믿고 있다	
because--<u>sells</u> *to sell: 팔다	팔기 때문에	파니까　*팔으니까
because--<u>will fly</u> *to fly: 날다	날 것이기 때문에/날 거기 때문에 *날겠기 때문에 *to be going to fly: 날겠다/날 것이다/날 거다	날겠으니까/날 것이니까/날 거니까
because--<u>opened</u> *to open: 열다	열었기 때문에 *to have opened: 열었다	열었으니까
because--<u>will be travelling</u> *to travel: 여행하다	날고 있을 것이기 때문에/날고 있을 거기 때문에 *여행하고 있겠기 때문에 *to be going to be travelling: 여행하고 있겠다/여행하고 있을 것이다/여행하고 있을 거다	여행하고 있겠으니까/여행하고 있을 것이니까/여행하고 있을 거니까
because--<u>shopped</u> *to shop: 쇼핑하다	쇼핑했기 때문에 *to have shopped: 쇼핑했다	쇼핑했으니까
because--<u>was reading</u> *to read: 읽다/독서하다	읽고 있었기 때문에/독서하고 있었기 때문에	읽고 있었으니까/독서하고 있었으니까

Korean Language: Grammar Pattern

	*to have been reading: 읽고 있었다/독서하고 있었다	
because--<u>shouts</u> *to shout: 소리치다	소리치기 때문에	소리치니까
because--<u>is heavy</u> *to be heavy: 무겁다	무겁기 때문에	무거우니까 *무겁으니까
because--<u>is tearing</u> *to tear: 찢다	찢고 있기 때문에 *to be tearing: 찢고 있다	찢고 있으니까
because--<u>will wait</u> *to wait: 기다리다	기다릴 것이기 때문에/기다릴 거기 때문에 *기다리겠기 때문에 *to be going to wait: 기다리겠다/기다릴 것이다/기다릴 거다	기다리겠으니까/기다리고 있을 것이니까/기다리고 있을 거니까
because--<u>will be working out</u> *to work out: 운동하다	운동하고 있을 것이기 때문에/운동하고 있을 거기 때문에 *운동하고 있겠기 때문에 *to be going to be working out: 운동하고 있겠다/운동하고 있을 것이다/운동하고 있을 거다	운동하고 있겠으니까/운동하고 있을 것이니까/운동하고 있을 거니까
because--<u>makes</u> *to make: 만들다	만들기 때문에	만드니까 *만들으니까

12. ALTHOUGH/THOUGH/EVEN THOUGH: 비록--지만

※although/even though = in spite of the fact that

※비록 is kind of optional.   In order to avoid the confusion with 'BUT' (지만), it is better to use 비록.   Drop 다 from the verb stem and add 지만.

1) 비록 + root verb stem ending in consonant or vowel + 지만 for present tense

•although--come: 비록 오지만   *to come: 오다

*오 ends in vowel ㅗ.   Drop 다 from root verb stem and add 지만.

•although--eat: 비록 먹지만   *to eat: 먹다

*먹 ends in consonant ㄱ.   Add just 지만.   Drop 다 from root verb stem and add 지만.

2) verb stem in past tense + 비록--지만

*verb stem in past tense ends in ㅆ다/았다/었다/웠다.   Drop 다 from verb stem and add 지만

•although--drank: 비록 마셨지만.   *to have drunk: 마셨다

•although--threw: 비록 던졌지만(던지었지만)   *to have thrown: 던졌다(던지었다)

3) verb stem in future tense + 비록 지만

*verb stem in future tense ends in 겠다/것이다/거다.   Drop 다 from verb stem and add 지만.

•although--will shout: 비록 소리치겠지만/비록 소리칠 것이지만/비록 소리칠 거지만

Korean Language: Grammar Pattern

*to be going to shout: 소리치겠다/소리칠 것이다/소리칠 거다

•although--will exchange: 비록 바꾸겠지만/비록 바꿀 것이지만/비록 바꿀 거지만
or 비록 교환하겠지만/비록 교환할 것이지만/비록 교환할 거지만

*to exchange: 바꾸다(pure Korean)/교환하다(Sino Korean)

4) verb stem in past progressive tense + 지만

*verb stem in past progressive tense ends in 고 있었다. Drop 다 from verb stem and add 지만.

•although--was eating: 비록 먹고 있었지만   *to have been eating: 먹고 있었다

•although--was fixing: 고치고 있었지만/수리하고 있었지만

*to have been fixing: 고치고 있었다(pure Korean)/수리하고 있었다(Sino Korean)

5) verb stem in present progressive tense + 지만

*verb stem in present progressive tense ends in 고 있다. Drop 다 from verb stem and add 지만.

•although--is writing: 비록 쓰고 있지만   *to be writing: 쓰고 있다

•although--is opening: 비록 열고 있지만   *to be opening: 열고 있다

6) verb stem in future progressive tense + 지만

*verb stem in future progressive tense ends in 고 있겠다/고 있을 것이다/고 있을 거다. Drop 다 from verb stem and add 지만.

•although--will be moving: 비록 움직이겠지만/비록 움직일 것이지만/비록 움직일 거지만

*to be going to be moving: 움직이겠다/움직일 것이다/움직일 거다

Korean Language: Grammar Pattern

※ NO irregular change rule applies to the verbs ending in ㄹ, ㄷ and ㅂ. Simply drop 다 from verb stem and add 지만.

•although--pushes: 비록 밀지만   *to push: 밀다

•although--walks: 비록 걷지만   *to walk: 걷다

•although--helps: 비록 돕지만   *to help: 돕다

•although--cold: 비록 춥지만   *to be cold: 춥다

Examples:

•although--was running: 비록 달리고 있었지만

*to have been running: 달리고 있었다

•although--closed: 비록 닫았지만   *to have closed: 닫았다

•although--walks: 비록 걷지만   *to walk: 걷다

•although--is choosing: 비록 고르고 있지만/비록 선택하고 있지만

*to choose: 고르다(pure Korean)/선택하다(Sino Korean)

*to be choosing: 고르고 있다/선택하고 있다

•although--will know: 비록 알겠지만/알 것이지만/알 거지만   *to know: 알다

•although--will be looking: 비록 보고 있겠지만/비록 보고 있을 것이지만/비록 보고 있을 거지만

*to be going to be looking: 보고 있겠다/보고 있을 것이다/보고 있을 거다

•although--taught: 비록 가르쳤지만   *to have taught: 가르쳤다

•although--was working: 비록 일하고 있었지만

*to have been working: 일하고 있었다

•although--pushes: 비록 밀지만   *to push: 밀다

•although--is singing: 비록 노래하고 있지만/비록 노래 부르고 있지만

*to be singing: 노래하고 있다/노래 부르고 있다

Korean Language: Grammar Pattern

•although--will begin: 비록 시작하겠지만/비록 시작할 것이지만/비록 시작할 거지만

*to be going to begin: 시작하겠다/시작할 것이다/시작할 거다

•although--will be paying: 비록 지불하고 있겠지만/비록 지불하고 있을 것이지만/비록 지불하고 있을 거지만

*to be going to be paying: 지불하고 있겠다/지불하고 있을 것이다/지불하고 있을 거다

•although--walk: 비록 걷지만   *to walk: 걷다

•although--disliked: 비록 싫어했지만   *to have disliked: 싫어했다

•although--was recovering: 비록 회복하고 있었지만

*to have been recovering: 회복하고 있었다

•although--asks: 비록 묻지만   *to ask: 묻다

•although--is holding: 비록 붙잡고 있지만   *to be holding: 붙잡고 있다

•although--will hike: 비록 등산하겠지만/비록 등산할 것이지만/비록 등산할 거지만

*to be going to hike: 등산하겠다/등산할 것이다/등산할 거다

•although--will be swimming: 비록 수영하고 있겠지만/비록 수영하고 있을 것이지만/비록 수영하고 있을 거지만

*to be going to be swimming: 수영하고 있겠다/수영하고 있을 것이다/수영하고 있을 거다

•although--cleaned up: 비록 청소했지만   *to have cleaned up: 청소했다

•although--is dirty: 비록 더럽지만   *to be dirty: 더럽다

•although--was driving: 비록 운전하고 있었지만

*to have been driving: 운전하고 있었다

•although--sells: 비록 팔지만   *to sell: 팔다

•although--is dancing: 비록 춤추고 있지만   *to be dancing: 춤추고 있다

•although--will help: 비록 돕겠지만/비록 도울 것이지만/비록 도울 거지만

Korean Language: Grammar Pattern

*to be going to help: 돕겠다/도울 것이다/도울 거다

•although--will be searching: 비록 찾고 있겠지만/비록 찾고 있을 것이지만/비록 찾고 있을 거지만

*to be going to be searching: 찾고 있겠다/찾고 있을 것이다/찾고 있을 거다

Exercise 47. Rewrite the English conjunction 'ALTHOUGH' in Korean.

conjunction 'ALTHOUGH'	conjunction ALTHOUGH in Korean: 비록--지만
although--<u>played golf</u> *to play golf: 골프 치다	비록 골프 쳤지만 *to have played golf: 골프 쳤다
although --<u>was receiving</u> *to receive: 받다	비록 받고 있었지만 *to have been receiving: 받고 있었다
although--<u>touches</u> *to touch: 만지다	비록 만지지만
although--<u>is selling</u> *to sell: 팔다	비록 팔고 있지만 *to be selling: 팔고 있다
although --<u>will like</u> *to like: 좋아하다	비록 좋아하겠지만/좋아할 것이지만/좋아할 거지만 *to be going to like: 좋아하겠다/좋아할 것이다/좋아할 거다
although--<u>will be studying</u> *to study: 공부하다	비록 공부하고 있겠지만/공부하고 있을 것이지만/공부하고 있을 거지만 *to be going to be studying: 공부하고 있겠다/공부하고 있을 것이다/공부하고 있을 거다
although--<u>fished</u>	비록 낚시했지만

Korean Language: Grammar Pattern

*to fish: 낚시하다	*to have fished: 낚시했다
although--<u>was asking</u> *to ask: 묻다/질문하다	비록 묻고 있었지만/질문하고 있었지만 *to have been asking: 묻고 있었다/질문하고 있었다
although--<u>folds</u> *to fold: 접다	비록 접지만
although--<u>is sending</u> *to send: 보내다	비록 보내고 있지만 *to be sending: 보내고 있다
although--<u>will hang</u> *to hang: 걸다	비록 걸겠지만 *to be going to hang: 걸겠다/걸 것이다/걸 거다
although--<u>will be buying</u> *to buy: 사다	비록 사고 있겠지만/사고 있을 것이지만/사고 있을 거지만 *to be going to be buying: 사고 있겠다/사고 있을 것이다/사고 있을 거다
although--<u>changed</u> *to change: 갈다/바꾸다	비록 바꿨지만(바꾸었지만) *to have changed: 바꿨다(바꾸었다)
although--<u>was opening</u> *to open: 열다	비록 열고 있었지만 *to have been opening: 열고 있었다
although--<u>hits</u> *to hit: 치다/때리다	비록 치지만/때리지만
although--<u>is respecting</u> *to respect: 존경하다	비록 존경하고 있지만 *to be respecting: 존경하고 있다
although--<u>will rain</u> *to rain: 비 내리다	비록 비 내리겠지만/비 내릴 것이지만/비 내릴 거지만

Korean Language: Grammar Pattern

	*to be going to rain: 비 내리겠다/비 내릴 것이다/비 내릴 거다
although--<u>will be travelling</u> *to travel: 여행하다	비록 여행하고 있겠지만/여행하고 있을 것이지만/여행하고 있을 거지만 *to be going to be travelling: 여행하고 있겠다/여행하고 있을 것이다/여행하고 있을 거다
although--<u>copied</u> *to copy: 복사하다	비록 복사했지만 *to have copied: 복사했다
although--<u>was attaching</u> *to attach: 붙이다(pure Korean)/첨부하다(Sino Korean)	비록 첨부하고 있었지만/붙이고 있었지만 *to have been attaching: 붙이고 있었다/첨부하고 있었다
although--<u>stops</u> *to stop: 멈추다	비록 멈추지만
although--<u>is tearing</u> *to tear: 찢다	비록 찢고 있지만 *to be tearing: 찢고 있다
although--<u>will wait</u> *to wait: 기다리다	비록 기다리겠지만/기다릴 것이지만/기다릴 거지만 *to be going to wait: 기다리겠다/기다릴 것이다/기다릴 거다
although--<u>will be working out</u> *to work out: 운동하다	비록 운동하고 있겠지만/운동하고 있을 것이지만/운동하고 있을 거지만 *to be going to be working out: 운동하고 있겠다/운동하고 있을 것이다/운동하고 있을 거다
although--<u>is easy</u>	비록 쉽지만

*to be easy: 쉽다	
although--<u>was light</u> *to be light: 가볍다	비록 가벼웠지만 *가볍었다 *to have been light: 가벼웠다
although--fought *to fight: 싸우다	비록 싸웠지만 *to have fought: 싸웠다

13. subjunctive mood 'IF': 만일/만약--면

*verb stem in all types of tense + 만일/만약--면: The use of 만일/만약 is optional. 만일/만약 sounds very formal.   It is better to say 만일/만약 if the sentence has something that needs to be emphasized.

※다 is NOT dropped from verb stem and 면 is added at the end of the verb stem. 면 is not combined with root verb stem.   Simply add 면 at the end of the verb stem in various tenses.   Refer to UNIT 7 for more information on verb stem and tense.

1) verb stem in present tense(NOT root verb stem) + 면

•if--flies: 난다면   *the verb stem in present tense is 난다

•If--comes: 온다면   *verb stem in present tense: 온다   오다면 is incorrect.   면 is NOT combined with ROOT VERB STEM.

2) verb stem in past tense + 면

*Past tense ends in ㅆ다 or 었다 or 았다.   Simply add 면 at the end of the stem.

•If--came: 왔다면   *to have come: 왔다

•If--knew: 알았다면   *to have known: 알았다

3) verb stem in future tense + 면 or 라면

Korean Language: Grammar Pattern

*Future tense ends in 겠다 or ㄹ(을) 것이다 or ㄹ(을) 거다. Simply add 면 at the end of the stem.

•If--will come: 오겠다면/올 것이라면(다면)/올 거라면(다면)

*to be going to come: 오겠다/올 것이다/올 거다

※In the case of future and future progressive tense, 면 is combined with either 것이라면/거라면 or 것이다면/거다면. However, 것이라면/거라면 is used more commonly and generally than 것이다면/거다면.

•If--will kick: 차겠다면/찰 것이라면(다면)/찰 거라면(다면)

*to be going to kick: 차겠다/찰 것이다/찰 거다

4) verb stem in past progressive tense + 면

*verb stem in past progressive tense ends in 고 있었다. Do not drop 다 and simply add 면.

•If--was breaking: 부수고 있었다면   *to have been breaking: 부수고 있었다

•If--was shaking: 흔들고 있었다면   *to have been shaking: 흔들고 있었다

5) verb stem in present progressive tense + 면

*verb stem in present progressive tense ends in 고 있다. Do not drop 다 and simply add 면.

•If--is reading: 읽고 있다면   *to be reading: 읽고 있다

•If--is dreaming: 꿈꾸고 있다면   *to be dreaming: 꿈꾸고 있다

6) verb stem in future progressive tense + 면

*verb stem in future progressive tense ends in 고 있겠다/고 있을 것이다/고 있을 거다. Do not drop 다 and simply add 면

Korean Language: Grammar Pattern

•If--will be blocking: 막고 있겠다면/막고 있을 것이라면(다면)/막고 있을 거라면(다면)

*to be going to be blocking: 막고 있겠다/막고 있을 것이다/막고 있을 거다

•If--will be showing: 보여주고 있겠다면/보여주고 있을 것이라면(다면)/보여주고 있을 거라면(다면)

*to be going to be showing: 보여주고 있겠다/보여주고 있을 것이다/보여주고 있을 거다

Examples:

•If--is coming: 오고 있다면   *to be coming: 오고 있다

•if--drink: 마신다면   *마시다면 is incorrect.   *verb stem in present tense: 마신다

•if--walked: 걸었다면   *to have walked: 걸었다

•if--will study: 공부하겠다면/공부할 것이라면(다면)/공부할 거라면(다면)

*to be going to study: 공부하겠다/공부할 것이다/공부할 거다

•if--was wearing: 입고 있었다면   *to have been wearing: 입고 있었다

•if--is selling: 팔고 있다면   *to be selling: 팔고 있다

•if--will be finding 찾고 있겠다면/찾고 있을 것이라면(다면/)찾고 있을 거라면(다면)

*to be going to be finding: 찾고 있겠다/찾고 있을 것이다/찾고 있을 거다

•if--live: 산다면   *살다면   *verb stem in present tense: 산다

•if--buy: 산다면   *사다면   *verb stem in present tense: 산다

•if--bought: 샀다면   *to have bought: 샀다

•if---will lose: 잃겠다면/잃을 것이라면(다면)/잃을 거라면(다면)

*to be going to lose: 잃겠다/잃을 것이다/잃을 거다

•if--was flying: 날고 있다면   *to have been flying: 날고 있었다

•if--is writing: 쓰고 있다면   *to be writing: 쓰고 있다

Korean Language: Grammar Pattern

•if--will be preparing: 준비하고 있겠다면/준비하고 있을 것이라면(다면)/준비하고 있을 거라면(다면)

*to be going to be preparing: 준비하고 있겠다/준비하고 있을 것이다/준비하고 있을 거다

•if--danced 춤췄다면   *to have danced: 춤췄다(춤추었다)

•if--will close: 닫겠다면/닫을 것이라면(다면)/닫을 거라면(다면)

*to be going to close: 닫겠다/닫을 것이다/닫을 거다

•if--was running: 뛰고 있었다면/달리고 있었다면

*to have been running: 뛰고 있었다/달리고 있었다

•if--helps: 돕는다면   *돕다면   *verb stem in present tense: 돕는다

•if--will be sleeping: 자고 있겠다면/자고 있을 것이라면(다면)/자고 있을 거라면(다면)

*to be going to be sleeping: 자고 있겠다/자고 있을 것이다/자고 있을 거다

Exercise 48. Rewrite subjunctive mood 'IF' in Korean.

subjunctive mood 'IF'	subjunctive mood IF in Korean: (만일/만약)--면
if--<u>wash</u> *to wash: 씻다	(만일/만약) 씻는다면 *씻다면 *verb stem in present tense: 씻는다
if--<u>received</u> *to receive: 받다	(만일/만약) 받았다면 *to have received: 받았다
if--<u>will believe</u> *to believe: 믿다	(만일/만약) 믿겠다면/믿을 것이<u>다면</u>(라면)/믿을 거<u>다면</u>(라면) *to be going to believe: 믿겠다/믿을 것이다/믿을 거다

Korean Language: Grammar Pattern

	※In the case of future and future progressive tense, both 것이다면/것이라면 and 거다면/거라면 are good to use. However, 것이라면 and 거라면 are more commonly used.
if--<u>was staying</u> *to stay: 머물다	(만일/만약) 머물고 있었다면 *to have been staying: 머물고 있었다
if--<u>is departing</u> *to depart: 출발하다	(만일/만약) 출발하고 있다면 *to be departing: 출발하고 있다
if--<u>will be working out</u> *to work out: 운동하다	(만일/만약) 운동하고 있겠다면/운동하고 있을 것이<u>다면</u>(라면)/운동하고 있을 거<u>다면</u>(라면)
if--<u>is difficult</u> *to be difficult: 어렵다 ※In the case of static verb, its root verb stem is the same as present tense.	(만일/만약) 어렵다면
if--<u>arrived</u> *to arrive: 도착하다	(만일/만약) 도착했다면 *to have arrived: 도착했다
if--<u>will throw</u> *to throw: 던지다	(만일/만약) 던진다면 *verb stem in present tense: 던진다
if--<u>was saying</u> *to say: 말하다	(만일/만약) 말하고 있었다면 *to have been saying: 말하고 있었다
if--<u>will be fixing</u> *to fix: 고치다	(만일/만약) 고치고 있다면 *to be fixing: 고치고 있다
if--<u>caught</u>	(만일/만약) 잡았다면

Korean Language: Grammar Pattern

*to catch: 잡다	*to have caught: 잡았다
if--<u>hates</u> *to hate: 미워하다	(만일/만약) 미워한다면 *verb stem in present tense: 미워한다
if--<u>will laugh</u> *to laugh: 웃다	(만일/만약) 웃겠다면/웃을 것이*라면*/웃을 거*라면* *to be going to laugh: 웃겠다/웃을 것이다/웃을 거다
if--<u>was traveling</u> *to travel: 여행하다	(만일/만약) 여행하고 있었다면 *to have been travelling: 여행하고 있었다
if--<u>is using</u> *to use: 쓰다/사용하다	(만일/만약) 쓰고 있다면/사용하고 있다면 *to be using: 쓰고 있다/사용하고 있다
if--<u>will be starting</u> *to start: 시작하다	(만일/만약) 시작하고 있겠다면/시작하고 있을 것이<u>다면</u>(라면)/시작하고 있을 거<u>다면</u>(라면) *to be going to be starting: 시작하고 있겠다/시작하고 있을 것이다/시작하고 있을 거다
if--<u>was cold</u> *to be cold: 춥다	(만일/만약) 추웠다면 *춥었다면 *to have been cold: 추웠다
if--<u>cries</u> *to cry: 울다	(만일/만약) 운다면 *울는다면
if--<u>will stop</u> *to stop: 멈추다	(만일/만약) 멈추겠다면/멈출 것이<u>다면</u>(라면)/멈출 거<u>다면</u>(라면) *to be going to stop: 멈추겠다/멈출 것이다/멈출 거다
if--<u>was cutting</u>	(만일/만약) 자르고 있었다면/끊고 있었다면

Korean Language: Grammar Pattern

*to cut: 자르다/끊다	*to have been cutting: 자르고 있었다/끊고 있었다
if--<u>is boiling</u> *to boil: 끓이다	(만일/만약) 끓이고 있다면 *to be boiling: 끓이고 있다
if--<u>will be climbing</u> *to climb: 오르다	(만일/만약) 오르고 있겠다면/오르고 있을 것이<u>다면</u>(라면)/오르고 있을 거<u>다면</u>(라면) *to be going to be climbing: 오르고 있겠다/오르고 있을 것이다/오르고 있을 거다
if--<u>was heavy</u> *to be heavy: 무겁다	(만일/만약) 무거웠다면 *무겁었다 *to have been heavy: 무거웠다
if--<u>lies down</u> *to lie down: 눕다	(만일/만약) 눕는다면 *verb stem in present tense: 눕는다
if--<u>will break</u> *to break: 부수다	(만일/만약) 부수겠다면/부술 것이<u>다면</u>(라면)/부술 거<u>다면</u>(라면) *to be going to break: 부수겠다/부술 것이다/부술 거다
if--<u>was sleeping</u> *to sleep: 자다	(만일/만약) 자고 있었다면 *to have been sleeping: 자고 있었다
if--<u>is taking a shower</u> *to take a shower: 샤워하다	(만일/만약) 샤워하고 있다면 *to be taking a shower: 샤워하고 있다
if--<u>will be placing an order</u> *to place an order: 주문하다	(만일/만약) 주문하고 있겠다면/주문하고 있을 것이<u>다면</u>(라면)/주문하고 있을 거<u>다면</u>(라면) *to be going to be placing an order: 주문하고 있겠다/주문하고 있을 것이다/주문하고 있을 거다

Korean Language: Grammar Pattern

if--<u>was happy</u> *to be happy: 즐겁다/행복하다	(만일/만약) 즐거웠다면/행복했다면 *즐겁었다면* *to have been happy: 즐거웠다/행복했다
if--<u>pushes</u> *to push: 밀다	(만일/만약) 민다면 *밀는다면*
if--<u>will paste</u> *to paste: 붙이다	(만일/만약) 붙이겠다면/붙일 것이<u>다면</u>(라면)/붙일 거<u>다면</u>(라면) *to be going to paste: 붙이겠다/붙일 것이다/붙일 거다
if--<u>was playing</u> *to play: 놀다	(만일/만약) 놀고 있었다면 *to have been playing: 놀고 있었다
if--<u>is grinding</u> *to grind: 갈다	(만일/만약) 갈고 있다면 *to be grinding: 갈고 있다
if--<u>will be waiting</u> *to wait: 기다리다	(만일/만약) 기다리고 있겠다면/기다리고 있을 것이<u>다면</u>(라면)/기다리고 있을 거<u>다면</u>(라면)
if--<u>asked</u> *to ask: 묻다	(만일/만약) 물었다면 *묻었다면* *to have asked: 물었다
if--<u>bit</u> *to bite: 물다	(만일/만약) 물었다면 *to have bitten: 물었다
if--<u>helped</u> *to help: 돕다	(만일/만약) 도왔다면 *돕았다면* *to have helped: 도왔다
if--<u>pushes</u> *to push: 밀다	(만일/만약) 민다면 *밀는다면* *verb stem in present tense: 민다
if--<u>turns off</u>	(만일/만약) 끈다면

Korean Language: Grammar Pattern

*to turn off: 끄다	*verb stem in present tense: 끈다
if--<u>was spicy</u> *to be spicy: 맵다	(만일/만약) 매웠다면 *_맵었다면_ *to have been spicy: 매웠다
if--<u>will board</u> *to board: 탑승하다	(만일/만약) 탑승하겠다면/탑승할 것이다<u>다면</u>(라면)/탑승할 거<u>다면</u>(라면) *to be going to board: 탑승하겠다/탑승할 것이다/탑승할 거다
if--<u>is raining</u> *to rain: 비 오다	(만일/만약) 비 오고 있다면 *to be raining: 비 오고 있다
if--<u>freezes</u> *to freeze: 얼다	(만일/만약) 언다면 *_얼는다면_ *ㄹ is dropped and 는다 is added for present tense.

About the Author

Cholho Choe, the author was born in Busan, the southern part of Korea. He earned B.A. and M.A. degree in English Language and Literature, M.A. degree in Translation of Korean to English and Ph.D. in English Language and Literature.

He taught English at secondary schools, college and university in Korea. He also served as an assistant professor at Defense Language Institute Foreign Language Center in Monterey, California.

www.ingramcontent.com/pod-product-compliance
Lightning Source LLC
Chambersburg PA
CBHW081141130726
47996CB00009B/2938